Peter Field Jefferson

DARK PRINCE OF SCOTTSVILLE

AND

Lost Jeffersons

Also by Joanne L. Yeck

"At a Place Called Buckingham"
The Jefferson Brothers
"At a Place Called Buckingham," Volume Two

PETER FIELD JEFFERSON:
Dark Prince of Scottsville

AND

LOST JEFFERSONS

Joanne L. Yeck

Library of Congress Cataloging-In-Publication Data

Yeck, Joanne L.
Peter Field Jefferson: Dark Prince of Scottsville & Lost Jeffersons/by Joanne L. Yeck
　　p. cm.
Includes bibliographical references.
ISBN: 978-0-9839898-9-9
1. Virginia—Albemarle County—History. 2. Virginia—Biography. 3. Virginia—Scottsville—History. 4. Virginia—Buckingham County—History. 5. Slavery—Virginia. 6. Historic Buildings—Virginia. 7. Historic Sites—Virginia. 8. Jefferson, Peter Field, d. 1861.
I. Joanne L. Yeck, 1954–II. Title.
F232.A3 Y43 2018

2018900784

Book production by Braughler Books, LLC
braughlerbooks.com

Published by Slate River Press Ltd.
slateriverpress.com
slate.river.press@gmail.com

For

All my Virginia kith and kin, including the Jeffersons

Contents

LOST JEFFERSONS

Preface

In *The Jefferson Brothers*, I strove to correct the persistent myth that Thomas Jefferson's only brother, Randolph, was an incompetent man, even a mentally handicapped one. A primary, and I believe powerful, argument against this are the successful lives of the majority of his children and grandchildren. He provided them with a solid start in life and most flourished.

Between 1782 and 1796, Randolph and Anne (Lewis) Jefferson had six children together: Anna Scott (Jefferson) Nevil, Thomas Jefferson, Jr., Isham Randolph Jefferson, Robert Lewis Jefferson, Peter Field Jefferson, and James Lilburne Jefferson. They came of age at the dawn of the 19th century, precisely when the culture along the James River in central Virginia began to flower. Over the course of their adulthood, their choices expressed not only their own personalities but also the values of this branch of the Jefferson family and Virginia's gentry class.

Little is known about Randolph Jefferson's children while they lived at Snowden. What is recorded survives in scattered sources. Much is confused, misleading, incorrect, and even fictitious. Many of these "facts" contradict each other.

At various times, all of Randolph and Anne Jefferson's children lived at or near Snowden or across the river at Scottsville. Peter Field Jefferson stayed to make the most significant impact on the town and its environs. The story of his life parallels that of the changing cultural landscape of the James River's Horseshoe Bend across seven decades—rising from virtual frontier in the early American Republic to the establishment of Scottsville in Albemarle County, through the building of the James River and Kanawha Canal, and culminating in the early months of the Civil War. Just as Scottsville mirrors the maturation of Virginia

Peyton Randolph McLean with his grandson, Hugh McLean Blumenshine, the great-great-great-grandson of Randolph Jefferson, June 1925. (Courtesy Mary Broach and Jane Eaton.)

and the American South, Peter Field Jefferson's turbulent life reflected those growing pains, becoming a personal, American tragedy.

Beyond Peter Field Jefferson's calamitous story, an even larger catastrophe unfolds in the decline of this Jefferson clan. A microcosm of multiple generations of cousin marriage, his family's story reveals how "undesirable" traits became concentrated in these Jeffersons. Hereditary insanity, alcoholism, and idiocy plagued succeeding generations. A steadily mounting number of suffering individuals, acts of criminal insanity, and increasing social burden of asylums to house Virginia's "degenerates" helped fuel the American Eugenics Movement and, ultimately, in 1924, led to Virginia's sterilization law.

By 1880, the federal government was deeply concerned about the growing number of unproductive Americans and created a special, supplemental schedule for the national census—"Defective, Dependent, and Delinquent Classes." By the end of the 19th century, asylums and other institutions kept statistics on whether or not their patients were the products of first cousin marriages.

Even in President Thomas Jefferson's generation, "inferior" genes were doubling up, particularly in the Randolph family. Outsiders noted that intelligence seemed unevenly distributed among the children of Peter and Jane (Randolph) Jefferson. Their daughter Elizabeth (1744–1774) was "feeble-minded" while their daughter Jane (1740–1765) was exceptionally bright. Both died unmarried and childless.

Virginians were experts on breeding, particularly of horses, but turned a blind eye to too much inbreeding in their families. Preservation of wealth and land took precedence. Thomas Jefferson, who observed the sometimes negative consequences of cousin marriage, still allowed his daughter Martha to marry her cousin Thomas Mann Randolph, and encouraged his daughter Maria to marry her cousin John Wayles Eppes.

Randolph and Anne Jefferson were first cousins and genetics might account for the alcoholism and unstable personalities which manifested in succeeding generations of the family. Sterility or genetic incompatibility was possibly another misfortune of inbreeding. Thomas Jefferson, Jr. and Polly Randolph Lewis were double first cousins. Married over thirty years, they produced no known living children.

Some of the grandchildren of Randolph and Anne Jefferson, most the product of further cousin intermarriage, suffered from ongoing incidences of low intelligence, idiocy, alcoholism, and even insanity. Their stories are told in the following essays. There may be others whose disturbed lives went undocumented or whose deficiencies were manageable enough not to be discovered in public records.

As in the previous generation, these genetic problems were not equally distributed among Randolph Jefferson's children and grandchildren. A bright spot, and an argument against multi-generational cousin marriage, are the descendants of Isham Randolph Jefferson, particularly his third family. His first two wives were his close cousins, while his third wife, Sarah Ann Mansfield, was not. Despite the fact that two of their sons died at a young age (one of typhoid fever), the couple produced an apparently healthy, intelligent, and successful family, including two attorneys and a physician.

I now believe that some of the uncomplimentary rumors of Randolph Jefferson's exceptionally low intelligence and possible alcoholism were actually based in the sad lives of Peter Field Jefferson and his unfortunate sons. Descendants and citizens of Scottsville long remembered this family and, as the years went by, perhaps, projected their deficiencies back on Randolph Jefferson—a strange case of the "sins" of the children being visited on the father.

The following biographical essays reveal how this web of Jefferson-Lewis-Randolph cousins intersected with the life of Peter Field Jefferson, and how his kinsmen faired in the larger world. Persistent myths about the extended family of Randolph and Anne Jefferson are debunked and, doubtless, more than one family skeleton is rattled. They are not meant as an exposé, but rather to be read with understanding and compassion for the values and behaviors of the Virginia gentry that sometimes "went wrong."

Joanne L. Yeck
Kettering, Ohio

Part One
PETER FIELD JEFFERSON: DARK PRINCE OF SCOTTSVILLE

If I had all the money in the world but one half dollar, and that was in New Orleans, I would ride there and get it.

PETER FIELD JEFFERSON

Peter Field Jefferson: Dark Prince of Scottsville

From his hilltop home, Mount Walla, high above Scottsville on the James River, Peter Field Jefferson gazed upon what he owned and on what he had lost. In 1826, he and his brothers were forced to sell Snowden, the Jefferson plantation which lay within his view just south of the James River. Neither he nor his brothers would ever reclaim the 2,000 acres which their grandfather, Peter Jefferson, had assembled in the 18th century. Apart from Snowden and his family, Peter Field Jefferson was determined to succeed on his own terms. He would be richer than his father, shrewder than his brothers. Unlike his uncle, President Thomas Jefferson, Peter Field had a head for business and would not die swimming in debt. He would prove that a Jefferson could capitalize on changing times.

Peter Field Jefferson was an unlikely founding father of a bustling river town. A brooding man, he kept to himself. Impatient and greedy, he often dismissed his wife and his children and hoarded his money. He shunned religion and flirted with the limits of the law. Despite his wealth and his achievements, he died confused and alienated. His money and local influence brought him no happiness. Ultimately and ironically, Peter Field Jefferson's dubious legacy would be carried on by a grandson who did not possess the Jefferson name.

Beginnings at Snowden

In the late 1780s, Peter Field was born to Anne (Lewis) and Randolph Jefferson. The family lived at Snowden, Randolph Jefferson's plantation, situated at the northern tip of Buckingham County, Virginia, on the south bank of the James River's Horseshoe Bend. No birth record nor family Bible survives documenting his birth. His name honored his grandfather, Peter Jefferson, and his great uncle, Field Jefferson. Their mother was Mary Field and her father was Maj. Peter Field of St. Peter's Parish, New Kent County, Virginia. Known as "Field" to his family, later in life, he went by Peter F. or P. F. Jefferson. He grew to be an ambitious man though he would never venture far from home, spending most of his adult life living at Scottsville within sight of his birthplace.[1]

Peter Field Jefferson's education was more than adequate. It likely included tutors and neighboring plantation schools, echoing his father's early education. His mother died in about 1800, leaving Randolph Jefferson with his younger sons still to rear, including Field. For nearly a decade, Randolph remained unmarried, surrounded by his children. In late 1802, his daughter, Anna Scott "Nancy" Jefferson, wed Zachariah Nevil of Nelson County, Virginia. In 1808, his son, Thomas Jefferson, Jr., married his double first cousin, Mary Randolph "Polly" Lewis. Baptist minister Rev. Martin Dawson performed both ceremonies.[2]

In about 1807, Zachariah Nevil joined Randolph Jefferson and his oldest sons in a business venture at Snowden. The exact nature of the enterprise is unknown, but it lasted for a few years until Jefferson married again. This time his bride was a much younger woman, Mitchie B. Pryor. The presence of the new Mrs. Jefferson at Snowden permanently divided the family. The business was dissolved. The Nevils and the Thomas Jeffersons left Snowden. Now an adult, Field openly expressed his disapproval at his father's choice in a second wife. Later, Randolph Jefferson would call Field an "undutiful and disrespectful" son.[3]

Despite hard feelings about his father's marriage, Peter Field initially remained in Buckingham County. He owned one slave, his personal servant. Beginning in 1812, Field disappears from the local records. Like his younger brother, James Lilburne Jefferson, he may have joined the Virginia Militia, participating in the War of 1812. The fight against the British satisfied many young men's call to adventure and sense of patriotism. Concurrently, Mitchie Jefferson had become the confident mistress of Snowden, making the plantation an increasingly unwelcoming place for Randolph Jefferson's first family.[4]

When Randolph Jefferson died on August 7, 1815 at the age of fifty-nine, the sons of his first wife and his widow fell into a long and vicious battle over his estate. Court hearings dragged on and, after two years, Mitchie left Virginia for Tennessee, taking her young son, John Randolph Jefferson, with her. There she remarried, leaving Randolph's first family to settle and divide the Buckingham County property. Their brother-in-law, Zachariah Nevil, was named Administrator of the estate. There were outstanding accounts to argue in court and, ultimately, it was necessary to sell Snowden to divide the remaining assets among the five Jefferson brothers. This process would consume the next decade of their lives. While the men waited for their inheritance, they operated Snowden, sought other forms of income, and borrowed from the estate.[5]

~

The war years reduced Peter Field Jefferson's circumstances. In 1815, the year his father died, Peter Field owned neither a slave nor a horse. He settled in Fluvanna County, just across the James River from Buckingham, to the north of Snowden. His older brothers, Thomas and Randolph, Jr., were already established there. Thomas and his wife, Polly, had purchased land located on the Hardware River, near the Fluvanna-Albemarle county line, close to Scott's Ferry and its growing commerce. In late 1813, Randolph, Jr. and his bride, Mary Anne Henderson, were married and settled in Fluvanna. Like Polly, Mary Anne was his Lewis cousin.[6]

Now in his twenties, Peter Field Jefferson was not interested in farming and sought another source of income, one that would eventually make him a rich man—"running goods" on the James River. Initially, Jefferson owned at least one boatman, a slave named Ned Henderson. In the late spring of 1816, Ned ran away and Field placed an advertisement in the newspapers, including Richmond's *Enquirer.* The advertisement reveals him to be a straightforward businessman.

> Thirty Dollars Reward. Runaway from the Subscriber in this City, a Negro Man named Ned Henderson. He is a spare made raw-bone negro, about 5 feet 8 or 9 inches high, had on when he went away a suit of yellow home spun clothes, and has been engaged in running the river for several years. I suspect he is gone to Fluvanna, where he has a wife, belonging to Mr. Henderson near Hardware river, in said County. I will give the above for the delivery of said Negro at Scott's Ferry, in Albemarle, or for securing him in any jail so that I (may) get him again. Peter F. Jefferson. June 8.[7]

Missing slaves were a universal problem in Virginia. Ned, in his privileged and mobile occupation as a boatman, had ample opportunity to slip away, even temporarily, for reasons of his own. His decision may or may not have reflected Peter Field Jefferson's demeanor as a slave holder. Peter Field's brothers, Thomas and Robert Lewis, also placed advertisements for runaway slaves. Thomas Jefferson, Jr. assumed a firm, formal, commanding tone in his advertisement:

> Twenty Dollars Reward–Runaway from the subscriber, on the fifteenth day of September last, a negro man slave, named Gary, aged about twenty-six years, light black complexion, height about six feet, stands quite erect, and when walking handles himself quite nimbly, his weight is one

hundred and sixty or seventy, countenance cast down when spoken to—the white of this [sic] eyes is unusually large, on being apprehended is very surly, he is a rough Cooper. On examination his shins will be found injured—he has probably obtained a free pass. About twelve years ago, Gary was brought from Brunswick county to Surry county in this state, by Mr. Travis Harris, where said boy lived for eight years, and was in the year 1808 purchased by myself of Thomas Edwards and Reuben Butlers ex'ors of said Harris, dec'd out of Surry, and brought to Buckingham, where said negro got a wife, and lived with me about two years on James river, not far from Scotts ferry, and was then brought by myself to Albemarle county, near Milton, from whom said negro eloped—said slave is probably harbored in Surry or some of the above places. I do hereby forewarn all person(s) from harboring said negro. Also, I do command all captains of vessels at sea, not to grant said slave his passage, or take him on board.

The above reward, with all reasonable charges, will be paid to any person taking said slave within this state, and bringing him to me, or else for confining him in any jail in this state, so that I get him again. An additional reward of ten dollars will be given to any person taking said slave out of this state, and for acting with him as above states.

Thomas Jefferson, Jr.
Albemarle county, Virginia. Feb 18, [1812].[8]

Brother Robert Lewis Jefferson, by contrast, wrote his advertisement in a colloquial style:

Runaway, from the Subscriber, living at Scott's Ferry, Albemarle County a negro man, named David, but has been in the habit of altering his name, sometimes passing by the name of Billy Logan. He is a small trim-made fellow, of a dark complexion, about five feet three or four inches high, small sunken eyes, and his forehead tolerably void of hair. This fellow has passed for a free man in August, but at this time it is likely he may be in the neighborhood of Buckingham Court house, or Bent Creek, as he has formerly lived with Mr. Cheek in that neighborhood. Any person who may secure the said fellow so that I may get him, shall receive a reward of Fifteen Dollars.

Robert L. Jefferson, June 18 [1811].[9]

 ⁓

Whether or not Ned Henderson was recovered, over the next few years, Peter Field Jefferson's responsibility for human property increased dramatically. Beginning in 1817, he was taxed on six slaves over the age of sixteen. In 1818, the number jumped to twelve adult slaves. The specifics behind this rapid increase in property are unclear. He may have borrowed against his eventual inheritance, actually purchasing slaves. He may have hired some of the slaves still held in Randolph Jefferson's estate.[10]

During 1816–1817, Peter Field established his residence in Albemarle County where he remained the rest of his life. His youngest brother, James "Lilburne" Jefferson, joined him, becoming postmaster at Scott's Ferry. It was a time and a place full of promise for two unattached men looking forward to a substantial inheritance. The bachelor brothers seized the opportunity to live differently from their parents, their elder brothers, their rural cousins, and the country folk they knew growing up at Snowden. The frontier west of Albemarle, Fluvanna, and Buckingham counties was about to make slow, but steady, steps forward. These two Jefferson brothers were poised to be among the first to move with it, helping establish a new town on the James River.[11]

The Birth of Scottsville on the James River

The summer of 1815 brought a convergence that would profoundly shape the lives of the Jefferson brothers—their father's death in August and the concurrent beginnings of a town at Scott's Ferry. Ironically, it was the Coles brothers not the Scott family who created the first grid of sixteen town lots and offered them for sale. Walter, John, Isaac, Tucker, and Edward Coles had inherited land along the James River from their father, John Coles II. William Woods, a.k.a. "Surveyor Billy," surveyed a fraction of it, roughly seven to eight acres, creating the lots that would become Scottsville.[12]

On October 7, 1815, Peter Field Jefferson was one of the first individuals to purchase a town lot, responding to the Coles' advertisement for a public sale:

Lots of land for sale, at Scott's Ferry.
FREQUENT application having been made to the Subscribers, for the purchase of Grounds at Scott's Ferry, in the County of Albemarle, for the purpose of erecting Lumber-Houses, &c. for the receipt of the produce

of this and many Counties beyond the Blue-Ridge—They will offer, at Public Sale, on Saturday the seventh day of October next, on the premises, from 15 to 20 lots of Ground, of different sizes, lying immediately adjoining the ferry, and extending from the River, (between the lots at present built upon,) to the top of the hill.

A credit of twelve months will be given the purchasers, upon their giving bonds with approved security.

WALTER COLES,
JOHN COLES,
ISAAC COLES.

At the same time and place, and on the same terms, will be offered at public sale, a TRACT OF LAND, in the property of Col. John Coles, dec'd. Containing 400 acres, lying in the County of Fluvanna, within two miles of Scott's Ferry, and on the road leading from thence to Richmond.[13]

On the deed to his purchased land, Jefferson was described as "Fields" Jefferson of the County of Buckingham. He agreed to pay $69.00 cash—"in hand"—for lot #6.[14]

The Jefferson clan had long known the Coles family. Col. John Coles, II did business with future president Thomas Jefferson and, when the British invaded Monticello in 1781, Coles gave refuge to Jefferson and his family at his home, Enniscorthy. There, Coles reared a large and prosperous family. Typical of Virginia's elite gentry class, his sons, who inherited a vast estate in southern Albemarle and Amherst counties, went on to become planters, enter politics, and serve in the national government.[15]

Walter Coles (1772–1854) was established at Woodville, where his father built a house for him in 1796. He also invested extensively in Scottsville. John Coles, III (1774–1848) lived at Calycanthus Hill and Estouteville at Green Mountain. Isaac A. Coles (1780–1841) inherited the original house at Enniscorthy, where their mother, Rebecca Elizabeth (Tucker) Coles (1750–1826), lived until her death. Isaac served as secretary to President Thomas Jefferson and, later, as private secretary to President James Madison. Tucker Coles (1782–1861), farmed Tallwood, originally the "Upper Quarter" of Enniscorthy, and entered Virginia state politics. The youngest brother, Edward Coles (1786–1848), inherited a farm on the Rockfish River in adjacent Amherst County. He replaced his brother, Isaac, as private secretary to President Madison. Later, Edward made a radical decision to remove to Illinois and free his slaves, becoming the first Governor of Illinois.[16]

~

When Peter Field Jefferson decided to invest in this new town, his father had been dead just two months and the Jefferson family was immersed in what would become a lengthy court battle with Randolph Jefferson's widow, Mitchie. Peter Field's home at Snowden was not a peaceful place and a single lot across the river held the promise of new beginnings for the ambitious twenty-seven year old. The parcel lay just east of Ferry Street. Like his grandfather and his father before him, Peter Field Jefferson would desire, and eventually own, the ferry landing and valuable parcels adjacent it.[17]

TAX RECORDS for SCOTT'S FERRY/ SCOTT'S LANDING TOWN LOTS — 1817
The Coles' Subdivision

Owner	Lot(s)	Value	Tax
Tucker Coles - Albemarle	water lot (?)	$25	$0.75
Tucker Coles -	8, 9	$20	$0.60
John Coles -	1, 7	$20	$0.60
Walter Coles -	2, 4, 12, 13	$80	$2.40
Sam'l Dyer, Jnr. -	¼ of lot	$20	$0.60
Fields Jefferson -	6	$25	$0.75
Jacob Moon -	10	$10	$0.30
Wm. Moon & Sam'l Dyer, Jnr. -	9	$25	$0.75
Martin Thacker -	10, 11	$25	$0.75
Randolph Turner - Kentucky	3	$50	$1.50[18]

The Coles lots sold quickly. Inspired by their success, John Scott, who was related to the Jeffersons through the Randolph family, soon followed their lead, petitioning the Virginia General Assembly for the right to establish a town, as well as a tobacco and flour inspection warehouse, on his property at Scott's Landing. His request was granted and, on January 22, 1818, the resulting Act declared:

> Fifteen acres of land, the property of John Scott, at a place on James River called Scott's landing, in the County of Albemarle, so soon as the

same be laid off into lots with convenient streets, be established a town by the name of Scottsville; and that Samuel Dyer, sen., Samuel Dyer, jun., Christopher Hudson, Tucker Coles and John Coles, gentlemen, be, and they are hereby appointed trustees thereof.[19]

On May 20, 1818, William Woods surveyed the Scott land, creating a second and larger grid of lots, alleys, and streets.[20] The new town lots were situated directly north of the tip of Buckingham County and the low lands of Snowden, still held in Randolph Jefferson's estate. By August 5th, John Scott was selling parcels which lay to the east of Albemarle's Old Courthouse. There Scott's Landing had been established in the 18th century on the land of Daniel Scott and, beginning in 1745, a ferry ran across the James River, from Scott's land to what would become Peter Jefferson's "Snowdon" on the south bank.[21]

In early 1818, shortly following John Scott's petition, Peter Field purchased his second, and considerably more expensive town lot, paying Scott $350.00 for a lot adjacent one belonging to Capt. John Harris of Viewmont. The deed describes him as Peter F. Jefferson of Albemarle County. At the end of the year, Lilburne Jefferson bought lots #43 and #44, paying $296.[22] By 1820, the Jefferson brothers, still awaiting their inheritance, had not developed their lots.

The distinction between the Coles and Scott subdivisions soon fell away and the place was referred to interchangeably as Scott's Ferry, Scott's Landing, and, ultimately, Scottsville. Gradually structures rose on the once empty lots, with various businesses catering to the traffic moving through the town and to the growing local population. John Scott built a stone warehouse on lot #12 at the eastern end of River Street and planned a second warehouse for lot #24, which backed up to #12. A tavern sat at the eastern end of Jackson Street and the Moon family erected a residence and a brick store house on lot #36, across Main Street from Scott's warehouses, firmly establishing the east end of Scott's subdivision as a commercial district.[23] By 1817, the Moons were the town's foremost merchants. "Moon, Perkins and Co.," William Moon, Jr., and "Jacob Moon & Co.," each paid $20.00 per year to Albemarle's High Sheriff for licenses to peddle their wares.[24]

Peter Field Jefferson Takes a Bride

On November 21, 1819, the up-and-coming and mature Peter Field Jefferson, wed his youthful cousin, Jane Woodson Lewis. Peter Field was about thirty years old; Jane had just turned twenty-one. They were married in Fluvanna County by local Methodist Episcopal minister, John Goodman. Both of Jane's parents were dead and it is likely that her aunt, Mary Randolph "Polly" (Lewis) Jefferson, and her new brother-in-law, Thomas Jefferson, Jr., hosted the wedding at their Fluvanna farm on the Hardware River. It is also possible that the Jefferson–Lewis family pressured Peter Field Jefferson to marry his young cousin. He had delayed, maybe even avoided, marriage and his cousin needed a home and protection.[25]

Born on October 10, 1798, Jane Woodson Lewis was roughly a decade younger than her new husband and a generation removed from him. Like his older brothers, Thomas and Randolph, Peter Field perpetuated a family practice by marrying his Lewis cousin. In Jane's case, both of her parents were Lewises, further narrowing the bloodlines of this intermarriage.

~

Lewis–Jefferson–Randolph

1. Peter Jefferson m.
   Jane Randolph

2. Randolph Jefferson m.
   Anne Lewis

3. Peter Field Jefferson

1. Charles Lewis, Jr. m.
   Mary Randolph

2. Col. Charles L. Lewis m.
   Lucy Jefferson

3. Lilburne Lewis m.
   Elizabeth J. Lewis

4. Jane Woodson Lewis

~

Jane's early life was a roller coaster of luxury, hardship and tragedy, giving her a shaky start. Born into comfortable circumstances in Albemarle County, Virginia, within a few years she was taken to Hanover County, Virginia where her family lived for two or three years, then was uprooted again and transplanted to far Western Kentucky along with many members of her extended Lewis family who were in search of a new beginning. This exodus included her grandparents, Charles L. and Lucy (Jefferson) Lewis, as well as her parents, Lilburne and Elizabeth Jane (Lewis) Lewis. They settled in Livingston County, Kentucky and established a farm with the decidedly unfertile sounding name of Rocky Hill.[26]

This move was primarily motivated by the family's financial collapse. President Thomas Jefferson, Charles L. Lewis' brother-in-law, witnessed and commented on the decline of the Lewis family. In 1792, he had observed, "C. L. Lewis is becoming one of our wealthiest people."[27] As the decade progressed, Jefferson watched the Lewis fortune plummet, eventually comparing the family's circumstances to a "shipwreck."[28]

By the turn of the century, Charles L. Lewis' debts had mounted to a debilitating degree. The family sold the majority of their slaves. In 1802, Lewis transferred 400 acres, including his manor house, to his son-in-law, Craven Peyton. He soldiered on, keeping up appearances, until July of 1802, when he and Lucy deeded half of their 1,300-acre tract to their son Charles, who was engaged to marry Peter Field Jefferson's sister, Anna Scott Jefferson. Almost a century later, Charles L. Lewis would be described as "taciturn, moody, abstracted and queer." At the very least, by 1807, as the family prepared to leave for Kentucky with no intentions of returning to Virginia, he was a beaten man.[29]

In the early days of the 19th century, this part of Kentucky, bordering the Ohio River, was mostly raw wilderness. Livingston County was a violent place, full of crude, brawling frontiersmen, who would just as soon gouge your eyes out as stab you. Unsurprisingly, the Charles L. Lewis family was outstanding in the neighborhood for their comparatively refined ways.[30]

Likewise, the Lilburne Lewis family was firmly established at their farm, Rocky Hill, when Jane's mother died on April 25, 1809. Elizabeth Lewis was twenty-seven years old. Her stunned widower was left with five young children to rear.[31]

As 1809 progressed, sickness plagued the Lewis household, including malaria. To what degree Jane suffered is unknown. In the fall of that year, Lilburne Lewis traveled to Lexington, Kentucky to request the job of enumerator for the 1810 census for Livingston County and was awarded the appointment. He also deposited his oldest daughters, Jane and Lucy, with a teacher in Mercer County, Kentucky, south of Lexington, in the kinder, gentler Bluegrass country. There, the girls would benefit from a more cultivated atmosphere, safe from the isolation of Rocky Hill and the violent nature of Livingston County.[32]

According to Boynton Merrill, author of *Jefferson's Nephews: A Frontier Tragedy*, the girls remained there for about eighteen months:

> [The region] not only had better schools than were available in Livingston, but also was comparatively free of malaria because of the excellent drainage of the limestone-based soil. It must have been in Lilburne's mind that

he, a widower, was not able to provide the feminine attending that girls of nine and eleven years required. In mid-December in Mercer County, probably in or near Harrodsburg, Lilburne made an agreement with one William C. Bradburn to board, lodge, and wash for the two girls at the cost of $100 per year "to be paid annually or at the end of their boarding." Lilburne agreed to pay Bradburn extra to have clothes made for the girls. Bradburn also, "at the special insistence and request of him the said Lilburne," sent the two girls to a dancing school for three months.[33]

The girls likely received conventional schooling appropriate to their ages in addition to the dancing lessons. In 1811, however, their stay was cut short. After eighteen months in William Bradburn's care, Lilburne Lewis had failed to pay his daughters' expenses. The girls were sent home to Livingston County. Now roughly thirteen and eleven years old, Jane and Lucy returned to a deeply unhappy household. Their father had married a "beautiful belle of the county," Letitia Rutter, who was pregnant with their first child.[34] According to Lewis family tradition, Lilburne, under increasing financial and domestic stress, began to drink heavily.[35] In addition to the mounting chaos at Rocky Hill, the girls returned to the painful absences of their grandmother Lucy (Jefferson) Lewis, who died in May of 1810, and their uncle, Randolph Lewis, who died in early 1811.[36]

Then, on a wild night in December of 1811, Lilburne Lewis' distress mounted, resulting in the gruesome murder of his young slave named George. His brother, Isham Lewis, was also implicated in George's death. The catastrophe culminated in Lilburne Lewis' suicide and Isham Lewis' escape from jail. Lilburne's shocking last will named his children and described his widow as his "beloved but cruel wife" Letitia.[37]

If George was killed and "cremated" in the Lewis kitchen, as early reports indicated, both the sounds and the smell of burning flesh would have reached the Lewis dwelling house. The night of the murder, the very pregnant Letitia was likely confined to her home. The children, including Jane, were probably at home and terrified in their beds.[38]

~

Concurrent with the calamity befalling the Lewis family, Jane's emotional shock was compounded by the reoccurring physical shocks of a trembling earth that lasted for weeks. All the Lewises in Western Kentucky felt the ongoing, jarring effects of the catastrophic New Madrid earthquakes, which continued into 1812.

The first quake was at 2:00 AM on December 16, 1811, just hours after the murder of the slave George. The epicenter was only 75 miles south of Livingston County. It was followed by what must have seemed like endless aftershocks and subsequent quakes, so relentless as to drive a sane person mad. The force was enough to make the Mississippi River run backwards.[39]

John Bradbury, a Fellow of the Linnean Society, was on the river on the night of the first quake and recorded his experience in his book, *Travels in the Interior of America in the Years 1809, 1810 and 1811*, writing:

> After supper, we went to sleep as usual: about ten o'clock, and in the night I was awakened by the most tremendous noise, accompanied by an agitation of the boat so violent, that it appeared in danger of upsetting. Before I could quit the bed, or rather the skin, upon which I lay, the four men who slept in the other cabin rushed in and cried out in the greatest terror, "O mon Dieu! Monsieur Bradbury, qu'est ce qu'il y a?" I passed them with some difficulty, and ran to the door of the cabin, where I could distinctly see the river as if agitated by a storm; and although the noise was inconceivably loud and terrific, I could distinctly hear the crash of falling trees, and the screaming of the wild fowl on the river, but found that the boat was still safe at her moorings. . . .
>
> By the time we could get to our fire, which was on a large flag, in the stern of the boat, the shock had ceased; but immediately the perpendicular banks, both above and below us, began to fall into the river in such vast masses, as nearly to sink our boat by the swell they occasioned. . . .
>
> At day-light we had counted twenty-seven shocks.[40]

The compounded effect of the quakes was tantamount to living in a war zone. Many believed it was the Wrath of God and the end times. Lilburne Lewis may have believed it was direct retribution for his murder of George. The extended experience was more than enough to put the fear of God into many residents of the mid-west and upper south. The Methodist Church, in particular, jumped in membership. Jane Woodson Lewis, who was old enough to make decisions of faith, ultimately abandoned her Lewis family's Presbyterianism, becoming a Methodist. It is entirely possible that her conversion happened during 1812.[41]

This natural cataclysm was echoed in the Lewis family, which sustained ever mounting personal shocks. In early 1812, Mary Howell (Lewis) Lewis, Randolph Lewis' widow, died leaving eight children, seven of whom were under twenty-one and in need of guardians. Jane's first cousin, Charles Lilburne Lewis, would soon turn twenty-one and would be able to rent his father's farm and hire one of the family's slaves, Andrew, maintaining a shred of continuity. The next son, Howell Lewis, was old enough to choose his own guardian following his mother's death, as was his brother, fourteen-year-old Tucker, who was close to Jane's age. Jane's younger cousins, Mary, Lucy, Susannah, Robert Randolph (called Randolph), and Warner, who was not yet two, became the responsibility of their grandfather, Charles L. Lewis, and his three unmarried daughters.[42]

Within weeks of Mary Howell Lewis' death, Jane's father, Lilburne Lewis, committed suicide, leaving a second set of Lewis orphans: Jane, Lucy, Lilburne, Elizabeth, and Robert. Letitia Lewis' son, James, had been taken away from Rocky Hill to live with her Rutter family. A year would pass before legal guardians were named for these Lewis orphans. While they awaited the Court's decision, they relied on the kindness of neighbors and their enslaved "family"—the men, women, and children who had witnessed George's murder. These men and women were no doubt fearful for their fate, as well as indignant in response to George's horrific death. At thirteen, Jane Woodson Lewis became, by default, head of this Lewis household. Her burdens and sorrows were great.[43]

It was not long before the murder of the slave George became national news. A report from Russellville, Kentucky, printed on April 22, 1812, under the lurid headline, "Murder! Horrid Murder!," was quickly reprinted in the *Kentucky Gazette* (Lexington) on May 12th and in Washington, D.C.'s *Courier* on May 27th.[44]

Russellville, April 22.

Murder! Horrid Murder!

A gentleman from Livingston county informs that the two brothers, Captain Lilburn and Isham Lewis, who were tried and admitted to bail during the last circuit court of that county, for murdering a negro boy, (the property of the former) and burning him on a kitchen fire on the night of the 25th [sic] December last, mutually agreed, the week before last, to destroy each other, and met with their rifles for that purpose on the plantation of Captain Lilburn Lewis. Lilburn stood on his first wife's grave—Isham a few steps from him—Lilburn received a ball through his heart and fell without discharging his gun, was found cocked and loaded on the ground with him. This shocking affair is said to have been occasioned by the flight of Captain Lewis' wife, who made her escape to save her life, as it was feared that her evidence would be admitted against Isham as an aider and abettor of the horrid deed with which her husband stood charged. Isham is confined in Salem jail, where it is said he confessed the above particulars, but at present, denies them.[45]

As the years went by, Lilburne Lewis' sordid tale would be used as anti-slavery propaganda, notably by abolitionist William Lloyd Garrison in his widely-read *Liberator*. The scandalous press no doubt humiliated Jane and her family. In 1841, journalists still stated that the Lewis crime would never be forgotten. They were remarkably correct.[46]

The Livingston County Court temporarily deposited the Lewis children in several households. Initially, Jane was sent to the Salem District to live with James Henderson, a blacksmith, Justice of the Peace, and one of the men who inventoried her father's property.[47]

In June of 1812, the auction of Lilburne Lewis' estate at Rocky Hill lasted for two days. Letitia secured one third of the estate—her dower right—and attended the auction, spending nearly $90.00, buying things she had enjoyed while she was Lilburne Lewis' wife. Some of the articles she purchased she may have brought into the marriage.[48]

Lilburne Lewis' personal property offers insight into Jane Lewis' life before her mother's death and the deterioration of her father's mind. In addition to farming and household basics, Lewis owned an impressive library, complete with bookcase. His books included the works of Benjamin Franklin; a volume of "Guthrie's Grammar" (*Guthrie's Grammar: A Geographical, Historical, and Commercial Grammar: and Present State of Several Nations of the World*, 1795) and a dictionary; the life of George Washington and Washington's letters; the life of Napoleon Bonaparte; the revised *Code of Virginia*; two volumes of *Bartram's Travels* (1791); a history of America; and Thomas Jefferson's *Notes on the State of Virginia* (c.1787). There were volumes on spelling, philosophy, and geography; eight volumes of the English publication, *The Spectator*; part of a Bible; and a copy of *Robinson Crusoe*.[49]

Following the estate sale, for the immediate future, there were sufficient funds to cover the childrens' expenses. Some of the monies that Letitia and the children might have inherited, once the land and slaves were sold, could have been claimed by the Livingston County Court. When Lilburne killed himself, he voided his $1,000 bail bond. Additionally, Isham Lewis' ultimate escape from jail meant that his $500 bond could be demanded from his brother's estate. There were other claims on the estate, including doctors' bills and the unpaid tuition and board costs for Jane and Lucy.[50]

Almost a year following the estate sale, in May of 1813, Jane and her siblings were finally assigned permanent legal guardians. Jane, now fourteen and one-half years old, became the ward of Gen. Jonathan Ramsey of Livingston County. In 1810, he owned fifteen slaves and had several young children of his own, plus two mature, unidentified women (age 26–44) living in his household. Apparently, there was room for one more and Jane had the opportunity to live with a family whose social position was commensurate with her Virginia origins.[51]

Gen. Ramsey was a founding father of Livingston County. A lawyer, surveyor, and one of the county's original Magistrates, his accomplishments read like those of Jane's great-grandfather Peter Jefferson. Ramsey was intimately acquainted with the Lewis family. Both Randolph and Lilburne Lewis served under him while he was Colonel in the Militia. Following the murder of George, he was one of Lilburne's original bondsmen and it was Ramsey who sent Isham Lewis to jail, following Lilburne's suicide.[52]

~

Jane was the only one among her siblings who returned to Virginia.[53] Changes in her grandfather's situation likely prompted her trip home. In May of 1814, Charles L. Lewis relinquished his guardianship of Randolph and Mary Howell Lewis' orphans, consequently, there was little left to hold him in Kentucky. Over the next year, he and his daughters became increasingly destitute, looking toward relations in Virginia for a solution.[54]

Back in Virginia, Jane's aunt Mary Randolph "Polly" Lewis had married Thomas Jefferson, Jr., eldest brother to Peter Field Jefferson. By 1813, these Jeffersons were living in Fluvanna County, on the Hardware River, not far from Scott's Landing on the James River. Sometime after August of 1815, Thomas Jefferson, Jr., went to Kentucky to bring his father-in-law back to Virginia. It is very likely that Jane Woodson Lewis returned with them.[55]

Awaiting them was another aunt, Jane (Lewis) Peyton, who had maintained the Lewis home, Monteagle, with her husband, Craven Peyton.[56] Monteagle should have been a welcome Virginia refuge for the Kentucky Lewises, however, beginning in 1814, family intrigue was brewing that would sever members of Charles L. Lewis family from the Peytons. Jane was blameless in this quarrel and, as such, was likely welcome at Monteagle. In the final analysis, even Charles L. Lewis was forgiven by the Peytons. According to his grandson, Charles L. Peyton, the old man died at Monteagle in 1828.[57]

Monteagle was one of Jane's childhood homes, a refined place compared to Rocky Hill. In 1799, Charles L. Lewis insured two dwellings, connected by a "wooden-covered way:" a one-story building, valued at $400, and a two-story building, 24x22 feet, valued at $800.[58] In Craven Peyton's day, the dwelling at Monteagle was beautifully appointed with both useful and decorative furniture. A desk, a secretary, and a bookcase were used by Peyton, a businessman, as well as a planter. A Mahogany tea table, three walnut dining tables and twenty-five chairs stood ready for the mistress of the house to entertain. Jane Peyton's many guests ate with silver spoons. Twenty paintings graced the walls.[59]

When Jane Woodson Lewis returned to Albemarle County, Craven Peyton owned approximately thirty-five slaves, seventeen of whom worked in agriculture. Others attended the family. Their enslaved children were coming of age at Monteagle, assuring the next generation of laborers. Horses and colts were plentiful. A dozen working oxen plowed the fields. Another dozen "milch cows" filled the dairy. Cattle and calves, fifty old sheep and twenty-five lambs dotted the rolling landscape. Hogs, shoats, and pigs fed the family and their servants. Wool was abundant and tobacco grew well at Monteagle, as did oats. There was a blacksmith in residence. A carriage awaited the Peytons' pleasure. Charlottesville was not far away, convenient for Court Day and shopping.[60]

If Jane Woodson Lewis ever had an opportunity to be carefree and comfortable, it was at Monteagle. She would never again enjoy this opulent life.[61]

∾

What was the character, personality, and countenance of this young cousin Peter Field Jefferson chose to marry? Many years later, as a woman in her sixties, Jane was described as an odd, withdrawn person. Understandably so. Her early life had been shaped by a cluster of traumas: beginning with her family's financial embarrassment and displacement to Kentucky; followed by the death of her mother and grandmother; the reported cruelty of her stepmother; and the shocking suicide of her father. She was thirteen when her father died, a murderer and likely insane.

Behind her Jefferson–Lewis heritage lurked the Randolph family's corrupted gene pool. Long after the murder of George, Lilburne Lewis' actions were reevaluated in light of the Randolph family history and "modern" psychology. In 1894, Atlanta H. Taylor Pool wrote: "It had occurred to more than one of the thoughtful men of the community that Lilburn's deed was the result of hereditary insanity."[62] Did Jane harbor fears of losing her mind? She could have and, maybe, should have, when she knew that the father of her children also carried a "double set" of Randolph genes.

As years went on, Jane's own marriage, particularly the role of motherhood, would prove challenging. In middle-age, she was described as a woman of low intelligence who kept to herself and was highly susceptible to the influence of others. According to neighbor George W. Dawson, "I don't think she was associated with anybody & I don't think she was a very intelligent woman."[63]

During her marriage, she co-signed deeds with her husband, though she may not have understood the details of his businesses or investments. It is even possible that, late in life, she was coerced into legal actions beyond her comprehension. In 1862, Jane acknowledged her last will with "her mark." Since she had signed deeds in the past, her inability to put her signature on her will may have been the result of infirmity, emotional stress, or mental diminishment due to age.[64]

Peter Field Jefferson's motivations for marrying his cousin are unknown; however, especially among this Lewis–Jefferson family, intermarriage with close cousins was deeply imbedded in the family culture. That he marry one cousin or another was probably assumed. Perhaps, the family agreed that Peter Field Jefferson, unmarried and well-established, was the man to care for Jane. Pity could have played a part in his decision. She had little wealth to bring to his household; it would be years before she received a distribution from her father's estate.[65] On the contrary, she brought with her personal liability, the effects of hardship and trauma, as well as shame. Jane may have been grateful and compliant, characteristics valued in a 19th-century wife.

In 1818, Peter Field Jefferson purchased two more lots in what would become Scottsville. One contained a structure valued at $120. It seems likely that this is where Jane and Peter Field Jefferson set up housekeeping in the fall of 1819. It had been a long road from Monteagle and Buck Island, to a log house in Western Kentucky, to the muddy streets of Scott's Landing.[66]

The Ongoing Responsibility of Snowden

By 1820, the Peter Field Jeffersons were settled in Albemarle County, awaiting the birth of their first child. Their immediate neighbors at Scott's Landing included several members of the Moon family and Thompson Noel, who ran a tavern and inn.[67]

Unlike the majority of his brothers, Peter Field did not aspire to the agrarian life of their youth. He was attracted to commerce. On October 26, 1821, he purchased a third town lot, though the deed was not recorded until the following spring. This lot was adjacent Richard Moon's "Store Houses." He paid John Scott a mere $15.00. Perhaps, this low price settled other financial agreements between the men.[68]

Despite Peter Field Jefferson's deepening commitment to the development of Scottsville, he still shared the responsibility for his father's estate and the management of Snowden. During 1822, he lived in Buckingham County, paying personal property tax there on himself, twelve slaves, and four horses. The majority of the real estate and, likely, much of Randolph Jefferson's personal and human property remained in the yet-to-be divided estate. That year, Field's younger brother, Lilburne, lived in Buckingham as well. Still a bachelor, Lilburne was taxed on two slaves and a horse. The following year, in 1823, their brother, Robert Lewis Jefferson, resided in Buckingham County, apparently taking over the management of Snowden. Peter Field returned to Scott's Landing while Lilburne remained in Buckingham.[69]

During this period, Jefferson's brother-in-law, Zachariah Nevil, acted as Administrator of Randolph Jefferson's estate, actively trying to sell the farm in total, scheduling an auction on November 1, 1822. If Snowden failed to sell for an acceptable price, he planned to rent it for a year.

Valuable James River Land For Sale.

Will be sold to the highest bidder in the town of Scottsville, Albemarle county, on the 1st of November next, the tract of land lying in Buckingham county, on James river, belonging to the estate of Randolph Jefferson, dec'd containing upwards of 1500 acres, of which 180 are river bottoms; a considerable proportion of the high lands is first rate. The tract abounds with a plenty of good timber. A further description is deemed unnecessary, as it is presumed purchaser will view the land prior to the day of sale; I will only add, the advantages that attend this land entitle it to rank of any tract of its size in the upper country. The payments will be accommodating, and made known on the day of sale. Those wishing to view the land are referred to Mr. Peter F. Jefferson, who lives on the premises.

Should the land not be sold on the above mentioned day, it will be RENTED for twelve months.

ZACH. NEVEL [sic], Adm'rer with the will annexed of Randolph Jefferson dec'd.[70]

That autumn, the farm did not sell. Peter Field Jefferson returned to Scottsville and, during 1824 and 1825, his brothers Robert Lewis and James Lilburne apparently resumed management of Snowden. Finally, during 1826–1829, the farm was conveyed to Capt. John Harris of Viewmont, Albemarle County. The first installment was paid to the estate on September 29, 1826; the last payment was to be collected on June 10, 1829.[71] Precisely how the funds from the sale were distributed among Randolph Jefferson's legatees is not known; however, at least one of the Jefferson brothers immediately invested his new funds. In about 1828, Robert Lewis Jefferson completed the purchase of a 531-acre plantation located in northeastern Buckingham County on Sharps Creek.[72]

Prior to the sale of Snowden, significant monies were borrowed from the estate not only by family members but also by Scottsville developers, John Scott and William Moon. On October 14, 1820, Administrator Zachariah Nevil attempted to recover $1,000 that Scott owed the estate. The Albemarle County Court settled the matter, demanding a payment of $500, with interest, from December 25, 1819. This claim was followed on May 7, 1822, when Nevil initiated another complaint against John Scott and William Moon, claiming a debt of $1,167.88 to Jefferson's estate. Again the debt was discharged with a lesser amount: $583.94 with interest from October 17, 1821.[73]

Both John Scott and William Moon were deeply invested in Scottsville's development. Scott sold his own land to establish the town and, in 1821, Moon significantly expanded his holdings, purchasing 655 acres known as Lower Plantation, located on Totier Creek, adjacent Scottsville and directly across the

James River from Snowden. The sellers were John Scott and Elizabeth (Scott) Wood. With this purchase, Moon overextended himself and soon sold the property to cover debts, some of which he owed Randolph Jefferson's estate.[74]

John Scott III (1796–1829) was a youthful entrepreneur, close in age to Peter Field Jefferson. They were distant Randolph cousins. Their family alliances soon tightened further when Scott married Susan Bathurst Bolling on May 15, 1823. Susan was the granddaughter of Mary (Jefferson) and John Bolling and the great-niece of Randolph Jefferson. Susan's parents, were John "Jack" and Mary Willis (Kennon) Bolling of Fairfields, Chesterfield County, Virginia. The family, however, maintained close ties to Albemarle County.[75]

The Scotts celebrated their wedding at Monticello, surrounded by their Randolph–Jefferson cousins. In a letter written from Monticello on June, 5, 1823, Thomas Jefferson's granddaughter, Virginia J. (Randolph) Trist, recounted part of the story:

> I must not omit my only piece of news, the marriage of Susan Bolling and John Scott and their intended removal to Alabama, in a few days. they dined with us the day before yesterday, and Susans Beauty is more resplendent than ever, and her countenance I think improves as she a[d]vances in life, which is a good sign of her intellect.[76]

Shortly after their marriage, the newlyweds moved to Somerville, Alabama. Their oldest daughter, Pocahontas Bolling Scott, was born there on July 22, 1825. John Scott died in Huntsville, Alabama on August 14, 1829. He was just thirty years old. His abrupt departure from Scottsville has never been fully explained. Like William Moon, Scott may have seriously overextended himself and creditors became a problem. Following his death, Scott's widow, Susan, and their three daughters returned to Scottsville where they were aided financially by Edward Harris Moon, great-nephew and heir of Capt. John Harris.[77]

～

The extended Moon family maintained a strong presence in Scottsville's commerce. Surviving journals and ledgers for William Moon's Stoney Point store, reveal that the Jefferson brothers—Peter Field, Thomas, Isham Randolph, and their youngest brother, James Lilburne—all did business with Moon. Located just north of Scott's Landing, Stoney Point was convenient to the Hardware River and Fluvanna County. By the 1820s, the Jefferson brothers were doing business with John Digges Moon, the eldest son of William Moon.[78]

John D. Moon's surviving store ledgers reveal his customers' debts and credits, while his journals list their purchases. In these pages, the Jefferson brothers come to life. On September 2, 1822, Isham Randolph Jefferson bought shot, powder, coffee, and brown sugar. Five days later, he was back at the store to purchase a pocket handkerchief. On September 24th, Peter Field stopped in to buy nails and ½ a gallon of whiskey. As the days grew cooler, he returned on October 5th to purchase a "Fine Furr Hat" for the impressive sum of $5.00.[79]

In July of 1822, widower Isham Randolph Jefferson married for the second time—his cousin, Margaret Gwatkins Peyton. That fall, he shopped at Moon's store, improving their kitchenware, buying plates and dishes. Either there was a flaw in the dishes or the new Mrs. Jefferson didn't care for his choice. Later that day, her husband was sent back to the store to return them![80]

The Loss of Snowden

In 1826, Snowden was taxed for the last time in Randolph Jefferson's estate. Though the exact details of the transaction between Zachariah Nevil, Administrator and Capt. John Harris, Grantee are lost, the Buckingham County land tax records for 1827 indicate that, during the previous year, the land remaining in Randolph Jefferson's estate was conveyed by the Administrator to John Harris of Albemarle, adding Snowden to Harris' expansive network of plantations, mills, and commercial ventures. In 1828, Harris was taxed on Snowden's remaining 1,445 acres, which he nearly lost in early 1829 when he was delinquent with a payment. On January 31, 1829, this advertisement began running in the *Richmond Enquirer*. In it, trustees for the Randolph Jefferson estate pressed Harris by threatening to put the property up for sale.

Valuable James River Land For Sale.

By virtue of a Trust Deed executed by John Harris to us, to secure to Zachariah Nevil certain sums of money, dated the 29th Sept 1826, and recorded in the Clerk's Office of Buckingham county 24th December 1828; in conformity to the request of said Nevil, in order to pay the two last installments secured by the deed, viz: four thousand dollars due the 10th of June 1828, and the same sum due the 10th June 1829; and to pay the charges of sale, we shall, on the premises proceed on the 21st day of March next, to sell for cash, the tract of land in the deed of trust mentioned, called Snowden, lying in Buckingham, supposed to contain (—) acres; the tract contains a large quantity of most valuable low grounds, and the high land is perhaps the finest tobacco land in Buckingham county; it lies on James River opposite Scottsville, and the late residence of Randolph Jefferson, dec'd. It is probable that the persons interested may make on the day of sale, some modification of the terms so as to allow some credit for a part of the purchase money, in which event the title will be retained till final payment. We believe the title good, but only convey as trustees.

JESSE JOPLING
THOMAS DANIEL[81]

In the end, Harris paid his obligation to the estate and, in 1829, at the advanced age of eighty-two, he became the new squire of Snowden. His plan was to establish his stepson, Thomas Jefferson Barclay, on the plantation.

~

With the sale of Snowden, Peter Field Jefferson received new capital from the estate. Importantly, any responsibility for its management was behind him. At forty, he was about to hit his stride. In 1829, he and Jane were expecting the birth of another child and his namesake, Peter Field Jefferson, Jr., joining daughter, Frances, and two older boys in the Scottsville household. In 1825, Jefferson had purchased another parcel, this time from Richard Moon, paying the top price of $400.[82] Then, concurrent with the final sale of Snowden, in 1829, Jefferson bought Scott's Ferry landing from Martin and Maria Tutwiler, paying $700 for this very valuable piece of Scottsville real estate.[83] The acquisition of the ferry not only provided Peter Field Jefferson with a steady income but also came with some personal satisfaction.

In the 1750s, Peter Field's grandfather, Peter Jefferson, owned the ferry land-ing on the opposite bank at Snowden, complete with an ordinary, offering food, drink, and lodging for those going to and passing through the newly established Albemarle County courthouse, which sat across the river on Daniel Scott's land. The Jeffersons owned the southside ferry landing through Randolph Jefferson's lifetime, Peter Field's boyhood, and beyond. Now, it was the property of Capt.

John Harris, included in the sale of Snowden. Significantly, just as Harris was paying his last installment on Snowden, Peter Field Jefferson acquired the ferry landing on the Scottsville side, evening the score. It would be the first, but not the last, time that Peter Field Jefferson and his family threw themselves into direct competition or confrontation with the large and wealthy Harris family. Peter Field may have taken the loss of Snowden to the Harrises very personally, for he was the only one of his brothers to remain in Scottsville, looking daily across the James at what was once his family's commanding home on the river. If he couldn't get it back, he would match it.

The loss of Snowden was not the only blow to Peter Field Jefferson's pride and family reputation. At precisely the same moment, his first cousin, Martha (Jefferson) Randolph, was in the process of selling Monticello, facing her father's massive debts, and suffering the public shame of auctioning the former President's property, both real and personal. Dozens of Monticello's slaves stood on the auction block. The eventual buyer of Monticello was none other than the adopted son of Capt. John Harris, Dr. James Turner Barclay. It must have seemed as though the Harris family wanted to own the best of what had once belonged to the Jeffersons . . . and they were succeeding [84]

On June 29, 1831, Thomas Jefferson's granddaughter, Cornelia Jefferson Randolph, wrote to her sister, Ellen Wayles (Randolph) Coolidge, recounting the despair at Monticello:

> We are none of us in very good spirits just now owing to the probability there is of Monticello being sold; Dr. Barclay (one of Mrs. Harris' sons) has offered brother Jeff. his house in Charlottesville (Mr. Hatch's house) and $9000 for the place. The thing is not determined yet; brother Jeff. will not make the bargain unless he can sell the house in Charlottesville; which they say he can do, nor do I believe that Dr. B. is positively determined on the purchase. His offer is quite a liberal one, brother Jeff asks about 12,000 for Monticello and Dr. B. offers him his house for what he gave for it $3500, although he has made improvements in it. . . . There remain $30,000 of the debts still to be paid and the creditors are pressing and he (brother J.) has made nothing from the publication of the manuscripts. . . . He thinks indeed Dr. Barclay will buy land enough around Monticello to make the sum $4000.[85]

On August 15, 1831, Mary Jefferson Randolph wrote to Ellen Wayles (Randolph) Coolidge:

> Monticello is at last sold . . . the house and 500 acres . . . [brother] Jefferson will receive Mr. Hatch's house in Charlottesville at $4000 for which Mr. Carr will . . . give him $3500 down and he will receive $3000 cash I believe from the purchaser Dr. Barclay, the second son of poor Mrs. Barclay that married old Harris. . . . You will say it was a dreadful sacrifice but the debts are pressing, the place going to ruin, and no other offer. . . . [86]

Reading between the lines, "old Harris" was not a family favorite with the Monticello Jeffersons. When Mary Randolph wrote to her sister, Ellen, John Harris was eighty-four years old and would be dead in six months. His wife, Sarah Coleman (Turner) Barclay, age fifty, was considerably younger and livelier. He was born in 1747, she in 1781. Capt. John Harris had been married to Frances Rowzee for forty-one years and, when she died, was left a childless widower. In 1818, when he married the widow, Sarah "Sally" Barclay, she gained financial security and he gained four stepchildren, age nine to fifteen. The Randolph girls may have pitied Sally Harris, but she was far from "poor." Her marriage to John Harris had guaranteed that!

Admittedly, Capt. John Harris was *nouveau riche* and lived accordingly. Harris made sure that his money showed, his dining service was made of gold and he traveled in a costly carriage. When he died, he was purportedly the wealthiest man in Albemarle County. He was not living on credit, he was making money hand over fist. His politics likely diverged widely from Thomas Jefferson's. Harris was friendly with Chief Justice John Marshall, Jefferson's "distant cousin and staunch political foe."[87] Harris was vocal about religion. A prosthelytizer, he gave away dozens of Bibles at his death. By contrast, Jefferson defended religious freedom and edited the Bible to suit himself.[88]

While John Harris and Thomas Jefferson may not have been enemies, they were not exactly friends. An accidental, and somewhat embarrassing, meeting at Warm Springs reveals the cordial distance between the two men. Jefferson had gone to the springs to treat his rheumatism but sitting too long in the sulphuric water resulted in painful boils on his backside. Jefferson, who had ridden his horse to the Springs, was unable to sit in the saddle when it came time to go home. John Harris happened to be there with his splendid carriage. On August 21, 1818, Jefferson wrote to his daughter, Martha:

> A large swelling on my seat, increasing for several days past in size and hardness disables me from sitting but on the corner of a chair. Another swelling begins to manifest itself to-day on the other seat. It happens fortunately that Capt. Harris is here in a carriage alone, and proposes to set out on the same day I had intended. He offers me a seat which I shall gladly accept.[89]

Significantly, four days earlier, Jefferson had written a gossipy letter to Martha, listing notables who were at the Springs, including Cols. John A. and Tucker Coles; Gen. James Breckenridge; and Col. Joseph Allstone. He had not mentioned Capt. John Harris.

Less is known about the relationship between John Harris and the Jeffersons of Snowden; however, even before he purchased the majority of the farm from Randolph Jefferson's estate, Harris had his eye on the rich soil on the Buckingham County side of the Horseshoe Bend. In 1816, Harris began purchasing land in the neighborhood. Initially, he acquired 178 7/8 acres from Charles A. Scott. Only months before his death, Randolph Jefferson had sold that property to Scott.[90]

In 1817, Harris purchased an additional 179 ½ acre tract known as "Murray's." Located on the James River, adjacent Snowden, the former owner was Richard Murray (d. 1772), tavern keeper and planter, who once leased the Snowden Ferry House from Peter Jefferson's estate.[91] In 1822, the structures at Murray's were valued at an impressive $2,400, likely including a substantial dwelling house and, possibly, a functioning mill site. Within a few years, Harris would successfully add Snowden to his expanding property on the south side of the Horseshoe Bend.[92]

Owned and Operated by Peter Field Jefferson

In the 1740s, Daniel Scott established the ferry service at Scott's Landing on the north side of the James River. During the 1750s, Peter Jefferson took over the southside landing at Snowden. Scott and Jefferson were married to sisters, Anne and Jane Randolph. Scott lived on his land, while Jefferson leased his tract on the James River, living about a day's ride north at Shadwell. They had the beginnings of a family business; however, when Scott died c.1754, his widow, Anne, moved back to her family home in Goochland County. Scott's land and the ferry were inherited by his brother, John Scott. Not long after, Peter Jefferson died in the summer of 1757.[93]

In 1789 and 1790, John Scott petitioned Virginia's General Assembly to establish an inspection station for agricultural products at his ferry. These requests were rejected by the legislature in favor of a warehouse and ferry a few miles upriver at the mouth of Ballenger's Creek on the land of Wilson Cary Nicholas to be called "Nicholas's Warehouse." The town of Warren grew up around the Nicholas warehouse and mill, beginning a long competition between Warren and Scottsville for dominance over this section of the James River.[94]

Next, Scott offered twenty acres of his land to establish a town at his ferry; this, too, was rejected. However, by 1792, Scott's petition was finally approved and he established "Scott's Warehouse" at the ferry. At his own expense, he was required to construct a substantial warehouse of "brick or stone, to be covered with slate or tile, and make the gates of iron." Additionally, the legislature established the ferry rates and described it as running "from the land of John Scott, over the Fluvanna, to the lands of Randolph Jefferson."[95]

Between John Scott's death in 1798 and Peter Field Jefferson's acquisition of the ferry at Scottsville, the property changed hands several times. First, it was inherited by Scott's grandson John Scott III (1796–1829).[96] At that time, a new survey of the Horseshoe Bend was completed, showing the "Road leading to the Ferry," with Capt. Randolph Jefferson's land on the south side of the Fluvanna (James) River, opposite Scott's Ferry.[97] In 1821, John Scott III sold the ferry to Thomas O. Henley for $750, who did not hold it long. In 1823, he sold it to Martin Tutwiler for $600. In 1829, Tutwiler profited when he sold it to Peter Field Jefferson for $700.[98] Eventually known as "Jefferson's Ferry," Peter Field Jefferson owned and operated it from about 1829 until his death in 1861.

When Jefferson purchased the ferry, he already owned a store at the ferry landing, selling a variety of goods typical to a country store, including groceries. In 1825, he purchased a Scottsville lot, with a store, from Richard Moon, who then held an Albemarle County Merchant's License. Subsequently, Jefferson paid $20.00 annually for his own license.[99] Men who knew Peter Field Jefferson and his habits commented that, for most of his adult life, he was actively involved in his ferry and store, spending much of his day there.[100]

Jefferson's initial business competition in Scottsville included Daniel Boatwright, Moon and Barclay, Woodson and Staples, and Benjamin M.

Perkins.[101] Interestingly, Scottsville store owners bought merchandise from each other. During 1832, Peter Field Jefferson purchased nails from fellow Scottsville merchant, Benjamin Dennis, who ran a general store, selling bacon, brandy, cotton, flooring, fodder, nails, plaster, salt, shoes, storage space, sugar, timber, tobacco, whiskey, etc. In turn, Mr. Dennis purchased plaster from Mr. Jefferson.[102] In years to come, there was impressive competition from T. K. Lyon & Co., a comparatively magnificent store, selling fancy imports, liquors, and staples such as sugar and coffee.

~

T. K. LYON & CO.
PRODUCE, COMMISSION AND FORWARDING MERCHANTS,
Dealers in Groceries, Wines, Liquors, &c.
SCOTTSVILLE, VA.

T. K. LYON,	W. & J. D. CHRISTIAN,
Scottsville	Richmond.

We have received by recent arrivals from New York Baltimore and Richmond, Via Canal, heavy additions to our stock of Groceries, Wines, Liquors, &c. which, with previous receipts, render our assortment extensive and complete, and to which we would solicit the attention of our customers and the public satisfied we can offer inducements in our line. We would call attention of Connoisseurs, Hotel Keepers, and the retail trade at a distance, particularly to our stock of pure Wines and Liquors of our own importation, and which we can confidently recommend.

The following comprises a portion of our stock, which we offer low for cash, or approved paper.

SUGAR—St. Croix, N. Orleans, Porto Rico, Havana White, Crushed and Refind Leaf.

MOLASSES—New Orleans, Porto Rico and S. H.

COFFEE—Old Java, Laguyra and Rio

WINES—Old L P Madeira, Brown Sherry, Old L Port, Claret, 'Medoc' and Malaga

BRANDIES—Champaigne, Old Cognac, Seignette, Old "3 ½ years" Peach and Apple

GINS—Old Holland, "J A J Nolet Scheidam," and "Rose" Rye

LIQUORS, Ass'd—N E Rum, Rye Whiskey, Cordials, London Porter

TEAS—Gunpowder, Imp., and Y H Teas, and Rice

SALT and FISH—Liverpool filled Salt; No 1 new Herrings

PLAISTER—Lump and Ground, (in tierces 500 lb)

BACON—Todd's Family, Cincinnati cured, hog round, Sides and Shoulders

SOAP—Hull's steam, Krikman's, and fancy Soap[103]

CANDLES—Patent refined hydraulic pres'd and Sperm

NAILS—Boston, Plymouth and Cumberland assorted Nails and Brads

LEATHER—Sole and upper, calf sides

COTTON—Cotton, Cotton Yarns, and Oakum for Calking

WINDOW GLASS—Assorted sizes, 5 and 10 gallon Demijohns, and Kegs

CROCKERY AND STONE WARE—Embracing every description in use

MALAGA RAISINS, Almonds, Pilot Bread and Crackers, Tobacco[104]

CIGARS, Mustard, Pepper, Starch, Nutmegs, Blacking

INDIGO, Bed cords and Lines, black and red Ink, Quills, wrapping, letter and cap Paper, Wafers, Curry Combs

COTTON CARDS, Knives, Scissors, Razors, Patent Threads, &c. &c.

DRY GOODS, 3-4,4-4, bleached and brown Shirtings, Checks, Domestic Plaids, Calicoes, very cheap; Ripka Stripes, Cottonades, Log Cabin Cords, Hdkfs, &c. &c.

HATS AND CAPS—Black Russia, coarse and fine Palm Leaf Hats; Seal and Fur Caps

SHOES—Men's peg'd and sew'd Brogans, Ladies' Seal Slippers, &c. &c. with a variety of other articles.

The highest market price is offered for every description of Country Produce, and our Western friends would do well to call on us before selling.

Having ample room for Storage, we shall devote particular attention to receiving and forwarding every description of Merchandize and Produce consigned to our care.

Advances made on Consignments of Produce addressed to our House in Richmond.

T. K. LYON & CO.

Scottsville, August, 1841[105]

~

Peter Field Jefferson definitely did not cater to connoisseurs. However, he sold whiskey at his store and he made a significant amount of money doing it. In the beginning, at least, he purchased some of his stock from local merchant, John D. Moon. Presumably, Jefferson took Moon's whiskey from the store at Stoney Point, carried it to the river front, and marked it up. On June 26, 1825, Peter Field Jefferson purchased "36 gallons of whiskey @ .34." The sale totaled $12.24. On July 23rd, an identical purchase appears on Moon's books, as well as on August 8, 1825 and on January 2, 1826. Though Peter Field enjoyed his whiskey, clearly, these purchases were not for personal consumption.[106]

In the August 1832 Albemarle County Court, held in Charlottesville, Peter Field Jefferson was granted a liquor license:

> On the motion of Peter F. Jefferson and it appearing to the satisfaction of the court that this is a man of good character, License is granted him to sell by retail spiritous liquors at his store in this county, it also appearing to the satisfaction of the court that his store is a convenience to the neighborhood for the retail of spiritous liquors.[107]

At least in 1832, Jefferson sold whiskey with a legal liquor license. Six years later, however, he was charged with *serving* ardent spirts without a proper license. He won the case, which raises more questions than it answers. On May 1, 1838, Jefferson was summoned by the Sheriff to appear before the Judge of the Circuit Superior Court of Albemarle County. He was charged with having sold "by retail ardent spirits to be drank at the place where sold without any legal license or authority for doing [so]." Evidently, his license allowed him to sell but not serve liquor; that required an ordinary license.[108]

The incident under consideration took place in October of 1837. The case was not settled in the May 1838 Court, continuing to the October 1838 Court. Misters Robert S. McCleland, George Darnielle, Charles A. Jopling, William Dawson, James W. Long, and John Atkinson were called as witnesses. There are no known surviving court transcripts to judge the evidence or Jefferson's defense. On October 11, 1838, the court ruled "not guilty." Court costs totaled $15.78: $5.18 (Clerk), $.60 (Sheriff), and $10.00.[109]

It is possible that Peter Field Jefferson was innocent of the charge. It is also possible that he failed to renew his liquor license, though friends Joseph Walker and Joseph Beal maintained he sold whiskey for years.[110] In the 1930s, R. E. Hannum surveyed the "Site of Store Run by Peter Fields [sic] Jefferson," for the Virginia Historical Inventory, preserving the local oral tradition concerning Jefferson's evasion of the county liquor laws:

> It is said that Mr. Jefferson sold whiskey here, but had a peculiar way of dispensing it. He kept it in a room separate from the store. When a customer wanted his jug filled Mr. Jefferson would enter the other room and close the door, slip a panel and reach out his hand for the jug, fill it and pass it through the hole to the purchaser. He was never seen during the transaction, and often stated that "No one ever saw me sell a drop of liquor."[111]

The store was located south of Main Street, on the west side of Ferry Street, making it the first building a weary traveler approached as he stepped off the ferry at Scottsville. Weary travelers are often thirsty travelers. R. E. Hannum described the structure they encountered:

> The building was of brick, about twenty feet square, a story and a half high, with a cellar, a shingled, [gambrel] roof, and four windows downstairs, two in front, one on each side of the central door. These had six panes to a sash, the two in the back had only four. There were four steps leading up to the door. There were two brick chimneys.
>
> As to the windows in the half-story above there seems to be a considerable difference of opinion. Some think there were four, one on each side of the chimney at each end; others that there were dormer windows, while some say there were small windows in the front and rear walls. Summing up the general ideas, it would seem they were in the ends.
>
> The cellar was divided into two rooms.[112]

Interestingly, by the 20th century, opinions differed about the design of the building, yet there was apparently no doubt in peoples' minds, seventy years after the fact, that Mr. Jefferson had illicitly sold whiskey at his store.

≈

During the 1830s, Peter Field personally operated his store on a dangerous river front. Years later, Joseph Beal remembered that "There were a turbulent set on this river at that time." Describing the store, Beal recalled something akin to the wild American West, where an industrious man could capitalize on river traffic and the easy flow of currency. The clientele was so unruly that he worked from behind a cage which ran from the floor to the ceiling, with bars running about three inches apart. According to Beal, Jefferson "chiefly sold whiskey, crockery ware, & tin ware, but mainly whiskey."[113]

> That was the time of his old grocery when they were running the little river boats, batteaux, before the canal was opened. There were a good many persons about drinking & fighting at times & he caged himself up—that was to protect himself from harm. . . . It was his general habit at that time to go in there, the grocery establishment, in the morning and remain generally all day, cold weather as well as warm. He had a small fire-place back of that counter where he kept a small fire just enough to keep his fingers warm . . . made with husks & chips that didn't cost him anything. He had on top of this counter near the entrance a small hole that would admit of a gallon & a half jug being passed in & out. He would pass out his goods bottles & drinks through this hole receiving the money first generally.[114]

By 1830, Peter Field Jefferson's family was complete. Living amidst the bustle of the steadily expanding river town, Peter Field and Jane Jefferson's household contained three boys under five and one girl, between five to ten years old. The little girl is Peter Field's only known daughter, Frances Ann, called "Fanny." The two younger boys were Thomas and Peter Field, Jr., called "Little Field" or "Fields."[115] The third boy, the eldest, died in 1833. The *Lynchburg Virginian* reported his death:

> Unfortunate Occurrence.—The eldest son of Mr. Peter F. Jefferson was unfortunately drowned yesterday in attempting to get across the river in a canoe. His body has not yet been found, tho' diligent search has been made.
>
> *Scottsville Farmer,* June 21.[116]

The unnamed son was about eight years old and likely ill-equipped to handle a canoe. Life in town and living right by the river was fraught with danger for the children. The loss of their first son was doubtless an emotional blow to both Jane and Peter Field Jefferson. Jane had already suffered so many personal losses, it is impossible to imagine the effect of this tragedy, however, a discussion doubtless began in the Jefferson household about moving away from the center of Scottsville.

In the early 1830s, Jefferson owned (and/or hired) a significant number of slaves, especially considering that he was not a planter. In 1830, he was taxed on seven adult males. Altogether, fourteen men, women, and children augmented his household and added to his responsibilities.[117] Some of these individuals may have been inherited from the division of Randolph Jefferson's estate. Only their gender and rough ages are known:

three males	age ten to twenty-four
three males	age twenty-four to thirty-six
two males	age thirty-six to fifty-five
one female	under age ten
one female	age ten to twenty-four
two females	age twenty-four to thirty-six
two females	age thirty-six to fifty-five[118]

It is not known how these people were employed, particularly the adult women. Joseph Walker, Jefferson's long-time associate, recalled that he "owned a good many slaves . . . sold about twelve men at the opening of the canal . . . when the little boats stopped running on the river. He had some five or six besides." While the tax records don't support Walker's numbers, Jefferson may have hired slaves, supplementing those he owned. In 1835, he was taxed on six slaves over the age of sixteen. By 1840, Peter Field owned two male slaves (age 36–55), one female (age 24–35), and two females (age 36–55). Only one slave was employed in "commerce." Interestingly, later in life, Jefferson expressed his reluctance to own slaves. Not because he found slavery objectionable, but because owning laborers, even skilled ones such as boatmen, was not as profitable as commerce.[119]

Prior to the building of the canal, Peter Field may have owned and operated many "little boats," or "batteau freight-boats," which ran on the James River between Richmond and Lynchburg. In *Scottsville on the James*, Virginia Moore refers to townsmen John O. Lewis and Peter Field Jefferson as "river barons," attributing some 200 river boats to these two Scottsville-based entrepreneurs. Both men were merchants in town. Two decades later, John O. Lewis would witness Jefferson's will, a testament to a long-time association between the men.

The Old Tavern

In the summer of 1834, Peter Field again expanded his Scottsville holdings, paying $206 for a portion of lot #35. Adjacent Scruggs' Tavern (formerly Noel's Tavern), the lot included a store house. Sold out of the estate of Robert Lewis, the property was associated with one of Scottsville's most public scandals.[120]

In 1821, Robert Lewis murdered Thompson Noel, the tavern keeper whose establishment sat on the western section of lot #35. The disagreement between Lewis and Noel may have had deep roots, possibly involving property rights. On August 6, 1818, John Scott sold the western part of the lot to Thompson Noel. The deed referred to a tavern already existing on the lot, making it one of the few developed spots in the new town. Noel paid a handsome $1,013 for the property. The same day, Scott sold the eastern part of the lot to Robert Lewis for $545. The lot ran between Jackson and Main Streets at the eastern edge of Scott's development. The lines and exact dimensions of the divided lot were vague in the original deeds, as well as in subsequent ones. It was the stuff feuds are made of. . . . [121]

In 1901, Rev. Edgar Woods wrote in his history of Albemarle County: "In 1821 Robert [Lewis] in a quarrel fatally stabbed Thompson Noel, a tavern keeper in Scottsville, and fled the country. It is said he went to Memphis, Tenn., and in course of time acquired a large fortune."[122] The tale of Lewis' amassing a fortune in Memphis may or may not be accurate, though it is certain that Robert Lewis escaped the authorities that September night. He died on August 26, 1832, in New Orleans, Louisiana.[123]

Accounts of the murder appeared in the local and Richmond newspapers. This lengthy version appeared in the *Richmond Daily Mercantile Advertiser* on September 11, 1821:

Charlottesville, (Alb.) Sept. 7.

FATAL RENCOUNTER.

A dreadful rencounter took place on Saturday last, near Scottsville, between a Mr. Lewis and Mr. Nowell, innkeeper at Scottsville, which eventuated in the death of the last mentioned. From the information we have, it appears that late in the evening of the above day Lewis came to the house of Mr. Nowell, where soon arose a quarrel about some trivial matter, which was followed by blows, from both parties. However, before either had received any serious injury they were separated and Nowell carried into the house and the front door fastened. He immediately broke out at a back door, armed with an auger, with which (our informant states,) he knocked Lewis down. The engagement was then renewed,—a gentleman standing near attempted to separate them, but Lewis drew a dirk, made several lunges at his antagonist, and inflicted two or three wounds on the gentleman who was exerting himself to disengage them; finding his own life in danger he thought proper to desist. Lewis then gave Nowell several severe stabs in the body, and a fatal one just above the left breast. He died in about four hours after, in great agony. A coroner's inquest was held over the body, whose verdict was "WILLFUL MURDER!" Lewis has fled. The accounts we have had of this affair, its origination, &c. are so various that we feel ourselves only at liberty to give a simple relation of what seems to be the most authentic.[124]

When Peter Field purchased this land from the Lewis estate his ultimate goal may have been to own the tavern and the adjacent lots. After all Jefferson loved his whiskey and, perhaps, he fancied himself becoming a tavern keeper with a legal license to serve "ardent spirits." Whatever his plan, he would have to wait until 1854 to acquire lot #36 which contained a three-bay, one-and-a-half-story frame house, one of the oldest buildings in Scottsville.[125]

Mount Walla

In the mid-1830s, Peter Field was one of several enterprising men taking advantage of the traffic flowing through a rapidly developing Scottsville as described in Joseph Martin's *Gazetteer of Virginia*:

SCOTTSVILLE, formerly Scott's Ferry, is 150 miles S. W. of Washington, and 83 W. of Richmond. It is situated on the N. bank of James river, 20 miles W. S. W. of Charlottesville. This place has improved rapidly in the last 4 years, and is yet a flourishing village. It contains 120 houses, chiefly of brick; one Methodist and one Presbyterian house of worship, a male and a female school, and two Sunday schools, nine general and five grocery stores, and one apothecaries shop. The principal manufactures are clothing, leather shoes, cabinet work, and earthen ware. An inspection of flour and tobacco is established in this place, of the former the average quantity inspected and sold is 3500 barrels. Scottsville carries on an extensive trade in flour, bacon, butter, lard, and other products, with the counties of Nelson, Augusta, Rockbridge, Rockingham, Bath, Pendleton, and Pocahontas; these products are exchanged for groceries, gypsum, coarse cotton and woollen cloths and money. The market of Scottsville is ready and tempting to the producer, the only fault of its enterprising merchants being that they pay prices too liberal for their own prosperity, and this cause only has lately given a temporary check to the rising of the town. A tri-weekly line of stages passes through it, communicating the Richmond and Staunton. Scottsville being situated at the extreme northwestern bend of the navigable water of the James river, would probably acquire an immense increase of trade, if the James and Kanawha [canal] improvement is carried in to effect. There is a savings institution in the town. It has two resident attorneys and four regular physicians; its whole population is about 600.[126]

The *Gazetteer* failed to mention Scottsville's Central Hotel Tavern, which in late 1835, was available to rent. An impressive establishment, its existence is an indicator of Scottsville's relative sophistication. An advertisement in the *Richmond Whig* read:

TAVERN IN SCOTTSVILLE, FOR RENT.

Will be rented, for one, two, or three years, the Central Hotel Tavern in the town of Scottsville, Albemarle county, lately occupied by William Lewis. The buildings consist of a large Tavern House, containing sixteen Rooms, convenient out Houses, Kitchen, Stables, Smoke House, &c. all in good order, and nearly new—constituting a very complete and commodious establishment for public accommodation—situated about the centre of the town. The active enterprising character of this place, the amount of travel to, and through it, both by private conveyance, and by stages, which arrive and depart twice a week from Staunton and

Richmond, with its present auspicious prospects, from the improvement of the James River, now in progress from its excellent Turnpike Road to Staunton; with some hope of a Rail Road to that place—a route for which has been already surveyed by the Engineer of the State, render this one of the most valuable and desirable Tavern stands in Virginia. Possession will be given on the 27th day of February next. Persons disposed to rent, will please make application in person, or by letter to Col. Martin Tutwiler, at the Middleton Mills, or to Horatio J. Magruder at the Union Mills, Fluvanna, or to the subscriber at the place.

BENJAMIN H. MAGRUDER.[127]

This advertisement for the Central Hotel Tavern vividly captures the steady movement of goods and persons passing through Scottsville as well as the anticipation of the coming of the canal, which was already in progress.

〜

By the mid-1830s, the Peter Field Jeffersons were more than ready to put a little distance between themselves and Scottsville's constant bustle. The loss of their eldest son was a stinging reminder that river towns were not a particularly safe nor peaceful place to rear children. In addition to drowning, fires were always a concern, like these reported in Richmond's *Daily Dispatch*:

Fires.—A workshop belonging to Messrs. Ferrell, near Scottsville, Va., was consumed by fires last Tuesday.[128]

Fires.—On Friday, the 10th inst., the broom factory of the Messrs. Littles, near this place, was entirely consumed by fire. Loss estimated $500. The fire was accidental. On the night of the same day the blacksmith shop of Mr. Lewis Mayo, seven miles from this place, was also consumed by fire. This makes the ninth shop the old gentleman has lost by fire.[129]

Transients filled the streets, including dangerous runaway slaves, and violent acts were reported in the Richmond newspapers.

The last *Charlottesville Jeffersonian* informs us that a runaway negro, belonging to Gen. B. Peyton, of this city, whose overseer he had murdered, and for whose apprehension a reward of $100 has been offered by the Governor, had been traced to a blacksmith shop, in the vicinity of

Scottsville, on Monday morning last, when Mr. Drumheller and Mr. Haskins of Albemarle endeavored to arrest him. The negro, however, escaped, after having inflicted severe wounds upon both of them with a knife, from the effect of which, it was feared, one of them (Mr. D.) would not survive.[130]

Decades later, escaped slaves remained front page news, such as this story of Kitty in Richmond's *Daily Dispatch*:

FIFTY DOLLARS REWARD.—Ran away from Warren, Albemarle county, on Saturday night, July 19th [1862], a negro woman named KITTY, in the employment of E. D. Purvis, and belonging to the estate of the late H. N. Templeman. Said negro is stout built, with a very bad scar (from a burn) on her neck. She is about 26 years old. She is thought to be lurking about Scottsville, Albemarle county. The above reward will be paid when delivered to Hector Davis, Richmond, or lodged in jail, where she can be got.

E. Templeman[131]

Public drunkenness and rowdy individuals populated the nearby taverns, fostering disturbing and, occasionally, serious incidents, like this one, that happened at Jefferson's ferry landing:

Accident.—One day during the past week whilst John Robertson, carpenter, of this place, was in a state of intoxication, he came near losing his life. He was sitting on the steep embankment at the ferry, when, it seems, he made a start to rise, but being in a delirious state, he plunged rapidly down the embankment about twenty feet, when he fell heavily against a sharp piece of wood—the wood penetrating the centre of his face, severing his nose, and producing a most ghastly wound. It was considered at first final, but we learn that he is now slowly recovering.[132]

~

In 1836, Peter Field Jefferson purchased Mount Walla, achieving the goal of lifting his family out of and above life at the river basin, placing them on the bluff high above Scottsville's business district. At an auction on October 8, 1836, he paid $2,800 for the property which included a dwelling house, out buildings, and over eighty acres of land.[133]

There, the Jeffersons lived in style, Federal Style to be precise, perched high on the bluff above potential flood waters. Their dwelling house and its dependencies were valued at $1,600. Unquestionably, Peter Field Jefferson had arrived. His hilltop house came complete with a view of his birthplace, Snowden, and eighty-eight acres—including orchards and timbered land—giving him and his family breathing space. He enjoyed his simple dwelling and his passion for gardening was evident on the grounds, especially his vegetable garden. He also kept bees and a large number of stock hogs.[134]

The name of the place, Mount Walla, may have been coined years after Jefferson's purchase of the house, possibly even after Jefferson's death. One version states that his grandson, Peter V. Foland, who inherited the property, named it after a Native American word meaning "high point overlooking a fertile valley." It has also been referred to as "Mount Wallow," sarcastically referencing Jefferson's hoarded wealth.[135]

In 1937, R. E. Hannum described the dwelling house at Mount Walla that had changed little since Peter Field Jefferson's day, writing:

> "Mount Walla" is situated on a hill above Scottsville and overlooks the "Horse Shoe Bend" of James River. Because the hill is so steep, it is necessary to approach the house from the rear. There are walnut and locust trees in the yard and small beds of flowering bulbs.
>
> The house is a rectangular, frame building, one and a half stories high, with gable roof, covered with metal; originally shingled. There are two brick chimneys, one on the east end and the other on the west. The house is covered with rather narrow beaded weatherboarding. The cornices are plain and of wood. There are twelve windows. . . .
>
> Both entrances, one on the north and one on the south, are exactly the same. A flight of steps leads up to each of two deep porches, which have the original pillars. Each door is very wide and [has] a single six panel door. The both open into the same room, about 16x16 feet. All of the woodwork is very massive—wide doors and frames with wide cornices over them. The wainscoting is wide and all of the woodwork has a strip of mantling to finish it off around the top. The stair is a closed one and goes up on the west wall next to the door on the north. Under the stairway and in the same wall a door opens into the only other room on this floor.

The fireplace is in the east wall and has a very pretty mantel, which has a sunburst in the center.

. . . Upstairs there are two small rooms with sloping ceilings. In the basement are located the dining room and kitchen. The original kitchen was in the yard at the west of the house. It as well as the old smoke-house is still standing.[136]

∼

Peter Field and Jane Jefferson had three children who lived to adulthood. Frances Ann, "Fanny," (born about 1820) and her brother, Thomas (born about 1825), were said to have good minds. The youngest, Peter Field, Jr. (born about 1829), had limited intelligence and remained illiterate throughout his life. His foolish behaviors caused some Scottsville citizens to label him idiotic. It is unknown where and to what degree Fanny was educated; however, she was handsomely dressed before her marriage, indicating that both she and her parents paid close attention to her appearance.[137]

∼

Tutors, as well as private schools, were available in and around Scottsville. For example, in the spring of 1845, a typical school for young ladies, operated by Miss Lucy P. M. Leake, opened near the Moon plantation, Stony Point. Though it opened too late to accommodate Fanny Jefferson, it was full of Jefferson connections and indicates the value the neighborhood gentry put on education. The *Richmond Enquirer* ran the following advertisement during February-March of 1845:

EDUCATION

MISS LUCY P. M. LEAKE will open a School for the education of Young Ladies at Stony Point, within one mile of Scottsville, Albemarle, on Monday, the 1st of April next. The course of tuition will comprise the usual branches of an English education, together with French, Music and Needle-work. After some years' experience, Miss Leake flatters herself that those who commit their daughters or wards to her care, will be gratified with the results. Satisfactory testimonials will be produced to those who may wish them; in the meantime, she refers particularly to the Rev. Wm. S. White, Charlottesville, Col. T. J. Randolph, Edge Hill, and Frank G. Ruffin, Esq. Shadwell.

Board, including all accommodations, may be had in the family of her brother, Mr. Samuel A. Leake, with whom she resides. He will have ample room for ten or twelve.

For ordinary English branches	$12.50
" " French (additional)	10.00
Music, with the use of Piano	18.00
Needle-work	5.00
Board, per month	8.00[138]

Miss Leake's references were first rate. Col. Thomas Jefferson Randolph, the son of Peter Field's first cousin, Martha (Jefferson) Randolph, operated a school at Edgehill, not far from Monticello. Shadwell was the birthplace of Peter Field's father, Randolph Jefferson. Rev. William S. White was at one time the pastor of the Scottsville Presbyterian Church and later founded Charlottesville Female Academy in the Old Manse.[139]

～

Fanny Jefferson's life remains shrouded in mystery, her reputation suffering from gossip which was still being repeated when Virginia Moore wrote *Scottsville on the James*. According to Moore, Fanny "had shocked Scottsville by marrying a man from the Union army: Peter V. Foland." This simple statement contains two glaring errors. Fanny married Valentine Foland. Peter Valentine Foland was her son, whose name honored his Jefferson grandfather as well as his father. Additionally, in 1840, when the Folands wed, there was no "Union army." If Scottsville was shocked, it was for completely other reasons.[140] It was widely known that Peter Field disapproved of the marriage and wrote Fanny out of his will when she persisted contrary to his wishes. Just why Jefferson disapproved of Foland is unknown, for in a few years, he would come to his son-in-law's aid.[141]

～

Valentine Foland was born on May 20, 1810, in the Shenandoah Valley. His grandparents, Johann Valentine and Anna Christian (Schuckmaenninn) Foland, settled in Rockingham County, Virginia during the first decade of the 19th century. Of German descent, the family name was originally "Voland" and their cultural background was markedly different from the planter class of the Jefferson and Lewis families. Valentine Foland was trained as a craftsman, becoming a skilled carpenter and cabinetmaker.[142]

How and when Valentine Foland met Fanny Jefferson is unknown; however, on April 23, 1840, they were married in Washington, D.C. Foland was almost thirty; Fanny was about twenty. They likely eloped, escaping Peter Field's disapproval. Other evidence suggests an even more complicated story behind the Jefferson–Foland marriage. On June 22, 1835, in Albemarle County, a man named Valentine Foland married a woman named Frances Smith, who gave her own written consent. Had Valentine Foland previously married another woman named Frances? Was this a different Valentine Foland? Or, did a fifteen-year-old Frances Ann Jefferson run away from home, giving a false name and age, only to marry again, legally, in 1840?[143]

By 1844, Valentine Foland experienced deepening financial problems, owing $125 to Alexander Rives and $125 to George W. Randolph. Foland's note, dated July 6, 1843 and recorded in Albemarle County, was payable on demand. Rives and Randolph apparently pressed Foland for the debt and, on May 27, 1844, Foland transferred his store inventory—"the lot of furniture now in the warehouse and shop"—to his father-in-law, Peter Field Jefferson, for the amount of $1.00. Foland's stock included a wide variety of valuable handcrafted furniture: bureaus, presses, wardrobes, folding tables, safes, cribs, bedsteads, cradles, wash stands, candle stands, ladies' work stands, stools, and chests. Foland was industrious even if he was overextended. His chest of tools, a lot of timber partly framed, a lot of plank in the cellar, a cow, and a calf were included in the transfer. If Rives and Randolph were not paid within six months, the lot would be auctioned to the highest bidder. Valentine Foland signed and sealed this new indenture.[144]

It is unknown if the auction took place, though likely it did. The Folands left Albemarle County, migrating west. On January 22, 1845, their son, Peter Valentine Foland, was born in western Virginia in Scott County.[145] The family was probably already en route to join the extended Foland family in Jefferson County, Tennessee. Fanny died sometime before March 7, 1855 when Valentine Foland married Jane Ann Smith in Jefferson County. Promptly, they started a new family and Peter Field Jefferson's grandson grew up far from Scottsville with his father, his stepmother, and a growing number of half-brothers and sisters. He would learn carpentry from his father, expected to be his life's occupation.[146]

The James River and Kanawha Canal

On July 24, 1835, the *Richmond Whig and Public Advertiser* announced that the James River and Kanawha Canal would be extended from Maiden's Adventure to Scottsville, from Scottsville to Tye River, and from Tye River to Lynchburg. Engineers and surveyors were listed by name, as well as Rodmen and Chainmen. Distant cousins of Peter Field Jefferson, Richard Field Archer and Junius L. Archer, were among the men supervising the segment running from Maiden's Adventure to Scottsville.[147] The presence of the canal would dramatically change the course of history for Scottsville, though not overnight. The business savvy Peter Field had time to shift his investments, reduce his involvement in bateau traffic, and consider how he might profit from the canal era to come.

In times of great change, there are always financial winners and losers. The quick and shrewd assess their assets and seize the moment. The coming of the James River and Kanawha Canal to Scottsville was no exception. In May of 1835, it was announced that the canal project would begin at Scottsville, a mixed blessing for the residents, though many doubtless profited. For Peter Field, his river front property, the ferry landing and the store, would be permanently affected by the creation of the canal basin where boats could be loaded and unloaded, turned, serviced, and stored.

As a result of the building of the canal, part of River Street was condemned. Jefferson, and others, appealed to the James River and Kanawha Company demanding restitution. On November 17, 1836, it was decided that he and other Scottsville property owners would be compensated for damage to their properties by the canal company:

> Lots nos. 113 & 117, belong to Peter F. Jefferson ... condemned 1 rod, 10 perches, 20 yards ... for injury to his ferry, Company agreeing to grade a road from ferry landing to the bridge across the canal, to be erected just above [Tucker] Coles' lumber house, and to construct a foot bridge across the canal opposite to the ferry and that they will remove his ferry house, where he may direct ... damage, $230.[148]

Others in Scottsville who were compensated included: N. H. Ragland, John D. Moon, William Brown, Samuel Tompkins, Tucker Coles, Richard Moon, the heirs of John Harris, Walter Coles, John Coles, Martin Tutwiler, and Robert

Carter. Tutwiler received $600 for injury to his tannery yard and destruction of his houses.[149]

The coming of the canal also meant many months of chaotic construction along the river. In the summer of 1836, the company advertised widely for workers. Some would be immigrants. Some would be free blacks. Many would be slaves.

NOTICE TO CONTRACTORS.

James River and Kanawha Canal.—Proposals will be received at the Office of the James River and Kanawha Company, in the city of Richmond, from the 15th to the 23nd day of August, of the construction of all the Excavation, Embankment, and Walling, not now under contract, together with nearly all the Culverts and the greater portion of the Locks, between Lynchburgh [sic] and Maidens' Adventure.

The work now advertised embraces the twenty miles between Columbia and the head of Maiden's Adventure Pond, the eight miles between Seven Island Falls and Scottsville, and about 20 isolated sections, reserved at the former letting, between Scottsville and Lynchburgh.

The quantity of masonry offered is very great, consisting of about two hundred Culverts, of from three to thirty feet span; nine Aqueducts, thirty-five Locks, a number of Wastes, with several farm and road Bridges.

General plans and specifications of all the work, and special plans of the most important Culverts and Aqueducts, will be found at the offices of the several Principal Assistant Engineers on the line of the Canal.

The work will be prepared for examination by the 25th July; but mechanics, well recommended, desirous of immediate employment, can obtain contracts for the construction of a number of culverts at private letting.

Persons offering to contract, who are unknown to the subscriber, or any of the Assistant Engineers, will be expected to accompany their proposals by the usual certificates of character and ability.

CHARLES ELLET, JR.,

Chief Engineer of the James River Kanawha Company.

Note.—The Dams, Guard-Locks, most of the Bridges, and a number of Locks and Culverts, are reserved for a future letting. Persons visiting the line for the purpose of obtaining work would do well to call at the office of the Company, in the city of Richmond, where any information which they may desire will be cheerfully communicated.

The valley of James River, between Lynchburgh and Richmond, is healthy. C. E. Jr.[150]

The building of the canal offered Jefferson a significant, unusual new business opportunity. Initially, several hundred Irishmen were "imported" to dig the canal trenches. Eventually, these laborers were replaced and/or supplemented with African Americans—both enslaved and free men. Even some of the overseers were African Americans. Hiring slaves out to the canal company could be lucrative.[151]

Locals who provided slaves to the crew included James Harris of Buckingham County, who hired out slaves from Snowden (then held in the estate of his uncle, Capt. John Harris, who died in 1831). Snowden, being directly south of Scottsville across the James River, provided a convenient source of labor. In 1835, three slaves from Snowden worked on the canal and, in 1836, Harris sent another a man. It is particularly interesting that the men requested to be hired out. The work was likely more stimulating and the company more diverse than agricultural work at home. Additionally, slaves who worked away from their home plantation often kept a percentage of their pay. During 1835–1836, Peter Field Jefferson owned six adult male slaves, some of whom likely worked on the canal.[152]

The canal workers were paid in State-issued scrip and Peter Field accumulated considerable amounts of it. He may have acquired some of it in exchange for the labor of his own slaves, as well as accepting script at his store and at his ferry. In 1900, the *Richmond Dispatch* article, "'Snowden' and Its Owner–Jefferson's Escape," stated that Jefferson saw unusual potential in the scrip and purchased it as an investment:

> [D]uring the building of the James river and Kanawha canal the operatives were paid off mostly in State "scrip," instead of money, and Mr. Jefferson bought up all of this he could get, and turned it into State bonds, from which he realized a good profit. Being an uncommonly shrewd and close businessman, he had, it is thought, when the war between the States broke out, accumulated from $75,000 to $100,000.[153]

When the *Richmond Whig* advertised for lockkeepers on July 10, 1840, the canal was nearing completion. During the month of July, men were stationed between Richmond and Scottsville and between Scottsville and Lynchburg "with the view of making a selection" of lockkeepers. The advertisement warned:

> The applicants must be of sober and steady habits. They will understand that the Company will require all their personal attention to the duties that will be assigned them, and subject to removal for any neglect of duty. They will also understand that they will not be allowed to sell groceries, or any other description of merchandize, along the line of the Canal—nor will they be permitted to raise animals or fowls to go at large, without the consent (in writing) from the owners of the lands adjacent to the Canal. At all places near a public highway or landing, there will be no objection to a lock-keeper having a shoe, harness, saddle, cooper's and tailor's shops.—The duties and salary to commence with the day the water is let into the Canal, unless some other duties may be required: in that case, the salaries will commence with such duties.

Samuel P. Parsons,
General Superintendent of the Canal.[154]

Peter Field Jefferson and other Scottsville merchants were no doubt relieved that they would not have new competition from the canal's lockkeepers, one of whom was his neighbor J. H. Briggs.

By the fall of 1840, Joseph E. Cabell, President of the James River and Kanawha Canal company, enthusiastically announced the canal's positive impact on Scottsville's commerce, "On the 18th of November 1840, a freight boat belonging to Messers Shepperson & Co. arrived in Richmond with a cargo of 300 barrels of flour from the town of Scottsville."[155]

Simultaneously, Peter Field Jefferson requested that the Albemarle County Court stop any further proceedings against the company, stating that his complaint had long been settled out of court. His business-like manner and his trained penmanship reflect both a temperate demeanor and a gentleman's education.[156]

Scottsville: Boom Town

The canal's promise of rapid growth resulted in new and varied business opportunities for Peter Field Jefferson. After withdrawing his investment in bateaux, he focused on the construction of the canal as a source of short-term profit. Once the canal was completed, Jefferson immediately reduced his investment in human property. By 1841, he owned only two slaves and one horse. His income from the ferry, the store, particularly his whiskey business, and his investments in "State Stock" provided a very comfortable life for himself and his family, without the headaches of managing a sprawling plantation and a large workforce. What Scottsville historian Virginia Moore called Jefferson's "streak of genius in business" was increasingly evident by his on-going success and his influence over the development of the town of Scottsville.

Concurrently, the wagon traffic which flowed overland through Scottsville to the river steadily increased. The Staunton to Scottsville turnpike bulged with commodities of every type bound for the James River. Unsurprisingly, Scottsville's population grew steadily in response to the increased traffic, as described by John Hammond Moore in his history of Albemarle County:

> Naturally enough, the canal brought substantial prosperity to the southern end of Albemarle. A petition seeking a branch bank (January 14, 1842) estimated the Scottsville community had some one thousand souls, together with twenty-one stores, "twenty-four mechanics' shops of various kinds," three taverns, a tobacco factory, and four churches. Canal transport eastward was conducted by nine freight boats and two packets. Produce and freight valued at over $1 million was being shipped annually . . . merchandise valued at $250,000 was sold in the town each year.[157]

By the mid-1840s, Scottsville, conveniently situated where the canal met the turnpike, had become a tourist hub. Packet boats advertised the ease of transferring from boat to stage. When passengers first alighted in Scottsville, coming or going, they found themselves at Peter Field Jefferson's store.

PACKET BOATS
For Scottsville and Lynchburg.
SUMMER ARRANGEMENT.

Our Mail Packet Boats, JOHN MARSHALL, Capt. Hull, and J. C. CABEL, Capt. Huntley, will leave Richmond from our landing, at the head of the

Basin, for the above places, on Mondays, Wednesdays and Fridays, at 8 o'clock A.M. precisely, and arrive at Scottsville by 1 A.M., next day, and into Lynchburg by 7 P.M.

RETURNING.

Leave Lynchburg, Mondays, Wednesdays and Fridays, at 7 A.M. and arrive at Scottsville by 10 P.M. and into Richmond next day by 4 P.M.

By this arrangement, passengers for Tennessee and Guyandotte [Western Virginia], will not be detained in Lynchburg, as heretofore. Our Boats will also connect with the lines of Stages from Scottsville to Staunton.

This is now the cheapest and best route to the different Virginia Springs, and offers many other inducements to travelers for preference.

The invalid will be pleased with his easy, comfortable and safe passage; the beautiful and romantic scenery will delight the admirers of nature, and the rich, far famed and highly cultivated James River low grounds and highlands, will gratify the agriculturist and man of taste.

On their arrival in Lynchburg, Passengers have a choice of two routes to the White Sulphur Springs, with an assurance that all shall be sent on—two lines of Stages running over the Natural Bridge and by Dibbrel's Springs, and the other by Liberty, Fincastle and Sweet Springs.

EDMONDS & DAVENPORT
Richmond, June 9, 1843[158]

~

Ten years after Peter Field Jefferson established his home on the hill above Scottsville, he reigned over a bustling and still growing river town. Others took notice as Scottsville and its citizens flourished. In 1846, Richmond's *Whig* published an article which captured the town as Peter Field Jefferson knew it. The growth over the previous decade was remarkable; the increased ease of transportation to and through the town was key to its development:

During the Fall and early part of the Winter until the road becomes impassable, a hundred waggons may be counted in one day between Scottsville and the Blue Ridge approaching the Scottsville market. It has been ascertained to be a fact which may be asserted without fear of confutation, that this great stream of trade would flow in a continuous current throughout the Winter and Spring months from the Parkersburg and Guyandotte turnpikes, and from various other directions, if it were not dammed up at the mountain, by the wretched state of the road leading to Scottsville. . . . Scottsville contains, according to the last census, about seven hundred inhabitants,—that there are thirteen mercantile and trading establishments in the village, besides three Taverns, two Boarding-Houses, four Churches, two Milliners, four Tailors, two Saddlers, one Tinner, two Boot and Shoemakers, one Carriagemaker, one Wheelwright, one Cabinetmaker, one Carpenter and one Lumber merchant. The Flour Inspector informs me, that the amount of flour inspected during the last ten years, has ranged at from fifteen to twenty six thousand barrels annually, besides about one-third of the quantity arriving, which goes off down the canal to Richmond without inspection; while the yearly receipts of wheat have averaged at from forty to fifty thousand bushels; and of butter, at from forty to fifty thousand pounds; besides a great variety of articles and products in smaller quantities, as tobacco, corn, oats, bacon, pork, lard, clover seed, honey, ginseng, &c. &c.—During the trading and marketing season from the first of Autumn to the latter part of Spring, when the road is in traveling order, an average of from fifty to a hundred wagons may be seen crowding weekly through the streets, and one of the most experienced, intelligent, substantial and respectable merchants of the place tells me, that from three to six thousand dollars are paid out every week for the various commodities exposed to sale in the village; whilst the sales of goods, wares and merchandise amount to one-hundred and twenty thousand dollars or upwards a year.[159]

The article favorably compared Scottsville with Charlottesville, Albemarle's county seat, stating:

Charlottesville is the gander that does the gabbling; Scottsville is the goose that quietly lays the gold egg for the James River Canal. . . . Scottsville, it appears . . . stays at home and looks to the affairs of her own household. Scottsville seeks neither to exalt nor depress others, but occupying her own position, she stands in her own defense.[160]

The same might be said of Peter Field Jefferson who both reflected his village and helped shape her. Apparently, he did not aspire to public office or a life of larger recognition. He enjoyed staying at home and making piles of money which the steady traffic brought to Scottsville, his store, and his ferry landing.

~

In 1843, Peter Field secured two more lots in Scottsville, #43 and #44, which had belonged to his younger brother, James Lilburne Jefferson.[161] These Jefferson brothers had led distinctly divergent lives. While Peter Field steadily gained wealth and business acumen, Lilburne was restless and rootless. Indebted to Peter Field, in 1835, Lilburne attempted to sell his undeveloped lots, enlisting his brother's aid, addressing him as "Dear Sir," which did not suggest a particularly close relationship. Still, he trusted him completely to represent him in business.

Lynchburg Jan 30 1835

Mr Peter F. Jefferson

Dr Sir

    I wish to sell my 2 unimproved lots in Scottsville as I never expect to improve them they lie on Jackson street and known by nos 43 and 44 and in the neighborhood of the lot I sold to George Scruggs separated by the cross street running to the river as I am oweing you a little debt sell them to the best advantage and pay yourself out of the sales of the lots and retain the ballance untill drawn [?] for if you cant sell them from this authority advertise them in the [Scottsville] Farmer I am about to embark largely in the Tobacco business this year and would be glad of all the aid that is in the power of you and my other friends

I am sir your
friend & brother
J. L. Jefferson[162]

It is unknown if James Lilburne Jefferson successfully launched his plan to involve himself in the tobacco business. The Scottsville lots may or may not have been advertised as he wished. In the end, they remained in his estate. Located below Mount Walla on a steep hill, they were essentially worthless for development.[163]

In October of 1836, James Lilburne Jefferson's death became national news, not for his own accomplishments, which had been few, but because he was a nephew of President Thomas Jefferson and because his death had been shocking. The *Lynchburg Virginian* printed the following:

Casualty–Mr. James L. Jefferson, of this place, died on last Friday afternoon. The Coroner's jury found a verdict of death by intemperance. The deceased was a nephew of the late President Jefferson, was intelligent, and possessed fine traits of character; and but for the unfortunate frailty to which he fell victim, would have been a useful member of society.[164]

Within days, the news appeared in a Baltimore newspaper, *American and Commercial Daily Advertiser*, and throughout November, the news of his shameful death was repeated and amplified in temperance-minded papers, such as the *Springfield Republican and Journal* in Massachusetts:

Melancholy.—A late number of Lynchburg Virginian mentions the death of James L. Jefferson, a nephew of the late Thomas Jefferson. He died, according to the verdict of the coroner's jury, from the effects of Intemperance! He possessed fine talents, learning, friends—but he could not withstand the temptation—He had never signed the pledge, and has gone down to the drunkard's grave![165]

Thus, in a very public way, it was revealed that Peter Field Jefferson was not the only one of his brothers who drank too much whiskey. Like his cousin, Lilburne Lewis, James "Lilburne" Jefferson's sad death was used as a cautionary tale.[166]

The youngest of Anne (Lewis) and Randolph Jefferson's children had died, without making a last will, unmarried, and with no known children.[167] In April of 1837, Peter Field Jefferson appealed to the Albemarle County Court to settle his brother's estate.

To the county court of Albemarle sitting in chancery.

Your orator Peter F. Jefferson begs leave respectfully to represent, that some time in the latter part of the year 1836 his brother James L. Jefferson died in the town of Lynchburg, intestate, leaving neither wife nor child, and that by due course of law his brothers and sisters [his parents being dead] succeed as his heirs to such estate as he left, as may not be required to pay his debts. Your orator has been informed and believes & charges that the personal effects left by the said James L. were more than sufficient to pay his debts. He left besides, two lots in the town of Scottsville in this county, numbered in the plan of said town Nos: 43 & 44 which are unimproved, and the precise extent of which is unknown to your orator. The said James L. left the following brothers & sisters, nephews & nieces etc: as his legal heirs viz besides your orator, Thomas Jefferson, Robert L. Jefferson, Isham R. Jefferson his brothers, and James L. Nevil, Jesse Mundy and Louisiana his wife formerly Louisiana Nevil, La Fayette Nevil and Jefferson M. Nevil, the said James L., Louisiana, La Fayette & Jefferson M. being children of Ann S. Nevil formerly Ann S. Jefferson, who was sister to the deceased. Your orator avers that the distributive portions of each of the said heirs of the decedent in said lots would be greatly less than $300: that Louisiana Mundy [one of them] is a femme covert—and he therefore prays that the court will direct a sale of the said lots and a distribution of the proceeds thereof among the heirs aforesaid according to their respective rights and to that end he prays that a commissioner may be appointed. He prays that the said heirs of the said deceased may be made parties defendant to this bill and required to answer the same and that such other & further relief may be granted in the premises as to the court may seem meet and proper. He would further represent that Isham R. Jefferson and James L. Nevil are not inhabitants of the state of Virginia & he prays that the usual order of publication may be made against them and the Commonwealth writ of subpoena may be awarded against the others.

P. F. Jefferson[168]

At a Court held for Albemarle County on September 2, 1839, Thomas W. Gilmer was appointed Commissioner for Lilburne Jefferson's estate and was directed to advertise and sell the two Scottsville lots, #43 & #44. Later, Thomas Staples replaced Gilmer as Commissioner. Though notices had been published in the Charlottesville's *Virginia Advocate*, and subpoenas were sent as Peter Field Jefferson had requested, the defendants Thomas Jefferson, Robert L. Jefferson and Jefferson M. Nevil (who had died on December 11, 1838) "failed to answer." On March 25, 1843, Commissioner Staples transferred lots #43 and #44 to Peter Field Jefferson for $40.00 and, on August 7, 1843, a final decree was entered. Here, the legacy of James Lilburne Jefferson sadly ended.[169]

Snowden For Sale

If Peter Field Jefferson had wanted to purchase Snowden from his father's estate in the 1820s, he did not possess the funds to do so. His share of the estate would be the seed money that launched his many investments in Scottsville and fueled his financial success. It is less clear, however, why he did not purchase the remaining 1,200 acres of Snowden when they were auctioned from the estate of Capt. John Harris. At that juncture, he had both the funds and plenty of collateral for credit.

The auction of Snowden was widely advertised. From July 15–August 20, 1843, a notice ran twice weekly in Washington D.C.'s *Daily National Intelligencer*. Concurrently, it appeared in the *Lynchburg Virginian*. The following version appeared in the *Richmond Whig* from July 14–August 18, 1843.

VALUABLE JAMES RIVER LAND FOR SALE.

By virtue of a Decree of the Circuit Superior Court of Law and Chancery for Albemarle County, in a cause therein pending, between Harris and Moon and others, pronounced on the 18th day of May 1843, we the undersigned, appointed Commissioners for that purpose, will sell at public auction, to the highest bidder, on the 18th day of August next, on the premises, a tract of land lying in the county of Buckingham, on the James River, called Snowdon, containing about 1200 acres—about 300 acres of which are James River bottom, of the best quality, admirably adapted to the growth of corn, wheat and tobacco—about 250 acres of the high land of great fertility are cleared, and the residue of the tract well timbered, and a large portion of fine tobacco land.

The improvements consist of a good overseer's house, large and commodious tobacco houses, barns, corn houses, stables, &c.

This farm is recommended as one of the most valuable and desirable in Virginia. It is remarkably fertile—it extends for several miles along the James River, having, by means of the James River canal, daily communication with Richmond, and is directly opposite to the very flourishing town of Scottsville, where an excellent market is at all times afforded for all the products of the farm.

This tract will be sold by us subject to the life estate of Mrs. Sarah C. Harris in about two-thirds of it, which have been allotted to her as a tenant in dower; but we are authorized by her estate, that her interest will be offered to the purchaser of the residue on the day of sale, on terms which cannot fail to be satisfactory, and which will be made known before the sale, so that the purchaser can at once obtain a fee simple in the whole tract. Possession will be given for the purpose of sowing a crop of wheat at the usual time of seeding next fall and full possession on January next.

Terms of sale—about $600 cash will be required, the balance to be paid in equal installments at the expiration of one, two and three years, the purchaser giving bond with approved security, and the legal title being retained as further security for the payment of the purchase money.

We will also, on the 19th of August next, on the premises, sell a House and Lots in the town of Scottsville on Main street, well situated for a Dwelling House and Store.

Also, on the 17th of August next, on the premises, we will sell a Lot in the town of Warren, Albemarle County, lately belonging to Capt. John Harris, dec'd.

These Lots will be sold on a credit of one, two, and three years, the purchasers giving bond with approved security, and the legal title being retained, as further security for the payment of the purchase money.
John H. Coleman, Edward H. Moon, Benj. H. Magruder, Commissioners[170]

Capt. John Harris' great-nephew, John L. Harris, a successful merchant and planter in Nelson County, bought the farm. On October 15, 1844, John L. Harris' first installment payment on Snowden, $5,466.66, was deposited in the Charlottesville Savings Institution. Identical installments were made in 1845 and 1846. On October 24, 1848, the deed to Snowden was executed to Harris.[171]

Gradually transitioning from Nelson to Buckingham County, by 1846, John L. Harris maintained seventeen horses at Snowden and, by 1850, Harris had finished building an impressive dwelling house valued with other structures at $5,000. He also owned a carriage worth $250. Unlike Peter Field Jefferson, John L. Harris openly displayed his wealth and his excellent, expensive taste.[172]

While no records have been found to indicate that Peter Field Jefferson bid on Snowden, a somewhat confused, though intriguing, oral tradition recalled that he wanted to purchase it. Though no source or author is credited, the information about Peter Field provided for an article published in the *Richmond Dispatch* in 1900, likely came from Peter V. Foland, Jefferson's grandson and heir.

After the death of his father, when in order to close up the matters of the estate, "Snowden" had to be sold at auction, Fields [sic] Jefferson intended to buy it; but another bidder, Mr. John L. Harris, offered him $1,000 not to bid against him, which Mr. Jefferson accepted, and Mr. Harris became the purchaser.

Soon after that, when the Winfrey place, a fine farm four miles below, was offered for sale, Mr. Jefferson bought it, and paid $20,000 cash down for it.[173]

By the time this account appeared in the Richmond newspaper, fifty-eight years had passed since John L. Harris' purchase of Snowden. The telling conflated Capt. John Harris' purchase of Snowden in 1826 from the estate of Randolph Jefferson with the sale to John L. Harris in 1843 from the estate of Capt. Harris. Later versions of Snowden's chain of ownership perpetuated this error. While it is doubtful that John L. Harris had a spare $1,000 to suppress Peter Field's intention to buy, Jefferson might have agreed not to bid up the price.

Dark Prince of Scottsville

By 1850, Peter Field Jefferson had out-lived his father by several years. He shared Mount Walla with his wife, Jane, and their sons, twenty-five-year-old Thomas and twenty-year-old Peter Field, Jr. A man in his early sixties, Peter Field remained robust, ever expanding his investments. Over the years, his personality had solidified around a single purpose—to accumulate wealth. Other aspects of his life necessarily suffered.

Randolph Jefferson had provided Peter Field with a good general education which was enhanced by either innate or acquired business acumen. Buckingham County planter Benjamin J. Harris, who was well-acquainted with the extended Jefferson clan, observed that "Peter F. Jefferson, Sr. was the most sensible, the most calculating and the most thrifty of his family." This Jefferson was, in fact, outstanding in his immediate family to favor business over farming. George W. Dawson, a Scottsville business and lumberman admitted, "He was a long ways ahead of some business men and probably not as shrewd as others."[174]

Like Randolph Jefferson, Peter Field led a comparatively simple life. Amassing wealth was Jefferson's occupation, not spending it. He invested sparingly in personal property, including slaves, and did not own luxury items. By contrast, his planter brother, Robert Lewis, enjoyed the typical refinements of the landed gentry, including a carriage valued at $200, a watch, a clock, and a piano.[175]

Peter Field's frugal nature protected him from debt, which plagued most of Virginia's gentry. His real estate holdings, however, did not protect him from devastating losses due to fire or natural disasters, like the earthquake reported in the *Alexandria Gazette* in 1852:

> The shock of the earthquake, which was felt in Richmond, on Tuesday evening, was, also very sensibly felt in Scottsville, Albemarle County. Every house in the village was shaken by the oscillation; the boats lying in the canal were tossed to and fro, and the waters gave evidence of being much trouble—at least, so says the *Scottsville Republican*.[176]

Though Jefferson feared robbery, particularly at his river-front store, he talked openly about his wealth and could be surprisingly gregarious when bragging about it. Jacob H. Briggs, a boat inspector who also operated a foundry in Scottsville and lived adjacent Jefferson's store at the ferry, knew him to be talkative and spoke with him often:

> I conversed with him on a great many subjects. He related to me for instance his history of his business here & his past life & how he had made a great deal of money. He told me how he had at one time bought up a good deal of canal script here when it was selling at a low rate against the advice of even some of his friends & had afterwards negotiated it for State bonds & had made a good speculation by it. He talked with me some about religion. He professed to disbelieve in a future state of existence for man. I don't remember ever conversing with him about mathematics or philosophy. I did not regard him as a literary man or scholar. . . . He was a democrat I think. . . . I talked with him on other matters than money making, but the main bent of his mind was on money & I thought he loved it better than anything else.[177]

Around the town of Scottsville, Peter Field Jefferson's wealth took on mythic proportions. Afraid to leave money at the store over night, he carried the cash home to Mount Walla in a shot bag, taking it back to the store in the morning. At home, he tucked the money in a desk with a sloping top and little drawers. Oddly, his makeshift safe was just as often open as it was locked.[178]

Tales of hidden treasure at Mount Walla persisted for decades after Jefferson's death and even made their way into the Virginia Historical Inventory survey for the house:

> Years afterwards when the place had changed hands many times, a man and his two sons were employed to repair the building. They were careful workmen and worked accordingly up to a certain point. The work was then hurried and they appeared anxious to get away. They were never known to work again and purchased considerable property. It is thought they found this hidden money.[179]

Even among his friends, Peter Field trusted no one person completely. Harriet Straton, whose daughter would eventually marry his grandson Peter V. Foland, knew Jefferson all of her life and observed that he would never turn his business over to just one man. He would engage another to see it was "done right." In Jefferson's mind, they were all "rogues" and he would get "one rogue to watch another."[180]

Peter Field was perceived as a solitary man, his obsession with money drove a wedge between him and most of the people around him. This self-imposed isolation could be viewed as merely eccentric or as deeply troubled. His reputation as a heavy drinker, who was often drunk by the end of the work day, suggests an unhappy man. Still, he had his close friends, among them his advisors— merchant Thomas Staples and attorney William M. Wade, well-respected men in Scottsville and beyond. Dr. James Wade was the family's physician. James "Madison" Noel, a tailor in Scottsville, and Joseph Walker, a carpenter who lived nearby at Driver's Hill in Fluvanna County, were his confidential companions. Madison Noel not only helped Jefferson with his store but also was trusted to manage some of his affairs.

Joseph Walker sometimes worked for Jefferson on building projects. Walker recalled, "I was intimately acquainted with him for a long time. He would advise with me about a good many small matters and some big ones too but I don't know whether he took my advice. I knew his ways pretty well & he had some rather curious ways." An Elder of the Scottsville Presbyterian Church, Walker remembered that Jefferson frequently stated that he would "die like a dog" but he thought that other people would be accountable in the hereafter. Clearly, Jefferson wasted no time reading his Bible and eschewed reading in general, both books and newspapers. Walker commented wryly, "Peter Field Jefferson was remarkable for not reading."[181]

As he aged, Peter Field increasingly disregarded his appearance. Born to deep-rooted lines of Virginia gentry, this had not always been the case. Jefferson was well aware of the expected behaviors of the planter class and, in his youth, "dressed up," as young men tended to do. As he climbed his way to the highest rungs of Scottsville's self-made mercantile class, it may have served him to shed some of the gracious customs of the previous generation. At the river front, he traded with the roughest kind of customers. What may have begun as rebellion, became first a lifestyle, then an obsession. For several winters, he was seen wearing the same, old blue blanket coat and linen breeches. This image of an unkempt Peter Field Jefferson was a far cry from the young man who spent $5.00 on a fur hat.[182]

Eccentricity in advanced age ran in the family. In his retirement, his uncle, former President Thomas Jefferson, also dressed as he pleased. In 1815, Francis Calley Gray visited Monticello and noted:

> Mr. Jefferson soon made his appearance. He is quite tall, 6 feet, one or two inches, face streaked & speckled with red, light gray eyes, white hair, dressed in shoes of very thin soft leather with pointed toes and heels ascending in a peak behind, with very short quarters, grey worsted stockings, corduroy small clothes, blue waistcoat & coat, of stiff thick cloth made of the wool of his own merinoes & badly manufactured.
>
> On looking round the room [at Monticello] in which we sat the first thing which attracted our attention was the state of the chairs. They had leather bottoms stuffed with hair, but the bottoms were completely worn through & the hair sticking out in all directions. . . .[183]

~

Peter Field Jefferson's family suffered from his peculiar habits. While Joseph Walker found him to be "a friendly man at his house," by 1850, the Jefferson household was far from peaceful. Since his marriage in 1819, his wife, Jane, had lived under mounting strain, coping with a difficult and distant husband; the death of her oldest son; and increasingly unmanageable children. Even when she first came to live in Scottsville, people thought her "strange," but in that respect, she and Peter Field were seen as a "good match." Reportedly, she had never been a woman of "good strong mind," some even went so far as to call her idiotic.[184]

Other, more generous onlookers, believed that Jane Jefferson became deranged as she aged, leaving her incapable of managing her domestic affairs. As a result, her husband was forced to take over the ordering of meals and other tasks that would normally be in a wife's domain. Nicey, the Jeffersons' female slave, doubtless was responsible for the household chores and the cooking, as well as looking after Mrs. Jefferson.[185]

W. W. Hamner, a carpenter living in Scottsville who knew both Peter Field and Jane Jefferson for over twenty-five years, told a strange and intimate story about the couple that began with a cry of "murder:"

> I can't tell you the date it was at the time of some political meeting here—someone was to speak here (in Scottsville) on that day who was kin or connected with Peter F Jefferson ... and I insisted on Mr. Jefferson coming down to hear him. There was a cry of murder and, when we heard it, myself and John Tyndall [sic] of Buckingham & various others went up to the house. I was the first one that went in the house, knowing Mr. Jefferson & his wife.
>
> When I went in there I asked Mrs. Jefferson what was the matter, she was bleeding a little around the mouth. She went on to tell me then that Mr. Jefferson had kicked her out of bed. Mr. Jefferson spoke up and said it was all a lie that she had been picking her teeth to make the blood come and that the truth was that she had kicked up a row because she wanted him to do something for her that he couldn't do just then.
>
> I was a little drinking and, to have some fun, told Mr. Jefferson to get up. He got up and had on nothing in the world but a short flannel shirt. There was a dim fire burning. I told him I wanted a light. He said he had no candle but told me to throw on some shingles and make a better light ... that was the best he could do. I put on some shingles and took one shingle burning at the end and shook it around him to examine him. ... He hopped and I told him he was pretty active to not really do anything—the old woman laughed and told me to touch him again.
>
> I was pretty drunk and made him trot around some time and treated him rather rough but it was on account of whiskey and all in a friendly way. Before we left, they went to bed—all parties satisfied. He at least went to bed. She may have been sitting up. She was in her night clothes too and promised to go to bed.[186]

Then, according to Hamner, everything was quiet in the household, no more disturbance, and the Jeffersons seemed to have enjoyed the proceedings. Hamner also noted that the couple had not been drinking. This was not always the case, for Peter Field had a wide reputation as an intemperate man. That he drank heavily and openly, perhaps engendering public disapproval, only added to Jane Jefferson's distress and social withdrawal.[187]

In 1851, Jane's increasing limitations were apparent when she co-signed a Fluvanna County deed with her mark. In her early fifties, possible cognitive loss proved temporary. Several years later, in the autumn of 1858, Jane co-signed and sealed an Albemarle County deed with her husband, indicating she had regained her composure and, at least some of, her faculties. After her husband's death, she devised a sensible last will.[188]

Despite a reclusive nature, Jane attended services at Scottsville Methodist Episcopal Church, possibly praying for her husband's redemption. When Scottsville town leader Joseph Beal suggested that Jefferson contribute to the church, since his wife enjoyed it, he declined, replying that while it was heaven for her to go to services, the same would be hell for him.[189]

Jane Jefferson's sons doubtless added to her distress and social embarrassment. Thomas was born with a "good mind," then "went deranged." By the early 1850s, he may have rarely left the house.[190] Peter Field, Jr. was generally thought to be a fool and could be a dangerous one. His low intelligence combined with volatile emotions even led to lawlessness.

In March of 1851, "Fields" Jefferson and George Herndon were accused of threatening Sally M. Seay, throwing rocks at her house. They made "threats against her person and figure," and threatened to "do her some bodily injury." The men were charged with disrupting the peace and the Albemarle County Court demanded that they "keep the peace for a year and be of good behavior towards all the citizens of this commonwealth and especially towards Susan M. Seay." Each was required to ensure that he obeyed the court order. In Peter Field, Jr.'s case, he committed to $100.00 towards the bond and his cousin, Elbridge G. Jefferson, guaranteed an additional $150.00. Peter Field, Jr. signed the bond with his "X," a sad reminder of his illiteracy.[191]

The disruptive young man, however, did not stay out of trouble and, on October 1, 1853, he was indicted by a Grand Jury for carrying concealed weapons. For a long time, he had been known to carry a pistol or a bowie knife. The summons was addressed to Field Jefferson, Jr., who offered an explanation for his behavior and asked that charges be dropped.[192]

~

While avoiding a social life, Peter Field Jefferson favored spending time at his work and in his gardens. He kept busy and had a "splendid hand to raise vegetables" both at his house and at his store.[193] Interestingly, on the 1850 Federal Census, he gave his occupation as farmer, instead of merchant, ferry keeper, or even speculator, all of which he was. While he owned over eighty acres of land at Mount Walla, much of it was wooded, with a little crop around the house for personal use. In middle age, had Jefferson become nostalgic for the life of a Virginia planter, with its accompanying status? He may have been looking ahead to his next significant investment—a plantation in Buckingham County.[194]

Soon, Jefferson completed an unprecedented purchase; he secured the title to 2,300 acres in Buckingham County from the estate of James Wiley Winfree. Known locally as "Winfrey's Tract," the spelling conformed to the branch of the family which resided in Buckingham. Situated twenty-three miles northeast of Buckingham Courthouse, the farm was adjacent Snowden and contained good bottom land running along the James River.[195]

The former owner, James Wiley Winfree (1781–1846), purchased the property in 1821 from Robert Craig's estate. Robert Craig, a long-time neighbor to Snowden, was one of the executors named in Randolph Jefferson's 1808 will.[196] Winfree probably never lived on the property. In addition to farming it, he may have used it to raise thoroughbred horses. In 1845, Winfree was taxed in Buckingham County for twenty-five slaves and fourteen horses. His full-time residence was in Chesterfield County, just south of Richmond, at Broad Rock. There, he owned at least another fifty slaves, bred race horses, and was, at one time, the Chairman of Broad-Rock Jockey Club. He also conducted business in Richmond, including shipping on the James River, and was a stock holder in the Bank of Virginia.[197]

In 1839, Winfree offered the property for sale, without success. His advertisement read:

James River Land for Sale
I AM determined to sell my PLANTATION in Buckingham, within sight of Scottsville, containing twenty-three hundred acres, about one

hundred and seventy five acres James River low grounds, and about one hundred acres Creek low grounds, about six hundred acres cleared land. It is the finest land for clover and plaster; the low grounds and some of the high lands are now covered with it. There is a small Grist Mill and Saw Mill on it. Any person disposed to purchase will please call on Mr. [Bledsoe], my Overseer, on the premises, and he will show the land. I will make the price reasonable, and the payments easy; for, as stated above, I am determined to sell. All who wish to purchase land are invited to view the premises. Letters directed to me in Richmond will meet immediate attention. Possession the 1st January, or before. The Purchaser will be permitted to sow a crop of wheat.

J. W. Winfree[198]

The land did not sell and, after Winfree's death in 1846, his widow and Administrix, Lucy Winfree, offered it at auction in the autumn of 1847:

VALUABLE JAMES RIVER ESTATE FOR SALE.

By virtue of a Decree of the Circuit Court of Chesterfield, of the 3rd of April, 1847, amended by another decree in July, 1847, in the suit of David C. Winfree, &c., against Lucy Winfree and others, the plantation on James river in the county of Buckingham, belonging to the estate of James W. Winfree, deceased, will be offered for sale, by public auction, on the premises, on TUESDAY, the 19th of October 1847, if fair, if not, the next fair day. The plantation contains, by survey, 2,300 acres, of which there are estimated to be about 600 acres of open arable land, including about 150 acres of river, and a small portion of creek low grounds. The residue of the land is in woods, and much of it well timbered. Nearly all the open land is in a high state of improvement from the use of clover and plaster, and is well adapted to the growth of tobacco, corn, wheat and oats. There is a grist mill on the place, and a site on which there has been a saw mill, the dam now standing in good repair. The mill was burnt last year, but may be rebuilt at a moderate cost, and rendered very profitable. The plantation adjoins the lands of Ro. Bolling, John and James Harris, Henry and Lorenzo Nicholas and others, and is about 5 miles from Scottsville and 8 miles from Virginia Mills. Produce may be carried across the river to the canal without any hauling on the opposite side. It is well watered by two creeks running entirely through it, and by a number of springs conveniently situated. There is a good orchard, and all necessary tobacco-houses, barns, &c. with a small dwelling and an overseer's house.

The purchaser will receive possession of the land, now in crop, so soon as the crops can be properly gathered and removed; and will take full possession on the 1st January next, reserving only the use of tobacco houses and necessary fuel until the tobacco crop can be cured and carried away.

The Terms are: One-fourth cash; and a credit of one, two and three years, equal instalments, for the residue—the credit payments to bear interest from the sale, and to be secured by bonds with good security, and by retaining the title until payment.

We are authorized to say, that it is not the intention of any of the persons now interested in the estate to purchase it.

Lucy Winfree, Holden Rhodes, Com'rs.[199]

Jefferson may have purchased the property at the 1847 auction; however, during 1851–1853, the James W. Winfree estate continued to pay taxes on the land and Jefferson did not assume tax payments until 1854. There are other indications that he took possession of the land earlier, possibly leasing it from the Winfree estate. By 1852, Jefferson owned one slave over the age of sixteen and a second slave between the ages of twelve and sixteen, living in Buckingham County.[200]

Additionally, Jefferson bought a mill site from William Henry and Lorenzo Nicholas. Situated on Big George's Creek, adjoining Winfrey's, this comparatively small tract greatly enhanced the value of his Buckingham County property.[201]

In 1854, the structures at Winfrey's were valued at $800, consisting of a dwelling house, overseer's house, and a small grist mill. Ever the good business-man, Jefferson had the tract surveyed, finding it to be only 2,270 acres, slightly reducing his tax obligation. He threw himself into an ambitious improvements project, hiring his friend, carpenter Joseph Walker, to build a new mill and cover a large barn. As a result, by 1855, the former Nicholas site had structures valued at $1,000. Two years later, Jefferson was taxed on dwellings totally $2,500, reflecting the extent of his improvements.[202]

Now in his mid-sixties, Peter Field had reached an age when thoughts of nostalgia and a leisurely life often creep into a man's mind. Did he feel a twinge of homesickness for agrarian life across the James River? Did he envision retiring in Buckingham County? Or, perhaps, he imagined enjoying a summer home in the country, away from town, providing a quieter domicile for his reclusive wife. He could not have either of his sons in mind to take over the plantation. His elder, Thomas, was now an adult dependent, and, his younger, Peter Field, Jr., was both mentally and emotionally incapable of operating a property of this scale. Until Jefferson was ready to occupy the plantation, if that was his plan, he needed a trusted manager. Ultimately, his nephew, Elbridge G. Jefferson, who lived on Sharp's Creek adjacent the Harris brothers in northern Buckingham County, took over the management at Winfrey's Tract while it awaited Peter Field Jefferson's pleasure.[203]

Whatever his plans for Winfrey's Tract, in the end, it might have been called Peter Field Jefferson's Folly. He would never enjoy the fruits of his much improved plantation in Buckingham County, rather, the property would significantly complicate his estate, as well as the estates of others, throwing his extended family into decades of legal conflict.

~

During 1850–1860, industry in Buckingham County expanded rapidly. It was certainly a place for Peter Field Jefferson to direct his entrepreneurial energy. In 1850, the Industrial Census for Buckingham County listed only five industries in the county, four of which were mills: Nicholas & Aldridge's saw mill, R. C. Nicholas & Bros.' flour mill, Samuel Putney's saw mill, and Carroll M. Shepard's saw mill and grist mill. Robert Carter Nicholas operated Virginia Mills and was also a merchant. His mill sat downstream from Snowden and Winfrey's, on the Slate River. Significantly, the mill was mentioned in the 1847 advertisement for Winfrey's Tract. The eight miles separating the two mills indicated they were not in direct competition with each other. By 1860, however, industry in Buckingham had radically changed. Twenty-eight individuals reported commercial property and over half of them were mills. Robert C. Nicholas was still operating a grist mill; however, no mill was operating on Winfrey's Tract. This may be because, before his death, Jefferson sold 15 acres to William H. Nicholas.[204]

~

In the spring of 1854, Peter Field Jefferson demonstrated a burst of energy, greatly expanding his real estate holdings. In Scottsville, he acquired multiple lots sold at public auction which were "knocked out" to him at a price of $2,361. He took immediate possession, offering the seller cash rather than the typical three or four installment payments. The fact that he possessed that amount in cash set him apart from the vast majority of Virginia gentry who relied on credit and were typically "cash poor." These lots were connected to other Jefferson-owned properties, located between Main Street & the Canal. The sale included two houses on Main Street.[205] The purchase was described as follows:

> Situated between Main Street and the canal in the corner formed by the street leading from Main Street to the ferry next to the store house then occupied by the said (John) McGrath including the old warehouse and all the recent vacant property on this locality belonging to the said Richard Moon (T) at the time of his death. Also two houses and lots on the opposite side of Main Street. . . .[206]

Peter Field Jefferson's Last Will

In September of 1854, Peter Field Jefferson wrote a new will. The acquisition of Winfrey's Tract and the valuable new property in Scottsville, in addition to the marriage of Peter Field, Jr., encouraged him to put pen to paper.[207]

On March 28, 1854, Peter Field, Jr. had married Elizabeth A. Wood, the daughter of Elizabeth and Thomas Wood, a millwright living in Fluvanna County. The couple was married in Fluvanna by Baptist minister Joseph H. Fox. Peter Field, Jr. was about twenty-five years old. The bride gave her age as thirty-five. Their age difference alone signals an unusual marriage for 19th century Virginia. Brides were rarely older than grooms and, if they were, they typically concealed their true age. The groom gave his occupation as "Gentleman," indicating he had none. Ultimately, it was an ironic self-description. Six years later, on the 1860 census, he was more accurately described as a laborer who could neither read nor write. On their mutual documents, Peter Field, Jr. signed with "his mark."[208]

Joseph Walker recalled that the primary purpose of the 1854 will was to include Jefferson's daughter, Fanny Foland, who had been disinherited by a previous will because she had married contrary to her father's wishes. Walker's memory was a bit inexact, though, and it may have been Fanny's death that prompted Peter Field Jefferson to revise his will. She is not mentioned in it; however, a significant inheritance is left to her only child, Peter Valentine Foland. If Jefferson had not made peace with his only daughter, who died far from her Virginia home, he could and did provide for her only child.

Walker remembered that he was asked to go up the hill to Jefferson's house to witness the new will. Jefferson was very drunk when he made the request, asking Walker to come up to Mount Walla the next morning. After breakfast, he did so, only to find the will already written out and witnessed.[209]

There is no indication that Peter Field was ill at this time or not of sound mind, rather, he noted "the uncertainty of life, and the duty of being prepared for death," as the "official" reason behind his decision to make a new will. A wise action for a man with a large estate. In his sixties, he was a man of considerable property and, naturally, wanted to divide it as he saw fit. In the will, as was customary of the day, he requested that his debts be met before his property was distributed and asked that any property not specifically named be distributed equally among his two sons and the children of his brother, Robert Lewis Jefferson, who was still living at the time. Clearly, despite his social peculiarities, Peter Field had remained close to his brother and his brother's children, Mary Elizabeth "Bettie" (Jefferson) Gantt and Elbridge G. Jefferson.

Jefferson gave the Buckingham County plantation, including the mill, to his wife, Jane, for the remainder of her life. He also gave Jane the household and kitchen furniture then in the Scottsville residence. The combination of these two gifts strongly suggested that Jefferson either planned to be living on the Buckingham County farm when he died or that he expected Jane to live there after his death. Additionally, he left Jane $1,500 in cash. At her death, her property was to be put in trust for the benefit of Peter Field, Jr., his wife, and their heirs.

A trust was created for the benefit of Peter Field, Jr., to be funded with $10,000. He was to be paid interest semi-annually and "in no case" was the principle to be invaded. After Jane's death, Jefferson wished that the Buckingham plantation would also be placed in trust for Peter Field, Jr., his wife, and their heirs. When Peter Field, Jr. came into possession of the land he had the right to cultivate it or to have it rented by the Trustees. Due to the fact that Jefferson sold the Buckingham County farm prior to his death, this part of the will was never implemented.[210]

Next, Jefferson provided $15,000 for his son, Thomas, "for and during his natural life." These funds were to be held in trust and interest was to be paid semi-annually. Again, the principle was not to be touched. Thomas was even less capable than his younger brother. In 1854, he relied on the full-time care of his parents.

Jefferson's grandson, Peter Valentine Foland, was to receive all of Peter Field's real estate "situated within the Town of Scottsville and immediately adjacent," including the ferry. The properties were to be rented and the income held until the boy reached his majority. In 1854, Peter Valentine Foland was just nine years old and living in Tennessee.

Jefferson also owned property in Nelson County, containing a store and dwelling that he rented out. These were to go to his nephew, Elbridge Jefferson.[211] Jefferson's personal servant, Winston, was left to Jane and then to Peter Field, Jr.[212] Should Jefferson's own children and his grandson die without issue, he wished his property to go to the children of his brother, Robert Lewis Jefferson—Elbridge Jefferson and Mary Elizabeth Gantt.[213] Jefferson's attorney, William M. Wade, and Elbridge G. Jefferson were named Executors.[214]

As the years progressed, William M. Wade was not only Peter Field Jefferson's general counsel, he also attended to a significant percentage of Jefferson's business affairs. While Wade did not serve as Jefferson's general agent overseeing properties, he did represent Jefferson in business. If Jefferson wanted "anything done," he would ask Wade to attend to it.[215]

Albemarle Mills

Peter Field Jefferson's next major purchase was Albemarle Mills. The deed transferring the mill site, with 82 acres, from James W. and Sarah B. Mason, was recorded on January 22, 1856. Located just outside Scottsville, on the Hardware River, near the Fluvanna County line, the property was significantly closer to Mount Walla and Scottsville than Jefferson's new mill in Buckingham County. Everything about Albemarle Mills was comparatively manageable and convenient. Importantly, its operation did not require acquiring more slaves, an additional investment that Jefferson was hesitant to make. Within the year, it was commonly known as Jefferson's Mill or Jefferson Mills.[216]

The mill site was developed long before Peter Field purchased the property. In 1823, one of Scottsville's biggest investors, Richard Moon, petitioned the county court to build a grist mill on the Hardware River.[217]

In 1837, Dr. Gilly M. Lewis purchased what had become known as Albemarle Mills, an extensive operation valued at approximately $6,000. One of forty gristmills in Albemarle County at that time, Albemarle Mills was impressive for its versatility and its privileged location close to the James River. A Magistrate in the county, Dr. Lewis lived at Cliffside, a beautiful, Federal-style, brick home sitting on a steep hill overlooking Scottsville. He died in 1842, and, in 1843, Albemarle Mills was advertised for sale by P. C. Lewis, Executrix of Gilly M. Lewis.[218]

LAND AND MILLS FOR SALE.

WILL be offered for sale, on the premises, on the 1st day of March, 1843, if fair, if not, the next fair day, thereafter, the Albemarle Mills and 240 acres of Land adjoining.—The above Mills are in good order and contain two pair of burrs for grinding wheat, one pair for corn, and one pair for plaster. Connected with the Mill is an excellent Wool Carding Machine, nearly new, which, with attention, could be made very valuable. There is also on the premises a Saw-Mill, and all the necessary houses for Coopers, Millers, &c.

This property is situated on the Hardware River, within 3 ½ miles of Scottsville, a flourishing town on James River, and in the vicinity of a fine wheat growing region, and affords to those who may desire to possess such valuable property, in a most desirable part of the country, and contiguous to an excellent market, an opportunity which but rarely occurs. All persons desirous of purchasing, will please examine before the day of sale. Mr. Davis, the Miller, who resides on the premises, will, with pleasure, show the property to any person disposed to examine it. TERMS—One-third of the purchase money to be paid on the 1st day of September, 1843, and the balance in 2 equal annual installments, with approved personal security and a deed of trust to secure the purchase money.

P. C. LEWIS,
Executrix of Gilley [sic] M. Lewis, dec'd.[219]

On September 19, 1851, 100 acres of the Gilly M. Lewis estate were sold to Henry T. Hartman, a Scottsville attorney. It was not long before the Hartmans experienced financial problems and, on November 14, 1854, they conveyed all but thirty acres in trust to Archibald McClung "to secure a debt of $3,410.07 to John Tyler and William Davis, lately merchants of the firm Tyler & Davis."[220] By December, Albemarle Mills was once again on the auction block.

TRUST SALE OF VALUABLE REAL ESTATE AND PERSONAL PROPERTY.

By virtue of two deeds of trust executed to me, by H. T. Hartman for the benefit of Tyler and Davis, and others, therein mentioned—and by order of the creditors, I will sell at public auction at the Albemarle Mills, on Wednesday, the 10th day of January 1855, if fair, if not the next fair day Sunday excepted, the following valuable property, viz: the Albemarle Mills, with about 100 acres of land, be the same more or less, situated on Hardware River, three miles North-East of Scottsville. This property has the advantage of a first rate water power, sufficient to operate a cotton and woolen factory. The grist mill commands a good custom, and has all the machinery for manufacturing flour, to the amount of from thirty to fifty bbls flour per day—the building, five stories high, is of the very best materials of brick and stone, and has been built with a view to strength and durability. There is also attached, and conveniently arranged, a first rate circular Saw-mill, with a good railway and yard for the reception of lumber.

Persons desiring to purchase, will find the property in possession of Henry T. Hartman, who will take pleasure in showing the same. Terms made know[n] on day of sale.

Archibald McClung, Trustee.[221]

The day of the sale, the property was purchased by James W. Mason, a prominent Scottsville businessman and president of the Scottsville Bank, who lived at Old Hall.[222] He paid $3,000 for the property. A year later, on January 22, 1856, he sold 82 ½ acres, including the mill, to Peter Field Jefferson.[223]

Jefferson was now ready to cash in on a booming flour market. A history of Scottsville written in 1902 describes the atmosphere:

In the early fifties Scottsville had the distinction of being the largest flour market in the State. Persons would come from Norfolk and buy as many as 600 barrels at a time. The mountain trade was fine. At least 100 large covered wagons would come over at a time from Augusta, Rockbridge, and other counties further west. These would be drawn by from four to six and sometimes eight of the finest draught horses. The teamsters took great pride in these splendid animals. Some wore bells, some wore none. If a team which had bells stalled, and was pulled out by horses that had none, the drivers of the latter transferred the bells to their own team. The wagoneers would bring their provisions with them and camp out in the vacant lots about the village.[224]

Did the enterprising Jefferson charge "rent" for the use of his undeveloped town lots as the wagons came and went from Scottsville? Certainly, his grocery provided food and drink to the hungry and thirsty teamsters.

During the 1850s, wheat wasn't the only product flowing into the village of Scottsville:

> All sorts of produce figured in their loads: venison, whiskey, dried fruits, nuts, etc., and these would be given in exchange for plaster and salt to take home with them. Good whiskey (if it ever can be), real old rye would be sold on the road for 12 ½ cents per gállon, and at this place for 25 cents. At one time, when the article was scarce, four wagon loads were bought on the road for 12 ½ cents....
>
> "This was as good a country as one would wish to live in then," say the oldest inhabitants—"healthy and prosperous." All the farmers owned slaves and laborers were plentiful. Business was brisk and the outlook cheering.[225]

In this booming atmosphere, how could a shrewd man like Peter Field Jefferson fail to prosper?

~

In the survey written for the Virginia Historical Inventory, R. E. Hannum recorded anecdotal material concerning "Jefferson Mills," including this confounding statement: "It is said that Thomas Jefferson gave his advise [sic] and helped superintend the work when his nephew Peter made some alterations." Since President Thomas Jefferson died in 1826 and Peter Field Jefferson purchased the mill in 1856, this anecdote could not possibly refer to President Thomas Jefferson. It could, however, be a confused recollection concerning Peter Field's brother, Thomas, and his intimate involvement with Peter Field's family during 1859–1861. It is just as likely another instance in which a Jefferson association is stretched to include the president. Other oral traditions erroneously connect the Jeffersons of Snowden and Scottsville to the great man and to Monticello. A bit like "George Washington Slept Here," any association with President Thomas Jefferson gives added value to a property, especially if that association includes architectural advice.[226]

When Hannum wrote his survey, the mill was standing and his detailed physical description of the place was based on first-hand observation:

The mill is located on the west bank of the Hardware river about four miles from Scottsville, Virginia. It is a brick structure, four stories high, rectangulare [sic] in shape being 65 by 40 feet. The walls are eighteen inches thick at the base but drop back to twelve inches at the second floor. The only door is in the center of the wall on the front of the building away from the river, there are two windows on each side of the door.

They are quite high having at one time nine panes in the top sash but at present there are six in each sash and the space that is left is boarded up.

The timbers in this building are well worth a trip to see, two of them run the full length and are 18 by 24 inches, on the second floor two others run across the building. They are the same size. The rafters are 4 by 4 except every fifth one which are 4 by 8's. All of the smaller timbers are whip sawed and hanging on the wall inside the door is a large saw that it is said cut the logs to get the timbers for the mill.

Originally the mill was run by an overshot wheel, fed from the stone dam which is eighteen feet above the water, and about twenty feet above the bed of the river. At present turbines are used, there being two of them. The original machinery was of course all hand made and some [of] the wooden tooth wheels are still to be seen although they are no longer used.[227]

Peter Field Jefferson had made another sound investment, the mill would generate revenue through rentals and continue to create income for his heirs. When Jefferson purchased Albemarle Mills in early 1856, Peter Field, Jr. (a.k.a. Little Fields and Fields) had been married for nearly two years. His first child, yet another Peter, was either on the way or an infant, and they needed a home of their own.[228]

On January 28, 1857, Peter Field purchased another tract on the Hardware River, not far from the mill, known as Bleak Hill, which became the home of Peter Field, Jr. and his family. The previous owner, Mahala Dawson, received $1,500 for the property, which contained about 65 acres in addition to the dwelling.[229] Living adjacent the young Jeffersons were James M. Dawson, carpenter; William F. Dawson, carpenter; R. P. Pace, miller; and William Pace, merchant, suggesting a mini service village around Jefferson Mills.[230]

Peter Field, Jr. and his wife, Elizabeth, had two surviving children: a son, Peter, and a daughter, Frances Anne Wade, called Fannie, whose name remembered her aunt, Fanny (Jefferson) Foland.[231] In 1937, R. E. Hannum wrote about Bleak Hill for the Virginia Historical Inventory. He dated the house c.1760, including an unusually long description of it and the grounds. It reads, in part:

> Today one can see that this place could be very easily called "Bleak Hill", but from the remains of the once well proportioned house, and beautiful old trees, one wonders how the name originated. The house sets [sic] on the hill well above the Hardware River and Jefferson, or as they are sometimes called, Albemarle Mill. The house faces the south, though the exterior entrances are alike. In the yard is an unusually large white pine, now badly broken by wind and storms. It is over a hundred feet high and three and three-quarters feet in diameter. There are other white pines but not so large, walnuts, cedars, alanthus and locust trees. There is a row of large cedars leading down the northern side of the hill and a tangle of rose bushes which was probably the flower garden in olden days. The barn and other remnants of out buildings were down the southern side of the hill.
>
> The house is rectangular in shape with a finished basement with brick walls. It is a frame house of two stories covered with very narrow weatherboards. The roof is gabled and now covered with metal roofing. The outside cornices are wood and plain. There are two brick chimneys, on the east and one on the west end.[232]

Hannum went on to describe the interiors, discussing the floor plan in great detail, the dormer windows, and the wide floor boards. His interest in the house may have been heightened due to its age, as well as the Jefferson connection. He closed his survey saying, "The house is in very bad repair, the basement walls are caving in and the roof leaks badly."[233]

This once charming house, the home of Peter Field Jefferson, Jr. and his family, bore similarities to Mount Walla, including its hilltop position above the river. The precise condition of the house, at the time of Jefferson's purchase, is unknown; however, the purchase price of $1,500 for the house and about sixty-five acres may not indicate top condition. If R. E. Hannum correctly dated the house, it was nearly 100 years old when the Jeffersons moved in.[234]

The Accident

Having settled his younger son at Bleak Hill, Peter Field Jefferson could look ahead to his next investment or, perhaps, retirement in Buckingham County. Then, in late 1855 or early 1856, Jefferson fell from a ladder that was braced against a locust tree (or a cherry tree) while attempting to hive a swarm of bees, dislocated his hip, and never regained full use of his lower limbs, becoming permanently lame. Jefferson may or may not have hit his head when he fell. At the time of the accident no disorientation or dementia was noticed by those closest to him.[235]

He was bed-ridden for several months, possibly longer, and had to be lifted from one bed to another. Permanently limited in his mobility, a "sick chair" was added to the household furniture. Eventually, he could walk and ride horseback, but could no longer do demanding work. Puttering in his garden gave him pleasure. From time to time, he suspiciously inspected his woodlands near Mount Walla to see whether anybody was "deprecating on the wood." When he went as far as Jefferson Mills, he rode his old grey horse.[236]

In light of Peter Field's physical impairment, the Jeffersons finally had to face the long-term mental health problems of their son, Thomas, who was an adult dependent, with no useful occupation. Family friend Joseph Walker simply, and rather kindly, described Thomas as "a curious sort of a fellow."[237] It is possible that Jane Jefferson was ill-equipped to care for both her husband and her son. She may have needed Peter Field's physical strength to control Tom. It is also possible that his condition worsened when his father became immobilized. Whatever the immediate cause, his mental deterioration had been a long time coming and, on August 7, 1857, "Thomas F. Jefferson," son of Peter Field Jefferson, was admitted to Western Lunatic Asylum in Staunton, Virginia.[238]

Twenty-nine years old, Thomas was diagnosed as a "masturbator." His condition had persisted for six years prior to his admittance, indicating that his issues began in his early twenties and that his parents, siblings, and others living at and near Mount Walla had long been coping with Thomas' problematic and socially unacceptable behavior. He was "medium" in build, with fair complexion. His hair was brown, his eyes were grey. Initially, he was treated three times a day. The asylum records do not disclose the nature of the treatment.[239]

In 1860, Thomas was enumerated on the Federal Population Census as patient #1484, age: thirty-three; occupation: none; diagnosis: masturbator. He is one of three such cases listed on that page of the census. Other diagnoses ranged from "domestic trouble," to epilepsy, to intemperance, to traumas (childbirth), and diseases (typhoid fever). One twenty-three-year-old woman called "Cinderella" was described as "disappointed in love."[240]

Jefferson made regular, annual payments of $250 towards his son's upkeep. After Peter Field's death, payments were made to the asylum from a trust created for Thomas' maintenance. Thomas outlived his father but preceded his mother in death, leaving his brother, Peter Field, Jr., and his nephew, Peter V. Foland, to inherit the lion's share of Peter Field Jefferson's estate. When he died from bronchitis on March 18, 1863, he had been institutionalized for six years, seven months, and twelve days.[241]

~

Unable to return to full-time work at the store or the ferry, Peter Field Jefferson hired his close friend, James Madison Noel, to assume the management of his properties in Scottsville. Noel was aided by Elbridge G. Jefferson, who looked after his uncle's interests in Buckingham and Nelson counties, particularly collecting any rents due. Peter Field frequently sent Elbridge on errands, even for minor matters, and some people thought he "abused" his nephew. Peter Field saw it differently and did not hesitate to tell his friends that he felt justified in working his nephew without compensation. His nephew would be "paid" through his inheritance of the store and lot near Faber's Mills in Nelson County. Elbridge also stood to inherit even more based on contingency terms in Jefferson's 1854 will. In advance of his death, the old man was determined to collect both work and personal attention from his nephew.[242]

A mature man in his early forties, Elbridge G. Jefferson's most important contribution to his uncle's estate was the management of Winfrey's in Buckingham County. Jefferson clearly trusted and liked his nephew, who was a stable and responsible gentleman, unlike his own sons. Elbridge's Buckingham County farm was convenient to Winfrey's and he could oversee both places with relative ease.

By 1857, however, Peter Field became displeased with his nephew's handling of the Buckingham property. According to family friend John T. Noel:

> Mr. Jefferson had been over to his farm and found his nephew Mr.
> Elbridge Jefferson farming the land as he said not according to agreement

& he then remarked that he should sell it that he should no longer abuse his place that way. . . . [He] found Mr. Elbridge Jefferson plowing his land too wet with the water running in the furrow.[243]

Immediately and, perhaps, impulsively, Peter Field called on John T. Noel's father, James Madison Noel, sending him to attorney William Wade with the request to make the necessary arrangements to sell Winfrey's. Jefferson's disapproval of his nephew's actions may have been an excuse to sell. A plantation meant either owning or hiring slave labor, which Jefferson believed was a poor investment of his capital.[244] It is also possible that, following his accident, he abandoned his original plans for the plantation and mill, his attention shifting back to expansion closer to Scottsville, including Jefferson Mills and Bleak Hill, which he could personally supervise.

In the autumn of 1857, Jefferson publically stated his reason for giving up Winfrey's when he advertised the forthcoming sale in the *Richmond Enquirer*. He also demonstrated his persuasive abilities when he opined that he would not sell such a valuable farm if it were not for "his inability to give it his attention."[245]

VALUABLE JAMES RIVER FARM, IN THE COUNTY OF BUCKINGHAM, FOR SALE.

The subscriber, of Scottsville, Albemarle county, will offer for sale of FRIDAY, the 6th day of November 1857, on the premises, in the county of Buckingham, at public auction, his farm, lying on James River, 8 miles below the town of Scottsville, containing 2,285 acres, and known as the Winfree tract. This is one of the most valuable and desirable farms on the River, and nothing could induce the subscriber to part with it but his inability to give it his attention.

About 700 acres of the tract are cleared and the balance heavily timbered. It includes about 175 acres of James River low grounds, and about 125 acres of flat land on the two creeks running through it—all of the finest quality. The high land is also of good quality.

There is a first rate grist mill, recently erected on the farm, commanding a large custom.

The improvements on the farm are good, and ample for all its purposes; and the society and health of the neighborhood unexceptionable.

TERMS:—One fourth of the purchase money in cash, and the residue will be divided into five equal annual instalments, bearing interest from date—the purchaser giving bonds, with good security, and a deed of trust on the premises as additional security.

PETER F. JEFFERSON.

Persons desiring to see the farm are referred to Elbridge Jefferson, who lives upon it; John Bledsoe, Esq., of Fluvanna, who lived upon it 10 years, will also give any information desired.[246]

Despite the fact that Peter Field Jefferson was "famous for not reading," he advertised Winfrey's Tract in both the *Richmond Whig* and the *Richmond Enquirer*. Did he actually subscribe to both newspapers? Reading the *Richmond Enquirer* would confirm Democratic leanings, whereas a subscription to the *Whig* would point toward conservatism. In either case, when it came to making money, Jefferson was likely indifferent to the buyer's politics.[247]

Apparently, no buyers came forward and, in the spring of 1858, Peter Field decided to sell Winfrey's Tract at public auction. He asked John T. Noel to be present at the sale and to "cry the property" for him. Noel remembered that he and "Old Mr. Jefferson" rode on horseback to the farm on the day of the auction, accompanied by Jefferson's attorney, William Wade. There was a "right smart gathering of the people," numbering two or three dozen. Noel "knocked out" the property to Elbridge G. Jefferson. Following the sale, Peter Field Jefferson told Noel that "he was willing to give his nephew a good long time to pay," indicating he was content with his nephew's purchase. Oddly, Elbridge Jefferson never processed the papers to finalize the sale.[248]

As a result, in October of 1858, in a private sale, Jefferson sold Winfrey's to James Harris of Buckingham County for $18,000, who took possession of the 2,285 acres on January 1, 1859. Jefferson and Harris had known each other for decades. They may or may not have been on friendly terms. Others were involved in the purchase, though, in the end, James Harris was the sole owner. Three bonds dated June 12, 1858 were signed collectively by James Harris, Samuel Allen (Harris' son-in-law), Henry St. George Harris (Harris' nephew), and J. W. Mason (who sold Albemarle Mills to Peter Field Jefferson in 1854). Installments of $2,700 were to be paid in January of 1861, 1862, and 1863—a total of $8,100 due on the Buckingham farm.[249]

Jacob H. Briggs, a boat inspector who also operated a foundry in Scottsville, lived adjacent Jefferson's store and the ferry. He and Jefferson had a friendly acquaintance, seeing each other daily.[250] Among other things, they discussed the sale of Winfrey's Tract.

> I had conversations with Mr. Jefferson himself about the sale of the
> place. He seemed satisfied with the price it brought—I think he said it
> cost him about $13,000 & that he sold it for about $18,000. I am not
> positive about the amounts. He gave as his reason for selling the property
> that he was himself old & physically unable to attend to it & his children
> were not competent to manage it.[251]

James Harris (1797–1872) was a close neighbor of Elbridge G. Jefferson and his property lay adjacent Winfrey's. His home plantation was on Sharp's Creek in Buckingham County and, in 1858, he was well on his way to becoming one of Buckingham's largest land and slave holders. A nephew of Capt. John Harris of Viewmont, during the mid-1830s, James Harris rented Snowden while it was still held in his uncle's estate and hoped to eventually inherit it, though he did not. Not surprisingly, the availability of a similar, adjacent plantation appealed to him.

Harris was widely known and respected. Joseph Walker called him as "honest a man as you would generally find." Joseph Briggs stated that he was a man of "very high character & bore a reputation rather remarkable for integrity & fair dealing in business." His nephew, Benjamin J. Harris (who eventually served as his Executor), called him a man of "great intelligence, prudence, and caution."[252]

James Harris put his son-in-law, Samuel Allen, in charge at Winfrey's and, when, Allen died in November of 1871, some of his personal property was inventoried there. Within a week of Allen's death, Harris sold the farm to Nathan T. Payne for $13,000. Later, this sale was long-contested in the estates of both Peter Field Jefferson and James Harris.[253]

Imbecile of Mind

Given his compromised physical state, Peter Field Jefferson began to limit his real estate to the immediate area around Scottsville. His nephew, Elbridge, looked after the Nelson County property and the sale of Winfrey's in Buckingham County freed Jefferson of a large responsibility. During 1857–1858, he focused once again on investing in Scottsville, buying and selling developed lots. He also engaged his friend Madison Noel to help supervise his considerable estate, agreeing to pay Noel $300 per year for his services.[254]

With son Thomas institutionalized in the asylum in Staunton and Peter Field, Jr. settled at Bleak Hill, Mount Walla may have experienced a momentary spell of quiet. The Jeffersons maintained a sparse household, furnished primarily with necessities. An ornamental clock, worth $80.00, was an outstanding exception. A writing desk, a large map, and a rifle belonged to Peter Field. A hanking reel and spinning wheel were among Jane's possessions. While the family owned a Bible and three volumes of history, there was a paucity of books in the household. Jefferson was, after all, "famous for not reading." Limited in his mobility, there was little for him to do besides brood and deteriorate.[255]

Following his convalescence from the accident, the old man continued to go about the streets of Scottsville, much as he had always done. Then, rather rapidly, his strength and health failed. Early in 1859, a decrepit Peter Field Jefferson now wandered aimlessly through the town. While people had whispered about disturbances at Mount Walla dating back five or six years, it was now clear to Jefferson's friends and business associates that he had lost his mental faculties. Unable to care for himself or for Jane, physician Ruben Lindsay observed, "He lived like a hog."[256]

By August of 1859, Jefferson was declared "imbecilic of mind," and his eldest brother, Thomas, was appointed his "Committee" (legal guardian). Almost two years earlier, in the autumn of 1857, Thomas Jefferson and his wife, Willie, had moved to Scottsville, making it convenient to oversee his younger brother's business. On August 31, 1859, Thomas completed an inventory of Peter Field's substantial property, both real and personal, which included typical household furnishings, plus a few luxury items such as a looking glass and the clock. Peter Field owned one horse, one cow, and twenty-five stock hogs. Two negroes were itemized: Henry, who was about forty years old and lame, and Winston, who was about fifty years old. Apparently, Nicey, the Jeffersons' female slave, had not been replaced when she died in 1855 and the crippled Henry may have served as their domestic servant.[257]

In over thirty years of investing in and around Scottsville, Jefferson had amassed significant real estate holdings, including the ferry and the grocery store near the landing; his residence, Mount Walla, described as "A tract of land in the Town of Scottsville containing about 84 acres;" Bleak Hill (65 acres); Albemarle

Mills on the Hardware River (100 acres); and lots #11, #12, #24, #35, #36 (the Tavern), #43, #44, #45, #47, #49, #50, #51, #52, #54, and #55.[258]

His investments, bonds, and loans to various Scottsville residents were sizable. He held $2,500 worth of guaranteed Virginia State Bonds, as well as the following personal bonds: James Harris et al. still owed significant installment payments for Winfrey's Tract, totaling $13,500; John T. Noel owed him $1,760, payable on demand; Mason & Lewis owed him $6,387; Staples & Martin's note totaled $5,500; William M. Wade's note was for $1,000; William B. Brady, O. W. Purvis, Spicy Napier, and William A. Woodward all owed Jefferson smaller amounts. That year, Jefferson had a contract with J. N. Gibbs, who rented the ferry and the grocery store. Gibbs paid $200 rent annually for the properties.[259]

The rather surprising number and size of loans to some of Scottsville's most prominent citizens reveals Peter Field Jefferson's hold on the local economy that may or may not have been common knowledge. In addition to his steady acquisition of real estate and accumulation of wealth, Jefferson possessed the power and control of a money lender. Importantly, both financially and psychologically, he was indebted to no one.

The bond with John T. Noel, made in 1858, provides an inkling of what a man would risk for a loan when he needed one. Noel had put up a significant amount of what he was worth as collateral:

> This deed made this 1st day of January 1858 between John T. Noel of the one part and Wm. M. Wade of the other part: Witnesseth that the said Noel hath granted unto the said Wade, his heirs and assigns, the following property viz: one house and lot in the town of Scottsville Albemarle County Virginia known in the plan of said town as lot No. 146. This is a wooden tenement lot adjoining the Eagle Hotel: also a brick tenement and lot adjoining the first mentioned one, in which Madison Noel now resides. This tenement is known in the plan of said town as part of lot No. 147 and both are situated on Valley Street—also the home and lot now occupied by Dr. Jas. M. Jefferies and which formerly belonged to the estate of Dr. Jas. Tompkins. This lot is also situated in the said town—also one negro woman named Martha and her child and also one negro boy named Jim together with the future increase of the female.

In trust to secure to Peter F. Jefferson the sum of Seventeen hundred and sixty dollars due by bond bearing xxxxx even date herewith. This deed shall not be closable until the first day of January 1859. The trustee in the event of sale is to have 5 per cent commission. Witness the following signatures and seals the date above written ~

Jno T. Noel
Notarized by James W. Mason, J. P.[260]

John T. Noel had hoped to have his finances settled by January of 1859. This, however, did not come to pass and, by the time Thomas Jefferson, Committee made an account of the bonds due his brother, Noel's debt was payable on demand.

⌒

There were now three households of Jeffersons in the vicinity of Scottsville. Peter Field, Jr. and his family were at Bleak Hill. Peter Field, Sr. and Jane remained at Mount Walla and, living adjacent them were Thomas and Willie Jefferson, who had married on January 4, 1858.[261]

In stark contrast to the Peter Field Jeffersons, Mr. and Mrs. Thomas Jefferson enjoyed life in Scottsville, displaying their affluence. Doubtless the town folk gossiped about the spending habits of Mr. Thomas Jefferson in contrast to his ever frugal brother, Peter Field. Two horses, valued at $200, and a pleasure carriage, valued at $150, were at his disposal. Peter Field's "old grey horse" was valued at $10. Thomas owned two watches valued at $100, one of which might have been Randolph Jefferson's highly prized silver watch.[262]

Between August of 1859 and August of 1861, Thomas Jefferson was an extremely active manager of his brother's wealth. Working with William M. Wade, Peter Field's trusted legal counsel, Thomas re-allocated a significant percentage of his brother's property. Among these decisions was the acquisition of slaves (which the outspoken Peter Field had avoided as "bad" investments) and a series of loans from Peter Field's considerable cash reserves, including one to himself for over $2,800; one to his mother-in-law, Anna C. Siegfried, for $300; and one to Mason, Martin, & Co. for $1,395.06.[263]

The purchase of the slaves and the loans may have been intertwined. In 1860, Thomas Jefferson reported six slaves on the slave census: a fifty-year-old man and forty-year-old female, a twenty-three-year old female and three boys, ages eight, six, and four. It is possible that they were purchased with his brother's money (the loan of $2,800) and were living with and serving the Thomas Jeffersons. A year later, a Negro woman Adaline ($500), Mariah Jane, a small girl, ($400), Wilson, a small boy ($300), Polly and child ($700) were listed as part of Peter Field Jefferson's estate; all purchased by Thomas Jefferson while he controlled his brother's funds.[264]

In 1860, nine individuals, including Jefferson-owned or hired-out slaves, appear to be connected with the Mason & Martin partnership. An Elizabeth Jefferson (there were at least three living in Albemarle County, however, this was likely Thomas Jefferson's wife Elizabeth "Willie" Jefferson) reported one twenty-five-year-old male, with the notation "M & M" (Mason & Martin). "P. F. Jefferson (Mason & Martin)" reported one fifty-year-old male. Also, in the vicinity of Bleak Hill and Jefferson Mills, a female slave with a five-year-old girl and an infant boy were credited to "(Peter Jefferson) Silas Dawson."[265]

The company of Mason & Martin was owned by James W. Mason (b. abt. 1834) and John S. Martin (b. abt. 1836). Mason, a justice of the peace, lived at Old Hall. In 1860, he owned $46,700 in real estate and $44,250 in personal property. Martin was a merchant, justice of the peace, and President of Scottsville Bank. He lived near Mount Walla and, in 1860, he owned $7,000 in real estate and $33,800 in personal property, including at least sixteen slaves. Why were these apparently wealthy men borrowing money from Peter Field Jefferson via Thomas Jefferson, Committee?[266]

≈

By 1860, the residents of Bleak Hill included the thirty-year-old Peter Field, Jr. and Elizabeth (who gave her age as thirty-four); Elizabeth's sister, Cynthia M. Singer, age thirty-two; and her daughter, Maria Singer, age sixteen. Little Peter was four and the Jefferson's daughter, Frances, was two. Cynthia Singer's occupation was "doctress" (midwife). With no livelihood, Peter Field, Jr. was completely dependent on his father's generosity. He had virtually no real or personal property in his own name. Now that his father was incapacitated, he was forced to rely on his uncle to pay his bills or provide funds for his expenses.[267]

By December of 1860, Peter Field, Jr. was furious with his uncle, accusing him of misuse of the funds entrusted to him. His Bill of Complaint, presented to the Albemarle County Court, paints a tragic picture of his current situation, emphasizing his delicate health and increasingly desperate financial situation; describing the alleged misdeeds of his uncle Thomas Jefferson (now referred to as Thomas Jefferson, Sr. to distinguish him from his nephew, Thomas Jefferson); detailing the mental downfall of his father, Peter Field Jefferson, Sr. and the confinement of his brother, Thomas, in the asylum in Staunton. The eloquent, four-page Bill, which does not reflect Peter Field, Jr.'s limited mental capabilities but rather the skill of an advocate, was signed by A. A. Pollack, his attorney.[268] The Bill asserted:

> Your orator's father while he possessed his mental faculties and the power and control over his Estate did aid by money and otherwise your orator to maintain support and take care of your orator and his family and your orator further charges and avers that since the committal of the Estate of the said Peter F. Jefferson to Thomas Jefferson Committee your orator has been deprived of any and all aid from any source whatever save his own individual exertions and that he is almost destitute of means to support himself and family. And educate his two children as he is himself a man of weak mental capacity and is not competent to obtain a comfortable support owing to his weak mental abilities. . . .[269]

Without his accustomed support, Peter Field, Jr. quickly accumulated debt. He requested that he receive payments from his father's holdings, essentially an allowance for the duration of the "lunacy" of his father. It would be as though his trust had been created pursuant to the terms of the will even though Peter Field Jefferson was still alive. It was, at best, an awkward situation between nephew and uncle.[270]

Despite the fact that Peter Field Jefferson had provided generously for both of his sons in his 1854 will, there was no provision for their care should he become incompetent in managing his affairs. The will established a trust fund for the illiterate Peter Field, Jr. and terms made it clear that he was incapable of handling large sums of money. The primary reason for denying him an outright inheritance was doubtless his low intelligence. Jefferson, Sr. may also have been concerned that his son was a wastrel or, knowing his poor judgement, that he could be easily swindled out of his fortune. While Peter Field, Jr. would eventually own Jefferson Mills, he was incapable of operating it. Until Peter Field Jefferson's death, any income from renting the property stayed in Peter Field, Sr.'s estate.[271]

~

Peter Field Jefferson died in Scottsville on August 25, 1861, at the home of his trusted friend Madison Noel. Old age was given as the cause of death. The record states he was seventy-two years old and born in Buckingham County. Randolph Jefferson was listed as his father; his mother's name was not written in the record. The informant was William M. Wade, Jefferson's legal counsel and Executor, who may not have known Jefferson's mother's name. No occupation was given on his death record, not even a previous one.

Somewhat unexpectedly, the death of Peter F. Jefferson was news across the South. The reclusive and eccentric man might have been surprised at the coverage, however, being the nephew of President Thomas Jefferson brought unexpected and not always desired attention. Nashville's *Tennessean* ran the announcement of his death under the headline, "Death of a Relative of Ex-President Jefferson." And, in a long column of national news, the *Memphis Daily Appeal* noted:

> Peter F. Jefferson, a nephew of President Jefferson, died recently in Scottsville, Virginia, at the house of Mr. J. Madison Noel, at the age of seventy-three years.[272]

Thomas Jefferson, Committee ceased to have any power over the contents of his brother's estate. Peter Field Jefferson's last will was recorded and put into action.[273]

Because the 1854 will was not rewritten before Peter Field became incapacitated, the estate was immediately complicated, especially the inheritance of Peter Field, Jr. The Buckingham County plantation, Winfrey's Tract, originally intended for him, had been sold and those assets had been reinvested by his uncle. Peter Field, Jr. would spend many years taking his grievances to Court, demanding the inheritance due him, and complaining that he and his family were suffering, lacking the necessities of life.[274]

Jane W. Jefferson, widow

Jane Woodson (Lewis) Jefferson, now a widow in her early sixties, remained at Mount Walla, her needs presumably met by her husband's Executors. It is not known who personally cared for her after her husband's death, though she likely had a domestic servant. Winston was hired out.[275]

Jane's elder son, Thomas, remained incarcerated in the Western Lunatic Asylum. Executor Elbridge Jefferson dutifully paid the bills for Thomas' care until he died of bronchitis on March 18, 1863.[276] He had resided at the asylum, with no improvement in his condition, for over six years. Her younger son, Peter Field, and his wife, lived on at Bleak Hill, could barely care for themselves, and were likely of little help to Jane.

Jane's brother-in-law, Thomas Jefferson and his wife, Willie, remained in Scottsville and watched as Peter Field's estate shifted from Thomas' control to Executors William Wade and Elbridge Jefferson. Additionally, there were a few family friends, like Joseph Walker, who had known Jane from the time of her marriage to Peter Field, and, perhaps, acquaintances from the Methodist Church, to whom she could turn for emotional support.

On March 8, 1862, Jane renounced her husband's will, claiming instead her 1/3 dower right under Virginia law. It is unclear who counseled her in this action, though the document was witnessed by J. S. Brady and notarized by James W. Mason. It is likely that, by claiming her dower right, her advisors attempted to solve the major complication with her husband's will. Due to the sale of Winfrey's Tract, she had "lost" the domicile intended for her. Mount Walla now belonged to her grandson, Peter V. Foland. Jane signed this document with her mark. While she was never characterized as completely incompetent, following her husband's death, she may have seriously declined. She made her brief will on March 4, 1864. In it, she requested that her debts be paid and what remained was to go to her son, Peter Field, Jr. She named James W. Mason her Executor. In 1869, Mason's bankruptcy would further complicate the Jefferson estate.[277]

Jane died early in April of 1864 and, on April 15th, the Jefferson household goods she had enjoyed since her husband's death were sold at auction. Elbridge Jefferson handled the sale and reported the proceeds to the Albemarle County Court, making numerous purchases himself, including the family Bible and his uncle's writing desk.[278]

A Dubious Legacy

By October of 1866, both William Wade and Elbridge Jefferson were deceased. James W. Mason next served as trustee for Peter Field, Jr. and was followed by Rev. John A. Doll, who became Executor of Peter Field Jefferson's estate and held power of attorney for Peter Field, Jr. Through the 1870s and into the 1880s, Rev. Doll collected debts and rents owed the estate, sold properties, and defended the estate against claims in court.

Ultimately, the total inheritance Peter Field, Jr. received from his father was significantly compromised. In the end, he owned his home, Bleak Hill (valued at $1,400) and Jefferson Mills (valued at $2,000), which was rented out, generating income. Like many Virginians who settled estates during the early 1860s, Executor Elbridge G. Jefferson accepted Confederate States Treasury Notes for the payment of debts, irrevocably devaluing the fortune held in trust for Peter Field, Jr.[279]

In 1870, Peter Field, Jr. (40), his wife, Elizabeth (46), and their two children, Peter (14) and Frances (12), remained at Bleak Hill. His real estate holdings were reported at only $600, presumably because the majority of his property was held in trust. Elizabeth (Wood) Jefferson lived long enough to see her daughter, Frances Anne, marry Hartwell Steven Moore on November 25, 1875. Then, on June 20, 1876, Elizabeth died from cancer, her death reported at "Albemarle Mills."[280]

During 1874–1875, Peter F. Jefferson, Jr. brought suit in Buckingham County against Benjamin J. Harris, the Executor of the estate of James Harris, in an attempt to recover Winfrey's Tract. His Bill argued that his father and mother had both been mentally incapacitated at the time the property was sold to James Harris and that William M. Wade had manipulated the sale. Numerous depositions were given as to the mental state of Peter Field, Sr. at the time of the sale. The Court concluded that Jefferson was of sound mind when he sold Winfrey's Tract to James Harris. As a result, in October of 1875, Peter Field, Jr. lost his case and any hope of regaining some of his father's "lost" wealth.[281]

Benjamin J. Harris, James Harris' Executor and one of the defendants in the case, called Peter F. Jefferson, Jr.'s accusations cowardly. In his eloquent answer to the charges against his uncle and the deceased Executors for the estate of Peter Field Jefferson, Sr., Benjamin Harris concluded:

> Your respondent further answering, says, that James Harris, William M. Wade & Elbridge G. Jefferson were in their lifetime and at the date of their deaths men of large means and their estates were ample to meet any demand which might be lawfully [brought] against them, and the impression that their action has been controlled by selfishness, improper & corrupt motives is unfounded and false. The said William M. Wade, James Harris & Elbridge G. Jefferson were in their day and generation

man of high integrity, spotless reputation and commanding influence, and the libelous charges made against them by the Plaintiffs in their bill are false, malicious & cowardly. Brave men sometimes assault the living, cowards alone assault the dead.[282]

Even without reclaiming Winfrey's Tract, Peter Field, Jr. had inherited significant property in Bleak Hill and Jefferson Mills, enough to support his family. In 1880, the widower "Fields" Jefferson remained at Bleak Hill, now rejoined by his sister-in-law, Cynthia Singer; her thirty-six-year-old, married daughter, Maria (Singer) Ellis; and Maria's five children: Susan, Mary, Laura, Eddie, and Wilber. Cynthia continued to work as a midwife. Maria was a cook and her husband, James Ellis, a photographer, was enumerated as the head of the household, while Jefferson was listed as a boarder. The illiterate and emotionally unstable Peter Field, Jr. was now described as "idiotic." Significantly, he was classified as idiotic rather than insane.[283] The instructions to the census enumerators were very specific concerning the difference:

> The word "idiot" has a special meaning which it is essential for every enumerator to know. An idiot is a person the development of whose mental facilities was arrested in infancy or childhood before coming to maturity. It is sometimes difficult to distinguish between the stupidity which results from idiocy and that which is due to the loss or deterioration of mental power in consequence of insanity. The latter is not true idiocy, but dementia or imbecility. The enumeration desired for the Census is of true idiots only. Demented persons should be classed with the insane. Enumerators may obtain valuable hints as to the number of idiots, and their residences, from physicians who practice medicine in their respective districts.[284]

Roughly fifty years old, Peter Field, Jr. had long been described as a person of low intelligence. Unfortunately, the enumerator did not fill in the additional, requested details. As a result it is impossible to know if his declined mental state was exaggerated due to early senility, the stress of protracted legal battles over his father's estate, or simply the result of a gradual disintegration of his fundamentally unstable personality. Whatever the specifics of his condition, it appears that Cynthia Singer and her family cared for him until he died of pneumonia in November of 1881.[285]

Additionally, in 1880, the Federal census described young Peter F. Jefferson, III as an idiot from birth, with a normal shaped head. Likely another casualty of the inbreeding of Virginia gentry, he could live with some degree of independence and was considered "self-supporting." Significantly, that year, he was not living at Bleak Hill in the Ellis-Singer-Jefferson household. Rather he was working as a farm laborer in Albemarle County, boarding with a widower named William D. Rudisill.[286]

In the summer of 1882, following the death of Peter Field, Jr., Jefferson Mills and Bleak Hill were advertised for sale by Administrator Rev. John A. Doll. This description reveals that Peter Field Jefferson, Sr. had provided a pleasant home for his son and extended family, complete with an orchard and well-timbered land, as well as an excellent source of income in Jefferson Mills. The properties had been carefully maintained. His grandson, Peter F. Jefferson, III, however, was mentally incapable of running them and they were put up for sale.

PUBLIC SALE OF
MILL AND FARM.

The undersigned, John A. Doll, administrator, c. t. a. of Peter F. Jefferson, deceased, and John B. Moon, special commissioner of Albemarle Circuit Court, both acting under decrees of said court in the cause of Peter F. Jefferson, &c., vs. Wm. M. Wade's ex'or, &c. will offer for sale at public auction on the premises on WEDNESDAY, THE 12TH, DAY OF JULY, 1882, that tract of land containing about EIGHTY-TWO AND ONE-HALF ACRES, on Hardware River, adjoining the lands of John L. Dawson, whereon is located the large brick mill on said River known as Jefferson's Mill, with abundant water power. . . .

And the said Doll, as administrator as aforesaid, will also at the same time and place, and on the same terms, offer for sale at public auction the farm known as "BLEAK HILL," adjoining the land above described and containing about SIXTY-SIX AND TWO-THIRDS ACRES, (about one third in timber), it being the same land where on the late Peter F. Jefferson resided, and having upon it a good orchard and framed dwelling with five rooms.

JOHN A. DOLL, Administrator.
JOHN B. MOON, Commissioner.[287]

~

Further fulfilling Peter Field Jefferson's wishes, as stated in his 1854 will, the ferry landing and other real estate in Scottsville became the property of Peter Valentine Foland, the son of Peter Field and Jane Jefferson's daughter, Frances Anne. Having never known his grandfather, Foland settled in Scottsville in 1865 and collected a handsome inheritance, complete with a steady income from the ferry. In 1867, the properties which would come to him included Mount Walla, valued at $2,500; the ferry and grocery store valued at $1,500; two lots in town below Mount Walla valued at $100; and the Poplar Spring house & lot (just across the line in Fluvanna County) valued at $500.[288]

On December 20, 1866, Peter V. Foland married Elizabeth "Bettie" Clarke Straton (1845–1921), the daughter of James and Harriet (Woods) Straton.[289] In less than three years, on July 3, 1869, Foland made an unusual decision concerning the ownership of Mount Walla, a brick store house, and the Ferry, gifting these to his wife and children—all who were born and those yet to be born. Despite the careful wording of the deed of gift, creditors may already have been knocking at Foland's door, a very common occurrence in post-war Virginia. The deed reads, in part:

> . . . Whereas, the said Peter V. Foland, is now but little in debt, his indebtedness, probably, being less than the value of his property, which is not embraced in this conveyance: And; Whereas the said Peter V. Foland, in view of the casualties of life, is desirous of providing, a comfortable house and subsistence for his wife and children, beyond the reach of misfortunes, which may hereafter befall him in business or otherwise: Now: Therefore for and in consideration of the love which he bears to his said wife and children, and for the further consideration of $5.[00] to him in hand paid, at and before the execution of this Deed, he, the said Peter V. Foland doth grant, bargain and sell, and convey, unto said Betty C. Foland, for and during the term of her natural life, a certain tract of land, called the "Jefferson Tract," lying and being in the county aforesaid, adjoining the town of Scottsville . . . containing by estimation 85 acres, be the same more or less—the said land being the same, on which the said Peter V. Foland now resides—also a certain brick Store House and the Lot on which it stands in said town near the Gauge Dock—also

the Ferry across James River, at the said town of Scottsville, and all its appurtenances. . . .[290]

Peter Foland was just twenty-two years old when he deeded this significant property to his wife and children. In 1870, the twenty-five-year-old grandson of Peter Field Jefferson operated the ferry and was credited with $8,000 worth of real estate. That year, Bettie's brother, James W. Straton, a twenty-four-year-old merchant, lived with the Folands and their two daughters, Frances (named after Peter's mother) and Hattie (named after Bettie's mother). Jacob H. Briggs still lived adjacent the ferry.[291] A few doors away, James M. and John T. Noel, old friends of Peter Field Jefferson, remained in Scottsville.

Operating Scottsville's ferry provided a steady livelihood, however, working as a ferryman could be a hazardous occupation. In 1871, the *Scottsville Register* reported the following tragedy involving Peter Foland and the ferry:

> One of the most exciting and distressing sights we ever witnessed, was on Christmas morning, at the Scottsville Ferry landing. The ferryman, Mr. Peter V. Foland, assisted by young Willie Patterson, had started to carry two colored men across the river, cutting the ice as they went, and getting within 75 yards of the other shore, they discovered to their horror, that the ice thus cut loose was slowly moving upon them, and in a moments time came upon the boat, when they jumped upon the ice and one of the colored men (Brightberry Toney) being more excited than the rest, ran upon the ice and broke through, drowning in a few minutes. Mr. Foland, Willie Patterson, and the remaining colored man (although they had fallen into the water) succeeded in climbing upon a large piece of ice and remained upon it until the citizens on this side had carried a large number of planks from the shop of the J. R. & K. Co., (which fortunately was near by) and laying them across each other, formed a walk to them, by which means they affected their escape from their perilous position.
>
> It is our duty to add, and we hope we will not be accused of discrimination, that the services rendered by our young friend, Mr. William S. Beal on this occasion, was most efficient, and deserves all praise. The boat in which the party attempted to cross the river and which was sunk by the ice, was found by Mr. John Butler, a few days since, one mile below town; but the body of the unfortunate colored man has not been heard [of].[292]

Peter V. Foland was one Jefferson descendant who was neither idiotic nor unbalanced. During the post-war years, he followed in his grandfather's footsteps, running the ferry, keeping the store, and enjoying a comfortable life at Mount Walla. By 1880, Foland cared for a growing family of six children, his wife, Bettie, and her widowed mother, Harriet Straton.

In 1894, the dwelling house at Mount Walla provided the setting for the marriage of Miss Fanny Foland:

> The town was enlivened on Thursday by a beautiful marriage, which took place at the residence of Mr. Peter V. Foland, the father of the bride, at 2 o'clock P. M. His lovely daughter, Miss Fannie, was united in marriage to Mr. Calvin Dunkum, of Bluefield, W. Va. Rev. J. W. Hildrup, pastor of the Methodist church, performed the ceremony very impressively. The happy pair took the east-bound train to visit the home of the groom's father, after which they will make their home in Bluefield.[293]

In 1889, Foland served as Scottsville's postmaster, earning $48.00 annually. He worked as a salesman, and was, eventually, elected Mayor of Scottsville in 1909. He died on July 27, 1915. His widow, Bettie, remained at Mount Walla, living with her daughters Frances Dunkum; Hattie A. Foland, who worked as a dressmaker; and Elizabeth Foland. Bettie died on March 22, 1921, leaving Mount Walla to the next generation of Jefferson descendants.[294]

~

Fortunately for this account of the life of Peter Field Jefferson, descriptions of his eccentric genius were preserved in numerous court depositions given by those who knew him best. His odd ways increased with age and, by 1850's, he was characterized, at the very least, as "a little odd about some things."

Jefferson's miserly ways stood out as a defining feature of his personality and his intense interest in accumulating wealth was integral with his financial success. Those who spoke of him kindly called him an economical man, a saving man, a hard-working man—always busy about something. Less flattering acquaintances found him shrewd and calculating. He was fast to collect rents owed him and did not hesitate to bring suit against competing Scottsville merchants indebted to him. Anyone in Scottsville could have told you, Peter Field Jefferson valued money above all else. He could find a way to "squeeze blood from a turnip."

Joseph Russell Beal put it succinctly; Peter Field Jefferson was a "great lover of money." Beal once warned Jefferson that hoarding money would bring him no pleasure in the end.

> You are laying up your money & it will do you no good hoarding
> it up here & denying yourself the comforts and pleasures of this world
> when you die somebody will be digging roads around the hills & riding
> up to your house in a carriage on the money you have saved & he said
> laying up money was his pleasure; that was his heaven while our heaven
> was going to church.[295]

Joseph Beal's words proved true. Jefferson lost his mind and much of his fortune to the mismanagement of his estate, lengthy court cases, and worthless Confederate currency. He never enjoyed the peace that his farm in Buckingham County might have provided him or even a quiet retirement at Mount Walla, looking down on the James River.

Jefferson's reputed wealth inspired curiosity, rumor, and, doubtless, envy, fueling Scottsville's gossip mill, and there is every reason to believe that a tight heart went with Jefferson's tight fist. Despite the fact that Jefferson maintained several long and trusted relationships, including his attorneys, he led a rather isolated life except with "home people." Even those relationships could be fractious. Jefferson and his son, Peter Field, Jr., were frequently at odds with each other and argued openly on the streets of Scottsville.

All agreed that Jefferson was not a church-going man. He did not believe in an afterlife, saying repeatedly that he would die in the street, like a dog. Claiming to be exempt from God's Final Judgement, he also skirted Man's laws, making considerable money selling whiskey, sometimes without a proper license.

Jefferson not only sold vast amounts of whiskey, he indulged in it. Widely known as an intemperate man, after a long day at the ferry or at his store, he was sometimes already drunk when he headed up the hill to his home. This fact does not suggest a man content with his fate.

In middle-age, he cared little about what others thought or said of him. As his eccentricities increased, there was a notable decline in his appearance. Some described his apparel as simple. To others, it was frankly shabby.

The solace Jefferson did not feel among Men, he found in Nature. He loved to grow things, tending to a "little crop" and to his bees. He maintained two vegetable gardens—one at home and one at his store—rooting about to his heart's content. He sacrificed his health to hive a swarm of bees. If cabbages and carrots could give depositions, we might be left with a somewhat different portrait of Peter Field Jefferson. Their silence, however, leaves us with his own actions and the opinions of those who knew him best.

NOTES

1   Some Albemarle County records give his name as Peter "Fields" Jefferson. His son, Peter Field Jefferson, Jr. is also called "Little Fields" or "Fields." When Rev. Edgar Woods confused Jefferson generations in his history of Albemarle County, he established a long chain of misinformation about Peter Field Jefferson of Scottsville. Woods wrote that Field was the grandson of Randolph Jefferson, rather than his son. Comparing two simple facts—that Randolph Jefferson married in 1780 and that Peter Field Jefferson of Scottsville was born between 1785 and 1789—should set the matter to rest. Peter Field Jefferson of Scottsville was President Thomas Jefferson's nephew, not his grandnephew as Rev. Woods suggested. Virginia Moore in *Scottsville on the James* and Boynton Merrill, in his widely-read book, *Jefferson's Nephews*, repeated Rev. Woods' error. It also appears in the application for Mount Walla to the National Register of Historic Places. See Albemarle County Deed Book 20, pp. 247–248; Rev. Edgar Woods, *Albemarle County in Virginia* (Baltimore, MD: Clearfield Co., 1997), 235–238; Virginia Moore, *Scottsville on the James* (Richmond, VA: The Dietz Press, 1994), 65; Boynton Merrill, Jr., *Jefferson's Nephews: A Frontier Tragedy* (Lincoln, NE: University of Nebraska Press, 2004), 420; "Mount Walla," National Register of Historic Places Registration Application, November 2000, p. 8.

2   Joanne L. Yeck, *The Jefferson Brothers* (Kettering, OH: Slate River Press, 2012), 199–211.

3   Ibid., 261–63.

4   Personal Property Tax, Buckingham County, VA, 1810. In 1811, Peter Field Jefferson still lived in Buckingham County and was taxed on four slaves over the age of sixteen, an inexplicable jump in personal property. During the War of 1812, Captain Gideon Massie's Company attached to the 8th Regiment, 4th Brigade included a man named Peter F. Jefferson. The company was stationed at Camp Carter, under General John H. Cocke, from August 26, 1814 to February of 1815. This Peter F. Jefferson served five months and twenty-one days and could be Randolph Jefferson's son or his cousin. See Personal Property Tax, Buckingham County, VA, 1811; Stuart Lee Butler, *Guide to Virginia Militia units in the War of 1812*, vol. 1 (Athens, GA: New Papyrus, 1988), 99.

5   Yeck, *The Jefferson Brothers*, 285–334.

6   Fluvanna County Deed Book 6, pp. 45–47, 260–261; Land Tax, Fluvanna County, VA, 1813–1815; Marriage Record, Fluvanna County, VA. In 1818, Isham Randolph Jefferson purchased his modest Fluvanna County farm (296 3/4 acres), located on Shepherd Creek, which flows into the Hardware River. Mary Ann (a.k.a. Mariann) Jefferson, the granddaughter of Bennett Henderson and Elizabeth Lewis, the sister of Anne (Lewis) Jefferson, died on December 3, 1821, leaving an infant son, Thomas Jefferson. On July 2, 1822, Randolph married Margaret Gwatkins Peyton, the granddaughter of Charles and Lucy (Jefferson) Lewis. See Fluvanna County Deed Book

7, pp. 186–87; Mary Ann Jefferson, obituary, 14 December 1821, *Central Gazette*; Marriage Record, Fluvanna County, VA; Joanne L. Yeck, "Isham Randolph Jefferson," *Lost Jeffersons* (Slate River Press, 2018).

7 *Richmond Enquirer*, 8 June 1816, p. 1. Ned Henderson's fate and his possible connection to Mary Ann (Henderson) Jefferson's family in Fluvanna County are unknown.

8 *Richmond Enquirer*, 18 February 1812, p. 1.

9 *Richmond Enquirer*, 18 June 1811, p. 1.

10 Personal Property Tax, Albemarle County, VA, 1817–1819.

11 Edith F. Axelton, compiler, *Virginia Postmasters and Post Offices, 1789–1832* (Athens, GA: Iberian Publishing Co., 1991), 6. James Lilburne Jefferson served as postmaster until 1819. See Ibid.

12 Richard Ludlam Nicholas, "The Early History of the Founding of Scottsville, Virginia and Surrounding Area 1732–1830, (Unpublished manuscript, 2009), 8, 71, 164–65; "The Coles Family," *Virginia Magazine of History and Biography* (July 1899), 101–2; "The Coles Family," *Virginia Magazine of History and Biography* (January 1900), 326–29; Richard L. Nicholas, "The first hundred years of the Scottsville community, 1728–1828," *Magazine of Albemarle County History* (2010), 1–23. According to Scottsville historian Richard Nicholas, "The lots were sold, and at least one substantial brick lumber house was erected on the property about this time. However, there is no record that the Coles brothers ever made an effort to have the development legally sanctioned by the State. In 1831 the original Coles' lots and adjoining tracts were officially incorporated into the Town of Scottsville when the town boundary was extended to include a substantial amount of land east of the ferry." See Nicholas, "Early History of the Founding of Scottsville," 8.

13 *Enquirer* (Richmond, VA), 27 September 1815, p. 1.

14 Albemarle County Deed Book 20, pp. 247–48. The deed was not recorded until January 6, 1817.

15 "John Coles, II," *Thomas Jefferson Encyclopedia*, accessed September 2017, http://www.monticello.org/site/research-and-collections/john-coles-ii; "Enniscorthy," National Register of Historic Places Registration Form, Delisted: loss of integrity, 1997.

16 Nicholas, "Early History of the Founding of Scottsville," 165; "Old Woodville," Historic American Buildings Survey, Library of Congress; "Tallwood," Historic American Buildings Survey, Library of Congress; Isaac Coles," *Thomas Jefferson Encyclopedia*, accessed September 2017, http://www.monticello.org/site/research-and-collections/isaac-coles; "Edward Coles, *Thomas Jefferson Encyclopedia*, accessed September 2017, http://www.monticello.org/site/research-and-collections/edward-coles; Kurt E. Leichtle, *Crusade Against Slavery: Edward Coles Pioneer of Freedom* (Carbondale, IL: Southern Illinois University Press, 2011), 7–29.

17 Nicholas, "Early History of the Founding of Scottsville," 97.

18 Ibid., 118. Randolph Turner emerged as an early developer in the Coles subdivision and, during 1819–1820, built an impressive structure valued at $1,200 on lot #3. See Ibid., 123.

19 Ibid., 15. In 1819, the Scottsville lots were taxed as such for the first time. The sixteen parcels originally owned by the Coles family were identified separately in the tax record. Although established in 1818, the "Town of Scottsville" was not incorporated until May 3, 1833. See Ibid., 8.

20 Albemarle County Surveyor's Book No. 2, p.145; Nicholas, "Early History of the Founding of Scottsville," 112.

21 Yeck, *The Jefferson Brothers*, 3–24. In 1818, Ferry Street was not identified on William Woods' survey of the town. It roughly constituted the boundary between the Scott and Coles properties, though, Richard Nicholas found good evidence indicating that the Scott/Coles dividing line actually lies about 160–170 feet east of today's Ferry Street. See Nicholas, "Early History of the Founding of Scottsville," 90, 96–7.

22 Albemarle County Deed Book 21, pp. 265–66, 340. The lot number is not mentioned in the deed between Scott and Jefferson; however, a plat created by the James River and Kanawha Canal Company indicates that lots #113 and #117 were owned by Peter Field Jefferson. Lots #114 and #118 belonged to John Harris. Lot #113, which sat to the east of Ferry Street, is likely Jefferson's purchase in 1818. See Richard Nicholas to Joanne Yeck, email, September 2013.

23 Nicholas, "Early History of the Founding of Scottsville," 121. George A. Scruggs owned lot #34, complete with residence. A series of confusing deeds and descriptions make it unclear whether the tavern sat on Scruggs' lot #34 or on Scott's lot #35. It may have been built prior to the division of the lots and straddled the line, explaining Scott's odd division of lot #35 when he sold to Robert Lewis and Thompson Noel in 1818. By 1820, Scott completed a dwelling house, with separate kitchen and smoke houses, on lot #40. It sat on the north side of Jackson Street, away from the bustle of the eastern end of town. See Ibid., 121–35.

24 Personal Property Tax, Albemarle County, VA, 1818. In 1820, "Moon, Anderson & Co.," owned lots #32 and #36. See Nicholas, "Early History of the Founding of Scottsville," 123.

25 Fluvanna County Marriage Registers, Book 1 (1781–1849), 108; Personal Property Tax, Fluvanna County, VA, 1819. The year 1819 was a turning point in the history of Albemarle County. Despite a nation-wide financial panic, on January 25, 1819, the Virginia General Assembly formally established what would become the University of Virginia at the site of Central College in Charlottesville, bringing former President Thomas Jefferson's vision of a publically funded college closer to reality. See "Funding the University of Virginia," *Thomas Jefferson Encyclopedia*, accessed September 2017, http://www.monticello.org/site/research-and-collections/funding-university-virginia.

26 Lucy (Jefferson) Lewis (1752–1810) died in Kentucky, is buried at the family cemetery in Livingston County, and is remembered with a state Historical Marker and an

obelisk erected by the Lucy Jefferson Lewis Chapter of the Children of the American Revolution. See Lucy Jefferson Lewis, Find A Grave, accessed September 2017, https://www.findagrave.com/memorial/17409353.

27 Thomas Jefferson to Philip Mazzei, 7 January 1792, *Founders Online*, accessed September 2017, https://founders.archives.gov/documents/Jefferson/01-23-02-0022; Merrill, 74–5.

28 Thomas Jefferson to Gideon Fitz, 23 May 1809, *Founders Online*, accessed September 2017, https://founders.archives.gov/documents/Jefferson/03-01-02-0180.

29 Albemarle County Deed Book 14, pp. 231, 506–7; Merrill, 48–50; Albemarle County Deed Book 14, pp. 506–7; Yeck, "Anna Scott Jefferson," *Lost Jeffersons*; Atlanta H. Taylor Pool, "Tragedies in Livingston," *Courier-Journal*, 10 June 1894, p. 18; Lucy Lewis to Thomas Jefferson, letter, 19 November 1807, *Founders Online*, accessed September 2017, https://founders.archives.gov/documents/Jefferson/99-01-02-3762.

30 Jay Feldman, *When the Mississippi Ran Backwards: Empire, Intrigue, and the New Madrid Earthquakes* (New York, NY: Free Press, 2005), 95; *New National Era*, 1 January 1874, p. 1.

31 Merrill, 163.

32 Ibid., 164–68. Today, Mercer County is home to the historic Shaker Village of Pleasant Hill. See Shaker Village, accessed September 2017, https://shakervillageky.org/.

33 Merrill, 167–68.

34 The Lewises had a son named James Randolph Lewis.

35 Merrill, 246–47.

36 Randolph Lewis wrote his last will on January 16, 1811. It was recorded in the Livingston County Court in February of 1811. He left a widow, Mary H. Lewis, and children: Charles L. Lewis, Howell Lewis, Tucker W. Lewis, Mary J. R. Lewis, Lucy J. Lewis, Susannah H. Lewis, Robert R. Lewis, and Warner Lewis. He named his "friends," Charles L. Lewis, Lilburne Lewis, Henry Williams, and Mary H. Lewis his executors. It was witnessed by Charles L. and Martha C. Lewis. ["Kentucky, Wills and Probate Records, 1774–1989," ancestry.com.] One error-ridden and fanciful newspaper article claimed that "Randall" Lewis died of a copperhead's bite. [*St. Louis Post-Dispatch*, 8 January 1899, p. 26] Despite the fact that Lucy Jefferson Lewis' monument records her death date as 1811, she probably died on May 26, 1810, as indicated in a letter from her daughters Martha, Lucy, and Ann to their uncle, Thomas Jefferson. They wrote on 17 September 1810: "no doubt You have before this, heard of the iraparable loss we have experianced, in the death of the best of mothers, and sister, which event took place on the twenty Sixth day, of last may, she graguley waisted away with little or no pain, for eighteen months enteirly sensable to here last moments, quite resind to meat the aughfull fate, her remains was intered the twenty Eigth on a high immenence, in view of that majestick river the Ohio." [Martha A. C.

Lewis, Lucy B. Lewis, and Ann M. Lewis to Thomas Jefferson, 17 September 1810, *Founders Online*, accessed September 2017, https://founders.archives.gov/documents/ Jefferson/03-03-02-0054.] For a romanticized version of Lucy Jefferson's life and death in Kentucky, see Atlanta H. Taylor Pool, "Tragedies in Livingston." In 1905, Lucy (Jefferson) Lewis was still pitied in the press, though misidentified as the President's sister, "Martha Lewis." A lengthy article repeated a century-old Jefferson myth: "Martha Jefferson was never happy in her Kentucky home, and according to tradition, used to sit for hours looking toward the river with the hope of catching sight of a flatboat that would bring her an old newspaper or some message from her beloved Virginia." [Ora V. Leigh, "Sister of Jefferson Neglected Grave of Mrs. Martha Lewis in Lonely Cemetery of Kentucky," *Grand Forks Daily Herald* (Grand Forks, ND), December 1905, Section 2, p. 7.]

37   Yeck, "Lilburne Lewis," *Lost Jeffersons.*

38   Merrill, 261–64.

39   Ibid., 249; Myron L. Fuller, "The New Madrid Earthquake," Department of the Interior United States Geological Survey, Bulletin 495, (Washington, D.C.: Government Printing Office, 1,913); Merrill, "Annus Mirabilis," 249–56.

40   John Bradbury, *Travels in the Interior of America in the Years 1809, 1810 and 1811* (Liverpool, England: Published for the author, 1817), 199–204.

41   Merrill, 254. According to Walter Brownlow Posey, "In the Methodist Church the Western Conference in 1811 was composed of the whole of Tennessee, Kentucky, and contiguous sections of Mississippi, Arkansas, Illinois, Indiana, Ohio, and West Virginia, nearly all of which lay in the seismical region of 1811 and 1812. In 1811 the Western Conference had a total membership of 30,741. This same territory (divided in 1812 into Tennessee and Ohio Conferences) at the next Conference reported 45,983, a net gain of 15,242." See Walter Brownlow Posey, "The Earthquake of 1811 and its Influence on Evangelistic Methods in the Churches of the Old South," *Tennessee Historical Magazine* (January 1931), 11.

42   Merrill, 303–6.

43   Ibid., 307.

44   "Murder! Horrid Murder!," *Kentucky Gazette*, 12 May 1812, p. 1; "Murder! Horrid Murder!," *Courier* (Washington, D.C.), 27 May 1812, p. 3.

45   *Kentucky Gazette*, 12 May 1812, p. 1.

46   *Liberator* (Boston, MA), 13 Oct 1832, p. 1; "Anti-Slavery. From the Anti-Slavery Lecturer," *Liberator* (Boston, MA), 21 June 1839, p. 97; "Hibernian Anti-Slavery Society Meeting at the Royal Exchange," *Liberator* (Boston, MA), 26 March 1841, p. 50; *Peoria Register and North-western Gazetteer* (Peoria, IL), 21 May 1841, p. 2. During 1873–1874, the murder of George resurfaced as a national story. See Yeck, "Lilburne Lewis," *Lost Jeffersons.*

47   Merrill, 307, 366.

48   Ibid., 308–9.

49   Ibid., 359–69.

50   Ibid., 308–10. In December of 1812, Governor Shelby remitted Isham Lewis' bond, stating that Lilburne Lewis' motherless children were "likely to suffer if the amount of the said judgement were made out of their estate." See Ibid., 310.

51   Federal Population Census, Livingston County, KY, 1810. Jonathan Ramsey died in 1860, his will was probated in Cole, Missouri. See "Missouri, Wills and Probate Records, 1766–1988," ancestry.com.

52   Merrill, 175, 180, 284, 298–99.

53   Ibid., 343.

54   Ibid., 313, 319. In the fall of 1815, the official guardianship of Warner Lewis, the youngest son of Randolph and Mary Howell Lewis, was transferred to Randolph Lewis' married sister, Martha Amanda Carr (Lewis) Monroe.

55   Ibid., 319–20. In 1820, a man (over 45) was living in Fluvanna County with Thomas and Polly (Lewis) Jefferson. This is almost certainly Charles L. Lewis who died in 1828. According to Lewis' grandson, Charles L. Peyton, Thomas Jefferson, Jr. escorted Charles L. Lewis back from Kentucky. See Federal Population Census, Fluvanna County, VA, 1820; *Atlanta Constitution*, 28 November 1874, p. 1.

56   In 1822, the Peytons' daughter, Margaret Gwatkins, became Isham Randolph Jefferson's second wife, further linking the Jeffersons with their Lewis-Peyton cousins.

57   *Atlanta Constitution*, 28 November 1874, p. 1. Over the years, Monteagle had several spellings, including Mount Eagle and Mt. Eagle. In May of 1815, Thomas and Polly (Lewis) Jefferson, along with her three sisters, Lucy, Nancy, and Martha, filed suit against their sister, Jane, and Craven Peyton. See "Thomas Jefferson, Jr., wife and others vs Craven Peyton & wife," Augusta County Superior Court Case 1818-001, Library of Virginia; Yeck, "Thomas Jefferson, Jr.," *Lost Jeffersons*.

58   The new dwelling house at Monteagle, built within sight of the old Lewis home at Buck Island. See David Anderson, deposition, "Thomas Jefferson, Jr., wife and others vs Craven Peyton & wife;" Mutual Assurance Society policy #339, Library of Virginia.

59   Albemarle County Will Book 12, pp. 381, 437–42; Albemarle County Will Book 13, p. 178.

60   Ibid.; Federal Population Census, Albemarle County, VA, 1820. Craven Peyton died in March of 1837. His obituary read: "Died, at Mount Eagle, Albemarle county on Thursday the 23d instant after a long and painful illness, Craven Peyton, Esq., was an old and respectable citizen of this county. Mr. P. was alike distinguished for warmth of feeling, ardent attachment to his friends, and kindness to his neighbors, and his hospitality was proverbial." See *Richmond Enquirer*, 7 April 1837, p. 3; *Alexandria Gazette* (Alexandria, VA), 10 April 1837, p. 3; "Monteagle for sale by Charles L.

Peyton, Executor," *Richmond Enquirer*, 2 January 1838, p.1; *Richmond Enquirer*, 14 August 1838, p. 1.

61   In the mid-19th century, a new dwelling house was built at Monteagle. It was surveyed by R. E. Hannum for the Virginia Historical Inventory. [R. E. Hannum, "Mount Eagle," 14 February 1938, Virginia Historical Inventory, Library of Virginia.] In January of 1870, advertisements ran in Charlottesville's *Tri-Weekly Chronicle* advertising the sale of Monteagle, reading: "Land Sales "MOUNT EAGLE FOR SALE— The mansion of MOUNT EAGLE a newly erected brick building, two stories high, with four spacious rooms on each and a wide passage, a basement with the same number of rooms, stands on a bluff rising four hundred feet almost perpendicularly from the Rivanna, presenting a magnificent view of the South-west mountains and the Blue Ridge for a distance of more than forty or fifty miles. Around this bluff, the centre of a half circle, extends the arable land, bounded on one side by the Rivanna, on the other by Buck Island creek. The Plantation contains 904 ACRES, of which 300 are inexhaustible low grounds. The upland is in fine heart and very productive. There is on it a large Orchard of choice fruit, in full bearing; an abundance of wood, and all the out buildings almost new, and in first rate order. It is two and a half miles distant from the C. and O. Railroad. The wharf on the river navigable for horse-boats—is four hundred yards from the barns. Albemarle Co., Va." See *Tri-Weekly Chronicle*, 27 January 1870, p. 1.

62   Atlanta H. Taylor Pool, "Tragedies in Livingston."

63   George W. Dawson, deposition, "B. J. Harris, Executor, etc. vs Jefferson," Buckingham County Chancery Case (October Term 1873), Buckingham County Courthouse. In 1860, George W. Dawson (b. about 1827) lived in Scottsville, four doors from Rev. John A. Doll. He was enumerated as a farmer; several craftsmen lived with him. See Federal Population Census, Albemarle County, VA, 1860.

64   Complaint Bill, "Peter F. Jefferson & wife, etc. vs James Harris Executor, etc.," 1875, Buckingham County Chancery Case, Buckingham County Courthouse; Final order, ibid.

65   In 1827, Jane Jefferson received 375 acres of Rocky Hill in Livingston, Kentucky. See Merrill, 343.

66   "Field" Jefferson, Land Tax, Albemarle County, VA, 1820.

67   Federal Population Census, Albemarle County, VA, 1820.

68   Albemarle County Deed Book 23, p. 65, dated 26 October 1821, recorded 6 May 1822.

69   Personal Property Tax, Buckingham County, VA, 1822–1823; Personal Property Tax, Albemarle County, VA, 1823.

70   *Richmond Enquirer*, 15 October 1822, p. 4.

71 *Richmond Enquirer*, 3 February 1829, p. 4; Yeck, *The Jefferson Brothers*, 332–34. The deed transferring Snowden from the Randolph Jefferson Estate to Capt. John Harris was lost in the Buckingham Courthouse fire of 1869.

72 Land Tax, Buckingham County, VA, 1828.

73 Albemarle County Law Orders Book, 1809–1821; Albemarle County Law Orders Book 1821–1831; Yeck, *The Jefferson Brothers*, 327–30.

74 Albemarle County Deed Book 26, pp. 178–79; Albemarle County Deed Book 25, pp. 148–50. Lower Plantation was also known as Belle Grove and, later, as Valmont.

75 John Vogt and T. William Kethley, Jr., *Albemarle County Marriages, 1780–1853, volume 1* (Athens, GA: Iberian Publishing Company, 1991), 278; "Mary Jefferson Bolling," *Thomas Jefferson Encyclopedia*, accessed September 2017, http://www.monticello.org/site/jefferson/mary-jefferson-bolling. Jack and Mary Bolling both died in Albemarle County. Susan Bathurst Bolling's sister, Evelina Bolling, married Alexander Garrett on April 15, 1808, in Albemarle County. Garrett was the long-term Clerk of Court in Albemarle and friend to President Thomas Jefferson. At the time of his death, John "Jack" Bolling was nearly destitute. His inventory, made on June 14, 1827, revealed his estate was valued at $227.74 ½. In 1838, his widow, Mary Willis (Kennon) Bolling died at Ash Lawn, the former residence of President James Monroe, then the residence of her grandson, Dr. John Bolling Garrett (1809–1855). It was Alexander Garrett (1778–1860), who renamed the property, Ash Lawn, when he purchased it in 1837. In Mary Willis Bolling's obituary, her husband is referred to as "Col. John Bolling." She was "in her 71st year." See Vogt and Kethley, *Albemarle County Marriages, volume 1*, p. 123; John Bolling, will, Albemarle County Will Book 9, pp.115–16; Christopher Fennell, "An account of James Monroe's Land Holdings," accessed September 2017, http://www.histarch.illinois.edu/highland/ashlawn1.html; "Alexander Garrett to Thomas Jefferson, 14 January 1813," *Founders Online*, accessed September 2017, http://founders.archives.gov/documents/Jefferson/03-05-02-0480; Mary Willis Bolling, obituary, *Richmond Whig & Public Advertiser*, 27 April 1838.

76 Virginia J. Randolph (Trist) to Nicholas P. Trist, 5 June 1823, "Jefferson Quotes & Family Letters," accessed September 2017, http://tjrs.monticello.org/letter/959.

77 John Scott III may have fled mounting friction in Scottsville caused by discontented investors, some of whom discovered they had purchased, sight unseen, un-buildable lots on Scottsville's steep hillside. Concerning Edward Harris Moon's generosity toward Susan Scott and her daughters, Scottsville historian Richard Nicholas wrote, "The connection between Edward Moon and the Scott family is unknown, but there must have been a special relationship to explain Moon's apparent generosity. By assuming ownership of the eight or nine lots from Scott's estate in 1834, purchasing the four and a half lots (131, 132, 133, 134, and half of 135) prior to 1840, and then donating the latter back to the family, he obviously relieved them of a significant financial burden." The financial problems of Edward Harris Moon's father, William Moon, may have had a negative impact on John Scott's wealth. Edward Moon, via

his marriage to John Harris' stepdaughter, Anna Marie Barclay, inherited a significant percentage of John Harris' wealth and could afford to be generous, perhaps, righting some of his father's financial "wrongs." See Nicholas, "Early History of the Founding of Scottsville," p. 28; Richard Nicholas to Joanne Yeck, email, 29 January 2010.

78 Journals and ledgers of Stony Point, Va., 1809–1829, Small Special Collections, University of Virginia; Stoney Point Journal 1816, pp. 83, 121, 128, 157, 207, 230, 283, 295, Small Special Collections, University of Virginia; Stoney Point Ledger 1820–1822, pp. 11, 27, 40, 76, Small Special Collections, University of Virginia; Ledgers of John D. Moon, 1826–1827, pp. 67, 68, 124, 142, 187, Small Special Collection, University of Virginia. In the early 19th-century ledgers, the store name was written Stoney Point. The spelling drifted to Stony Point and, on late 19th-century maps, is labeled without the "e." In addition to selling merchandise, William Moon provided cash loans. By at least mid-1817, Thomas Jefferson, Jr. was involved with Scottsville speculators Littleberry Moon and Charles A. Scott. Jefferson owed Moon $466.22 and his partners paid off most of the obligation. By comparison, Peter Field Jefferson maintained the comparatively modest debt of $90.92.

79 Journal Scottsville Store [John D. Moon], 1822–1826, pp. 62, 64, 70, Small Special Collections, University of Virginia.

80 Ibid., 75.

81 *Richmond Enquirer*, 3 February 1829, p. 4. Within the year, Jesse Joplin of Nelson County became an executor for Zachariah Nevil's estate. Nevil died on April 8, 1830 in Nelson County. See Death Record, Nelson County, VA.

82 Albemarle County Deed Book 25, p. 237.

83 Albemarle County Deed Book 28, p. 202. Later, during the building of the canal, Martin Tutwiler's lumber house was compromised by the new embankment. According to Virginia Moore, he was awarded $600 and "the company agreed to build him a passageway, at both back and front of his warehouse, wide enough to accommodate four-horse teams." See Virginia Moore, *Scottsville*, 65.

84 "Dr. James Turner Barclay, Minister and Missionary," Scottsville Museum website, accessed September 2017, http://scottsvillemuseum.com/church/homeJB01cdJB01. html.

85 "Sale of Monticello," Thomas Jefferson Encyclopedia, accessed September 2017, http://www.monticello.org/site/house-and-gardens/sale-monticello.

86 Ibid.

87 "First Inauguration," *Thomas Jefferson Encyclopedia*, accessed September 2017, http://www.monticello.org/site/research-and-collections/first-inauguration.

88 John Harris Will, Albemarle County Will Book 11, pp. 168, 228; Thomas Jefferson, with Dickinson W. Adams and Ruth W. Lester, *Jefferson's extracts from the Gospels: "The philosophy of Jesus" and "The life and morals of Jesus"* (Princeton, NJ: Princeton University Press, 1983).

89   Edwin Morris and James Adam Bear, Jr., *The Family Letters of Thomas Jefferson* (Columbia, MO: University of Missouri Press, 1966), 426.

90   Roger G. Ward, *Land Tax Summaries & Implied Deed 1815–1840, volume 2* (Athens, GA: Iberian Publishing Company, 1994), 158.

91   Ibid. A man named Murray, likely Richard Murray's son and heir, Anthony Murray, sold to Charles A. Scott in 1810. County land tax records locate these two tracts as twenty-five miles north of Buckingham Courthouse, owned by Capt. John Harris of Albemarle. See Roger G. Ward, *Land Tax Summaries & Implied Deed 1782–1814, volume 1* (Athens, GA: Iberian Publishing Company, 1993), 219, 226.

92   Land Tax, Buckingham County, VA, 1819, 1822; Lyndon H. Hart, "Three Buckingham County Wills," *Southside Virginian* (April 1985), 122–29. In 1822, land taxes records included the value of dwellings. By comparison, the 1,649 acres remaining at Snowden were assessed at $32,980, including $1,200 worth of structures, with no dwelling house.

93   Yeck, *The Jefferson Brothers*, 17–18. Sometime after 1761, the ferry landing moved around the bend to the east near the modern bridge, likely about the time John Scott attempted to establish a town on his land. In 1936, R. E. Hannum wrote the following for the Virginia Historical Survey, "After the court house was moved to Charlottesville the site of the ferry was moved down the river to the point just below the present iron highway bridge." See R. E. Hannum, "The Old Ferry" (Warren, VA), 30 November 1936, Virginia Historical Survey, Library of Virginia.

94   Nicholas, "Early History of the Founding of Scottsville," 7–8.

95   Ibid., 8, 13–14.

96   Albemarle County Will Book 4, p. 1.

97   Buckingham County Surveyor's Plat Book, 120.

98   Albemarle County Deed Book 22, p. 428; Albemarle County Deed Book 24, pp. 24, 58; Albemarle County Deed Book 28, p. 202.

99   Albemarle County Deed Book 25, p. 237; Personal Property Tax, Albemarle County, VA, 1826–1827. Peter Field Jefferson bought several properties from Richard Moon and/or his estate. Historian Richard Nicholas identifies Richard Moon (c.1803–1847) as the son of William Moon (1770–1840). Local records often refer to him as Richard Moon (T) or "Tennessee Dick" to distinguish him from other men named Richard Moon. He owned numerous lots in Scottsville and extensive property adjacent to town; was a partner in the merchant firm of Moon, Anderson & Co.; and, later, was involved in the concern known as "Moon Perkins" probably located on lot #36. See Nicholas, "Early History of the Founding of Scottsville," 168.

100   John T. Noel, deposition, "Peter F. Jefferson & wife, etc. vs James Harris Executor, etc."

101   Personal Property Tax, Albemarle County, VA, 1826–1827.

102 Benjamin Dennis Ledger (1832–1834), 24 March 1832, [13] June 1832, 16 July 1832, 24 July 1832, Scottsville Museum, Scottsville, VA.

103 For a history of Kirkman soap, see "The Kirkman Soap Shop," accessed October 2017, http://www.chriskirkman.com/kirkman-soap-company.html.

104 Pilot bread is another term for hardtack.

105 *Richmond Whig*, 3 September 1841, p. 3.

106 Merchant License, Personal Property Tax, Albemarle County, VA, 1826; Journal Scottsville Store [John D. Moon] (1822–1826), 383, 391, 396, 449; Joseph R. Beal, deposition, "Peter F. Jefferson & wife, etc. vs James Harris Executor, etc.;" Virginia Moore, *Scottsville*, 56.

107 Albemarle County Minute Book, 1832, p. 96.

108 During the 19th century, liquor licenses were issued at the county level. Susan B. Chiarello writes, "There are separate business license indexes for grist mills, restaurants, liquor sales, ordinary licenses and a category called Retail Licenses. The last index contains licenses issued to the man who wanted to sell drugs, jewelry, dry goods or merchandise manufactured outside the US. Even the man who wanted to run a circus had to have a license and can be found in this index." See Susan B. Chiarello, "Featured Website: A Case Study in Court Loose Papers: Loudoun County Clerk of the Circuit Court Archives," accessed September 2017, http://www.vgs.org/research-aids/featured-websites/182-fw-a-case-study-loudon.

109 "Commonwealth vs Peter F. Jefferson," Criminal Records 1838, Albemarle County, VA, Library of Virginia.

110 Joseph Walker, deposition, "Peter F. Jefferson & wife, etc. vs James Harris Executor, etc.;" Joseph R. Beal, deposition, ibid. A life-long associate of Peter Field Jefferson, Joseph Walker was a farmer and a carpenter; served as a Magistrate in Fluvanna County; and as an Elder in Scottsville Presbyterian Church. In May of 1834, Peter F. Jefferson, Assignee for Joseph Walker, was the plaintiff in a case against Charles Grillet and James Brady. Grillet was a fellow merchant in Scottsville. The argument involved a debt of $377.66. The nature of the debt is not disclosed in the court minutes. On October 11, 1834, the complaint was settled in favor of Jefferson and Walker, discharged by a payment of $211.77, plus legal fees from May 29, 1834. Late in life, Jefferson hired Walker to supervise the construction of a mill on his Buckingham County farm. See Law Order Book, 1831–1837, Albemarle County, VA, pp. 220, 239.

111 R. E. Hannum, "Site of Store Run by Peter Fields Jefferson," 29 October [c.1937], Virginia Historical Inventory, Library of Virginia. The properties of the ferry landing and the store were contiguous. In 1830, Peter Field Jefferson was taxed on 92 poles adjoining Scottsville, with structures valued at $500. As part of Jefferson's estate, on December 24, 1861, Scott's Ferry ($500) and "Grocery House at Canal Bridge in Scottsville" ($300) were appraised separately. See Land Tax, Albemarle County, VA,

1830; Peter Field Jefferson Estate Appraisal (1861), Albemarle County Will Book 26, pp. 330–33.

112 Hannum, "Site of Store Run by Peter Fields Jefferson."

113 Joseph R. Beal, deposition, "Jefferson and wife, etc. vs Harris Executor, etc."

114 Ibid.

115 Federal Population Census, Albemarle County, VA, 1830.

116 *Lynchburg Virginian*, 1 July 1833, p. 2. To date, no family Bible or public records have been discovered revealing birth dates for the children of Jane and Peter Field Jefferson.

117 Federal Population Census, Albemarle County, VA, 1830.

118 Ibid.

119 Joseph Walker, deposition, "Jefferson and wife, etc. vs Harris Executor, etc.;" Federal Population Census, Albemarle County, VA, 1840.

120 Albemarle County Deed Book 31, p. 467; Nicholas, "Early History of the Founding of Scottsville," 127–35. The sale to Peter Field Jefferson, handled by George C. Gilmer, Commissioner, was a result of a chancery case between Howell Lewis, plaintiff, and Zachariah Lewis and the heirs of Robert Lewis. In the deed, the word "Tavern" was crossed out and the word "store" was inserted. Formerly, the store house was occupied by Benjamin M. Perkins, nephew of Sarah (Perkins) Lewis, who was the mother of Robert Lewis. When Jefferson purchased Lewis' fraction of the lot, George A. Scruggs had been residing at what had been Noel's Tavern since at least 1831. Scruggs was an early developer in Scottsville, owning a residence on lot #34 since 1818. On December 12, 1825, he married Frances Noel, daughter of Thompson Noel, tavern owner. The ownership of these properties remains a puzzle today. It seems likely that lot #34 mentioned in the bond is actually Noel's fraction of lot #35. According to Richard Nicholas, "Thompson Noel, the son of Thompson Noel, deceased, used lot number 34 as security for a bond of $45 given by Noel to George A. Scruggs and describes the property as " '... the same lot whereon the said George A. Scruggs now resides purchased by the said Thompson Noel, deceased of John Scott together with all the buildings and improvements thereon. ...' Noel conveyed the lot in trust to Benjamin H. Magruder to secure the debt to Scruggs." See Nicholas, "Early History of the Founding of Scottsville," 26, 121, 127–35; Vogt & Kethley, *Albemarle County Marriages, volume one*, 278.

121 John Scott to Thompson Noel, Albemarle County Deed Book 21, p. 339; John Scott to Robert Lewis, Albemarle County Deed Book 21, pp. 339–40.

122 Woods, 257.

123 LaFaye C. Sutkin, Ph. D, Lewis family history, accessed September 2017, http://archiver.rootsweb.ancestry.com/th/read/LEWIS/2001-06/0993544055. Dr. Sutkin wrote: "In New Orleans Public Library, we found the kind of documents of which

genealogists dream: one which gave us the names of parents, siblings—with birth order—and a little insight into the family history: Our John Lewis had a brother named Robert, who had been mentioned in guardianship papers of John's son Robert Nicholas Lewis as 'Robert Lewis of New Orleans.' We located Robert's Will, Inventory, and about 151 pages of Succession Pages (Probate.) We learned that the parents of John were Owen Lewis and Sarah Perkins." [See Ibid.] This Lewis family was well-known to Peter F. Jefferson. Robert Lewis' mother, Sarah Perkins, grew up adjacent Snowden in Buckingham County and married Owen Lewis in Fluvanna County in about 1776. Their son, Robert Nicholas Lewis, was born in 1786, in Albemarle County. His brothers included Howell, Zachariah, and Hardin Perkins Lewis. Their grandfather, Hardin Perkins of Buckingham County, was a neighbor and friend of Randolph Jefferson. Their Lewis grandfather, John Lewis, a contemporary of Peter Jefferson, was an early settler and developer of the area around Albemarle's first courthouse. In 1742, John Lewis acquired land on Totier Creek and kept an ordinary at the courthouse. See "Lewis," accessed September 2018, http://www.blankensteingenealogy.net/lewis.htm; Woods, 257; Albemarle Order Book 2, p. 317.

124 "Died—Near Scottsville on Saturday, September 1, Mr. Nowell, innkeeper at Scottsville, killed by Mr. Lewis," *Richmond Daily Mercantile Advertiser*, 11 September 1821, p. 3; "Fatal Rencounter," *Enquirer* (Richmond, VA), 11 September 1821, p. 2. Decades later, Virginia Moore summarized the incident, relying on an article printed in the *Central Gazette* which also identified Thompson Noel as Nowell. See Virginia Moore, *Scottsville*, 52; Nicholas, "Early History of the Founding of Scottsville," 130.

125 Albemarle County Deed Book 52, pp. 404–5. According to Richard Nicholas the structure which stands at 380 Main Street in Scottsville, once The Old Tavern, was originally owned by John Scott. Later known as the "Doll House," it was occupied by Rev. A. J. Doll, a trustee for Peter Field Jefferson's estate. Nicholas believes the building at 360 Main Street in Scottsville has been mis-identified as The Old Tavern: "According to local tradition, the two-story brick building that exists today at 360 Main Street is considered to be an historic structure that probably originated in the early years of the 19th century about the time of the founding of the Town of Scottsville, or perhaps even earlier. A local brochure published in 1991 points out that while the 'Exact date of construction is unknown,' it was 'probably late 1700's or early 1800's.' Another folder states that the 'Old Tavern' was built in 1840, a third gives a date of 1820, a fourth reference suggests it that was built circa 1800–1825, and yet another states that 'The Scottsville Tavern on Valley [sic] Street dates to the second quarter of the nineteen century.' Unfortunately, no historical architectural analysis or other documented study of the building has ever been done, and therefore its origin and history must be determined today by other methods without the benefit of a detailed onsite investigation." See Nicholas, "Early History of the Founding of Scottsville," 130–31.

126 Joseph Martin, *A New and Comprehensive Gazetteer of Virginia, and the District of Columbia* (Charlottesville, VA: Moseley & Tompkins, 1835), 117.

127 *Richmond Whig*, 1 December 1835, p. 3. This William Lewis was likely the brother of Robert N. Lewis. See "Owen Lewis & Sarah Perkins," accessed September 2017, http://www.blankensteingenealogy.net/owen_lewis_&_sarah_perkins.htm.

128 *Daily Dispatch* (Richmond, VA), 9 January 1860, p. 2.

129 *Daily Dispatch* (Richmond, VA), 20 February 1860, p. 2.

130 *Richmond Whig*, 28 September 1847, p. 4.

131 *Daily Dispatch* (Richmond, VA), 1 August 1862, p. 1.

132 *Daily Dispatch* (Richmond, VA), 20 February 1860, p. 2.

133 Albemarle County Deed Book 35, pp. 59–61. On October 12, 1836, an Indenture of Release was filed at the courthouse. Nathaniel Garland and John Coles, Trustees were authorized by Tucker Coles to convey the title to Peter Field Jefferson. Versions vary concerning the property's previous owners, as well as the date Jefferson owned the property. Several sources erroneously repeat that Jefferson acquired it from John Scott. In 2009, Richard L. Nicholas made a detailed study of the ownership of Mount Walla (a.k.a. lot #54), concluding that while John Scott III and James B. Holeman at one time owned the land, Richard Moon first built a house there sometime between 1821–1828. This was Richard Moon (T), the son of William and Charlotte (Harris) Moon, who removed to Bledsoe County, Tennessee as a young man, later returning to Albemarle County. In 1828, Moon deeded the house and 93 acres in trust to secure debts. See Nicholas, "Early History of the Founding of Scottsville," 81, 89–91, 142–52; R. E. Hannum, "Mount Walla: Home of Mrs. Hattie F. Moulton," 30 March 1937, Virginia Historical Inventory, Library of Virginia; "Monograph of a Plantation Home," a sales brochure created by Stevens & Company, Mount Walla vertical file, Albemarle Charlottesville Historical Society; Virginia Moore, *Scottsville*, 97; "Mount Walla," National Register of Historic Places Registration Application, October 2000, p. 8; "John Scott House, Jackson Street, Scottsville, Albemarle County, VA," HABS, 1974, Library of Congress.

134 Jacob H. Briggs, deposition, "Peter F. Jefferson & wife, etc. vs James Harris Executor, etc.;" Joseph Walker, deposition, ibid.; Peter Field Jefferson Inventory (1859), Albemarle County Will Book 26, pp. 4–5. The tax records for the property have compounded the confusion. In 1838, when Peter Field Jefferson was initially taxed for the property, the value of buildings on the parcel was given as $.00. In 1839, the value of buildings increased to $300, and, in 1840, the structures were valued at $1,600. See Land Tax, Albemarle County, VA, 1838–1840.

135 Hannum, "Mount Walla: Home of Mrs. Hattie F. Moulton."

136 Ibid. Because of the uncertainly surrounding the original date of the house and its improvements during Peter Field Jefferson's ownership from 1836–1861, it is impossible to attribute the design or appointments to the sensibilities of the Jefferson

family. Hannum's survey also relates several unconnected oral traditions concerning the house, including this incongruous statement: "It is said that Professor Blatterman [sic] lived here while his effects were being transferred from London by way of Scottsville, Va., to the University of Virginia where he was a professor." Dr. George W. Blaettermann (1782–1850) arrived in Albemarle County c.1825, when Richard Moon still owned the property and long before Peter Field Jefferson's brother, Thomas Jefferson, married Dr. Baettermann's niece, Elizabeth Siegfried, in 1858. Hannum's primary informant was Peter Field Jefferson's descendent, Hattie (Foland) Moulton.

137 M. B. Harris, deposition, "Peter F. Jefferson & wife, etc. vs James Harris Executor, etc." In 1860, M. B. Harris was a merchant and, at one time, postmaster in Scottsville. See John T. Noel, deposition, ibid.

138 *Richmond Enquirer*, 11 March 1845, p. 4.

139 Jean L. Cooper, *A Guide to Historic Charlottesville & Albemarle County, Virginia* (Charleston, SC: The History Press, 2007), 140.

140 Virginia Moore, *Scottsville*, 97. Virginia Moore's confusion of the facts is rooted, in part, in multiple errors made by Rev. Edgar Woods concerning the descendants of Randolph Jefferson, including the statement that the daughter of Peter Field Jefferson married Peter Foland. See Woods, 237.

141 Joseph Walker, deposition, "Peter F. Jefferson & wife, etc. vs James Harris Executor, etc."

142 "Descendants of JOHANN VALENTINE VOLAND/FOLAND," accessed September 2017, http://familytreemaker.genealogy.com/users/s/a/n/Sandra-Lee-Sanchez/GENE6-0003.html#CHILD3; June La Moine, editor, Harry Miller Strickler and Hudnut Rader, contributors, Christopher Henry Droegemuller, translator, *Record Book of the Rader Lutheran Church, Timberville, Virginia* (Sarasota, FL: W. A. Rader, 1990); Federal Population Census, Rockingham County, VA, 1810. Precisely when Peter Field Jefferson's son-in-law, Valentine Foland, came to live in Albemarle County is unknown. The county's personal property records erratically report the following taxpayers: Valentine Foland (1832), Valentine Foland, Sr. (1837); Valentine Foland (1838); Valentine Foland, Jr. (1839); Valentine Foland (1840). [See Albemarle County, VA, Personal Property Tax, 1832, 1837, 1839, 1840.] During the 19th century, there were at least four men called Valentine Foland. They were: Johann Valentine Foland (b. abt. 1756), Valentine Foland (b. 20 August 1789), Valentine Foland (b. 1806–1810), and Valentine Foland (b. 20 May 1810), who married Frances Ann Jefferson. He was interred on November 2, 1893 in Crown Hill Cemetery, in Indianapolis, Indiana. [See Valentine Foland, Find A Grave, accessed September 2017, https://www.findagrave.com/memorial/45939396] The Valentine Foland (August 20, 1789–May 1, 1875) buried in Wayne County, Indiana, is likely his uncle. [See Valentine Foland, Find A Grave, accessed September 2017, https://www.findagrave.com/memorial/23414116] The Valentine Foland buried in Perkinsville, Madison County, Indiana, who died age forty-three on May 31, 1853, is likely his cousin. [See

Valentine Foland, Find A Grave, accessed September 2017, https://www.findagrave.com/memorial/34189517]

143 Vogt & Kethley, *Albemarle County Marriages, 1780-1853, volume two*, 630. Witnesses were [L.] R. Hamner, Robert Roberts, and J. M. Johnston. Roberts doubled as the bondsman and Alexander H. Arthur witnessed the marriage. [See Ibid.] Other evidence suggests that Fanny Jefferson could be the second Mrs. Valentine Foland. In 1840, Fanny was not residing in her father's household. That year, a "Valen" Foland, age twenty to thirty, was enumerated in Albemarle County. Living with him were one male child under five, one female under five, and two females age fifteen to twenty. Fanny would have been about twenty years old. Valentine Foland was about thirty years old. See Federal Population Census, Albemarle County, VA, 1840; "Washington, D. C. Marriages, 1826-50," ancestry.com.

144 Albemarle County Deed Book 42, pp. 28–9.

145 Enlistment records, Company F, 9th Tennessee Calvary, CSA, 15 September 1863. Peter Valentine Foland's obituary says he was "a native of Richmond, Virginia." This remains unverified. See "Peter Valentine Foland," *Richmond-Times Dispatch*, 30 July 1915, p. 3.

146 "Tennessee State Marriages, 1780–2002," ancestry.com; Federal Population Census, Jefferson County, Tennessee, 1840–1860. Foland family members who migrated to Jefferson County, Tennessee potentially included Valentine Foland's parents, Jacob and Mary Elizabeth (Hinkle) Foland; his brothers George, Nimrod, William, and Jacob; and his sister, Harriet. To date, the Valentine Folands have not been located on the 1850 census. Fanny (Jefferson) Foland may have died before September 9, 1854, when her father made his final will; in it, Fanny's only child, Peter Valentine Foland, was included as a legatee. By 1870, Valentine and Jane Ann Foland lived in Indianapolis, Indiana, with five children aged twelve to six months. Valentine Foland died on October 31, 1893 in Indianapolis. He was eighty-three years old. See "Descendants of JOHANN VALENTINE VOLAND/FOLAND," Jacob Foland, accessed September 2017, http://familytreemaker.genealogy.com/users/s/a/n/Sandra-Lee-Sanchez/GENE6-0003.html#CHILD3; Federal Census Population Census, Indianapolis, IN, 1870; "Indiana Deaths, 1882–1920," ancestry.com.

147 *Richmond Whig*, 24 July 1835, p. 1.

148 James River and Kanawha Company, "Extracts from the proceedings of the board of assessors: 1836–1840," Special Collections, Library of Virginia; Virginia Moore, *Scottsville*, 64–66.

149 James River and Kanawha Company, "Extracts from the proceedings of the board of assessors: 1836–1840;" Ruth Klippstein, "The Booming Scottsville of the 1840's," Scottsville Museum website, accessed October 2017, http://scottsvillemuseum.com/transportation/hometutwiler.html.

150 *Pittsburgh Gazette*, 4 June 1836, p. 3.

151   Virginia Moore, *Scottsville*, 65–66.

152   James Harris to John Harris Exr et al., letter, 31 July 1838, "Sarah Harris vs Edward H. Moon, etc.," Albemarle County Chancery Case 1849-014 Csc, Library of Virginia; James Harris, deposition, ibid.; Personal Property Tax, Albemarle County, VA, 1835–1836; John J. Zaborney, *Slaves for Hire: Renting Enslaved Laborers in Antebellum Virginia* (Baton Rouge, LA: Louisiana State University Press, 2012).

153   *Richmond Dispatch*, "'Snowden' and Its Owner–Jefferson's Escape," 25 February 1900, p. 9. Virginia Moore paraphrased this article in her book *Scottsville on the James*. [See Virginia Moore, *Scottsville*, 66; Yeck, "Jefferson Myths," *Lost Jeffersons*.] In 1843, Jefferson paid $16.30 tax on $660.00 interest generated by State Bonds and, in 1859, an inventory of his property noted that he still owned: "State bonds including bonds guaranteed by the state amounting in all to $2,500." While the bonds were a fraction of his overall wealth, they certainly added to it and provided a steady income.

154   *Richmond Whig*, 10 July 1840, p. 3.

155   "Old Canal Warehouse," Scottsville Museum website, accessed September 2017, http://scottsvillemuseum.com/business/homeB35cdB14.html.

156   "Award James River and Kanawha Company & Peter F. Jefferson," filed 10 October 1839; James River and Kanawha Company, *Extracts from the Proceedings of the Board of Assessors: 1836–1840* (C&O Railroad Company, 1981), 17; "Letter from Peter F. Jefferson to Clerk of Superior Court of Albemarle," 2 March 1841, "Peter F. Jefferson vs Thomas Jefferson, etc.," Albemarle County Chancery Case 1843-007, Original case number 572-11, Library of Virginia.

157   John Hammond Moore, *Albemarle: Jefferson's County, 1727-1976* (Charlottesville, VA: Albemarle County Historical Society), 185.

158   *Raleigh Register*, 18 August 1843, p. 4.

159   "Scottsville and Staunton Turnpike. No. IV," *Richmond Whig*, 24 November 1846, p. 1.

160   Ibid.

161   Yeck, "James Lilburne Jefferson," *Lost Jeffersons*; Nicholas, "Scottsville," 167.

162   James Lilburne Jefferson to Peter Field Jefferson, letter, "Peter F. Jefferson vs Thomas Jefferson, etc."

163   According to Scottsville historian, Richard Nicholas, "The topography was so steep on the hillside immediately below the Mount Walla property that it must have been obvious to prospective buyers from the very beginning that it would be impractical to build there. As a consequence, there is no evidence that Holman Street was ever opened. Furthermore, the topographic hindrance to development on the precipitous hillside apparently also included the six eastern-most lots (43–48) on the north side of Jackson Street as well." See Nicholas, "Early History of the Founding of Scottsville," 89.

164 *Lynchburg Virginian*, 24 October 1836, p. 3.

165 *Springfield Republican* (Springfield, MA), 26 November 1836, p. 2.

166 Yeck, "Lilburne Lewis," *Lost Jeffersons*.

167 The Lynchburg Court appointed an administrator, William L. T. B. Jones, to make an inventory of Lilburne Jefferson's "goods, chattel, and credits." See Lynchburg Will Book "B," 292, 295.

168 Bill of complaint, 7 August 1843, "Peter F. Jefferson vs Thomas Jefferson, etc." Notably, James Lilburne Jefferson's half-brother, John R. Jefferson, was not named in the Chancery Case, though he was alive and living in Tennessee.

169 Albemarle County Deed Book 41, p. 29; Albemarle County Court Minutes, 1839–1842, pp. 100–1; Yeck, "James Lilburne Jefferson," *Lost Jeffersons*.

170 *Richmond Whig*, 21 July 1843, p. 4. The men placing the advertisement were John Harris Coleman, Executor of the John Harris Estate; Edward Harris Moon, Sarah C. Harris' son-in-law; and Benjamin Henry Magruder (1808–1885) of Fluvanna County. While Snowden and its accompanying property remained in Harris' estate, Magruder acted as Executor, involved with the hiring out of Snowden's slaves, some of whom worked on the canal. Magruder studied at Winchester Law School (1828–1829), as did Robert Hill Carter, who acted as Curator for the John Harris estate. See "Sarah Harris vs Edward H. Moon, etc."

171 Receipts, "Sarah Harris vs Edward H. Moon, etc."

172 John L. Harris sold his farm on the Rockfish River in Nelson County to John S. Davis, whose first payment was due in October of 1844, coinciding with Harris' first payment on Snowden. See Nelson County Deed Book 11; pp. 253–54; Personal Property Tax, Nelson County, VA, 1844; Personal Property Tax, Buckingham County, VA, 1846; Land Tax, Buckingham County, VA, 1850.

173 "'Snowden' and Its Owner–Jefferson's Escape," *Richmond Dispatch*, 25 February 1900, p. 9; Yeck, "Jefferson Myths," *Lost Jeffersons*.

174 Joseph Walker, deposition, "Peter F. Jefferson & wife, etc. vs James Harris Executor, etc.;" Benjamin J. Harris, deposition, ibid.; George W. Dawson, deposition, ibid.

175 Personal Property Tax, Albemarle County, VA, 1845.

176 *Alexandria Gazette*, 6 November 1852, p. 2.

177 Jacob H. Briggs, deposition, "Peter F. Jefferson & wife, etc. vs James Harris Executor, etc."

178 W. W. Hamner, deposition, ibid.; Harriet Straton, deposition, ibid.

179 Hannum, "Mount Walla."

180 Harriet Straton, deposition, "Peter F. Jefferson & wife, etc. vs James Harris Executor, etc.,"

181 Joseph Walker, deposition, ibid.

182 Ibid.; Joseph R. Beal, deposition, ibid.

183 "Francis C. Gray's Account of a Visit to Monticello," 4–7 February 1815, *Founders Online*, accessed September 2017, https://founders.archives.gov/documents/Jefferson/03-08-02-0189.

184 Joseph Walker, deposition, "Peter F. Jefferson & wife, etc. vs James Harris Executor, etc.;" W. W. Hamner, deposition, ibid.; Ruben Lindsay deposition, ibid.

185 Joseph R. Beal, deposition, ibid.; Federal Slave Census, Albemarle County, VA, 1850. Nicey was born in Buckingham County in about 1805 and may have been one of the slaves in Randolph Jefferson's estate. See Death Record, Albemarle County, VA.

186 W. W. Hamner, deposition, "Peter F. Jefferson & wife, etc. vs James Harris Executor, etc."

187 Joseph Walker, deposition, ibid.; Jacob Briggs, deposition, ibid.

188 Fluvanna County Deed Book 16, pp. 133–34; Albemarle County Deed Book 57, pp. 216–17.

189 Joseph R. Beal, deposition, "Peter F. Jefferson & wife, etc. vs James Harris Executor, etc." According to the Scottsville Museum's website: "In March 1832, the Scottsville Methodist Episcopal congregation purchased Lot 26 from Martin and Mildred Thacker for $150. This church property sat two lots east of Valley Street on the north side of Main Street and was deeded to the following church trustees: Lewis Mayo, Beverly Staples, Nathaniel Moon, Lelan Morris, Martin Tutwiler, Horatio I. Magruder, and William C. Adams. . . . *The Scottsville Sun*, dated November 8, 1951, reported that the Methodist Church first belonged to the Albemarle Circuit, and its first pastor was Reverend Albert C. Burton." See "Scottsville Methodist Church," Scottsville Museum website, accessed September 2017, http://scottsvillemuseum.com/church/homeB58dcdB16.html.

190 M. B. Harris, deposition, "Peter F. Jefferson & wife, etc. vs James Harris Executor, etc." According to Joseph Walker, "Peter F. Jefferson, Jr. was a foolish sort of a fellow never had much sense at least it was thought so & I reckon I thought with the balance of the folks." See Joseph Walker, deposition, ibid.

191 Commonwealth vs Fields Jefferson & George Herndon, Albemarle County, VA, Criminal Cases, 1851, Library of Virginia.

192 Commonwealth vs Field Jefferson, Jr., Concealed Weapons, Albemarle County, VA, Criminal Cases, 1853, Library of Virginia.

193 Joseph Walker, deposition, "Peter F. Jefferson & wife, etc. vs James Harris Executor, etc."

194 Federal Population Census, Albemarle County, VA, 1850. Jane W. Jefferson was incorrectly enumerated as sixty-five rather than about fifty-two years old.

195 Roger G. Ward, *Land Tax Summaries & Implied Deeds, volume 3*, (Athens, GA: Iberian Publishing Company, 1993), 149.

196 Ward, *Land Tax Summaries & Implied Deeds, volume 2*, p. 395; Yeck, "Buckingham County: A Contest of Wills," *The Jefferson Brothers*, 289–318.

197 "Shipping News," *Richmond Whig*, 2 June 1843, p. 2; "Broad-Rock Races," *Enquirer* (Richmond, VA), 24 April 1832, p. 1; "Directors of the Bank of Virginia and [—] for 1840," *Richmond Whig*, 10 January 1840, p. 4; Federal Population Census, Chesterfield County, VA, 1840. In 1840, James W. Winfree was enumerated in Chesterfield County, owning fifty-two slaves, and in Buckingham County, owning twenty-one slaves. See Federal Population Census, Buckingham County, VA, 1840.

198 *Enquirer* (Richmond, VA), 10 September 1839, p. 4.

199 *Enquirer* (Richmond, VA), 8 October 1847, p. 3.

200 Land Tax, Buckingham County, VA, 1852–1854; Personal Property Tax, Buckingham County, VA, 1852. The deed transferring James W. Winfree's land to Peter Field Jefferson was lost in the 1869 Buckingham County courthouse fire.

201 Ward, *Land Tax Summaries & Implied Deeds, volume 3*, p. 149. William "Henry" Nicholas (1803/05–1867) and Lorenzo Dow Nicholas (1808–1867) were the sons of Ann "Nancy" (Scott) Nicholas of The Hermitage, a farm sitting to the south of Snowden. In 1850, Henry and Lorenzo were enumerated as farmers, living adjacent John L. Harris. Nancy Nicholas was seventy-eight years old and her wealth was estimated at $17,000. She died in 1853, leaving Henry and Lorenzo "all the land [356 acres, less 35 acres] I bought of Walter L. Fontaine lying on James River in Buckingham." See Federal Population Census, Buckingham County, VA, 1850; Buckingham County Will Book 1, pp. 42–4.

202 Land Tax, Buckingham County, VA, 1855–1857. In 1875, Joseph Walker remembered building a mill on the property in about 1852, shortly after Jefferson acquired it. See Joseph Walker, deposition, "Peter F. Jefferson & wife, etc. vs James Harris Executor, etc."

203 Initially, Peter Field Jefferson's niece, Mary Elizabeth, and her husband, Albert W. Gantt, may have lived at Winfrey's Tract, either leasing it or managing it for Peter Field Jefferson. In mid-September of 1850, the Gantts and their young son were enumerated in northern Buckingham County on a farm valued at $14,000, managing the labor force. Twelve black men, women, and children were enumerated under Gantt's name. That year's agricultural census detailed the development at the farm. There were nine horses, a milk cow, and pigs. They grew a mixed crop of wheat, corn and oats, as well as producing 10,000 lbs. of tobacco. If all of this was being managed for Peter Field Jefferson, he was indeed a farmer as indicated on the 1850 census. In November of 1850, Albert W. Gantt and his family were also enumerated in Albemarle County, living with his father-in-law, Robert Lewis Jefferson. During 1851–1852, Gantt did not pay personal property taxes in Buckingham, his family having returned to Albemarle. On March 13, 1858, Robert Lewis Jefferson died of cancer, leaving his middle-aged widow, Elizabeth Ann "Bettie" (Moorman) Jefferson, in charge of their plantation, Rock Castle. Gantt reported Jefferson's death.

See Federal Population Census, Buckingham County, VA, 1850; Industrial Census, Buckingham County, VA, 1850; Agricultural Census, Buckingham County, VA, 1850; Slave Census, Buckingham County, VA, 1850; Federal Population Census, Albemarle County, VA, 1850; Death Record, Albemarle County, VA.

204 Industrial Census, Buckingham County, VA, 1850–1860; Buckingham County Deed Book 1, pp. 531–33. This deed from Peter Field Jefferson to William H. Nicholas was lost in the Buckingham County courthouse fire, however, the transaction was mentioned when James Harris sold Winfrey's Tract to Nathan T. Payne in 1871.

205 Albemarle County Deed Book 52, p. 404–5; Nicholas, "Early History of the Founding of Scottsville," 127. The lots were not identified in the deed; however, the purchase included lot #34 (which Jefferson sold in 1858) and the so-called Doll House, lot #36. See Nicholas, "Early History of the Founding of Scottsville," 168; "The Doll House," Scottsville Museum website, accessed September 2017, http://scottsvillemuseum. com/homes/homeRoll7Neg4A.html.

206 Albemarle County Deed Book 52, pp. 404–5.

207 Peter Field Jefferson Will, Albemarle County Will Book 26, pp. 245–46.

208 Marriage Record, Fluvanna County, VA; Federal Population Census, Albemarle County, VA, 1860. Elizabeth A. Wood's age varies in the public record. Her marriage license suggests a birth date of about 1819. Her death record states that she was sixty when she died on June 20, 1876, suggesting she was born about 1816. On the 1860 census, Elizabeth's age is recorded as thirty-four, placing her birth in 1826, while the 1870 census, stated she was forty-six, placing her birth in 1824. All of these dates make her older than Peter Field Jefferson, Jr. How they met is unknown, though, Elizabeth's father, Thomas Wood, lived in the neighborhood of Nancy Pollard, the future wife of Peter Field Jefferson's brother, Thomas. See Federal Population Census, Fluvanna County, VA, 1850.

209 Joseph Walker, deposition, "Peter F. Jefferson & wife, etc. vs James Harris Executor, etc."

210 During 1874–1875, Peter F. Jefferson, Jr. and others sued the estate of James Harris concerning the sale of the Buckingham County farm in 1858, claiming that Peter F. Jefferson, Sr. was not in his right mind when he sold the property and was unduly influenced by attorney William M. Wade, who might have profited from the sale. The settlement of the suit was delayed by several deaths. See Final Order, "Peter F. Jefferson & wife, etc. vs James Harris Executor, etc."

211 John T. Noel, deposition, "Peter F. Jefferson & wife, etc. vs James Harris Executor, etc."

212 Slave Census, Albemarle County, VA, 1850. In 1850, Peter Field Jefferson owned only two slaves: a twenty-year-old man, likely Winston, and a forty-year-old woman. Winston's surname is currently unknown. In 1870, a Winston Cabell, age 57, resided in Fork Union Township, Scottsville Post Office, Fluvanna County. His sixteen-year-old

son was named Peter. [See Federal Population Census, Fluvanna County, VA, 1870.] The forty-year-old woman is probably Nicey, who was born c.1805 in Buckingham County. On February 15, 1855, Jefferson reported her death in Albemarle County. By 1860, Jefferson owned only Winston who was enumerated as fifty years old. See Slave Census, Albemarle County, VA, 1850, 1860; Death Record, Albemarle County, VA; Roger G. Ward, *Buckingham County, Virginia Natives Who Died Elsewhere, 1853–1896* (Athens, GA: Iberian Publishing Co., 1994), 103.

213 When Peter Field Jefferson wrote his will, his brother, Robert Lewis Jefferson, was still living; however, Lewis would precede Peter Field in death on March 13, 1858.

214 Peter Field Jefferson Will, Albemarle County Will Book 26, pp. 245–46. Previously, Peter Field Jefferson had replaced his counsel Thomas Staples with the younger William Wade. After Wade died on April 5, 1862, Elbridge G. Jefferson served as the primary executor of Peter Field Jefferson's estate until his death in September of 1865. See Administrator of Peter F. Jefferson, etc. vs Executor of William M. Wade, etc., Albemarle County Chancery Case 1870-031 Cc, Library of Virginia; "Octavia Bowcock, etc. vs John T. Blair, etc.," Albemarle County Chancery Case 1881-016 Cc, Library of Virginia.

215 William D. Davis, deposition, "Peter F. Jefferson & wife, etc. vs James Harris Executor, etc." William D. Davis was William W. Wade's uncle and, at one time acted as Wade's personal representative.

216 Albemarle County Deed Book 55, pp. 81–2. Sources vary as to the property's distance from Scottsville, placing it between two and four miles north of the town. Today, Route 618 (a.k.a. Brick Mill Road) leads to the property. In the application for "Mount Walla" to the National Register of Historic Places, the authors erroneously suggest that Albemarle Mills might have been purchased by Peter Field Jefferson, Jr. About twenty-five years old when the property was acquired, Peter Field, Jr. had no funds of his own. See "Mount Walla," National Register of Historic Places Registration Form, 13 September 2000 (VLR), 22 November 2000 (listed NRHP).

217 Albemarle County Deed Book 23, p. 475; Nicholas, "Early History of the Founding of Scottsville," 81.

218 Albemarle County Deed Book 34, p. 394; "Cliffside," Scottsville Museum website, accessed September 2017, http://scottsvillemuseum.com/homes/homeEEcdEE01.html; Woods, 378, 403.

219 "Land and Mills For Sale," *Richmond Whig*, 17 January 1843, p. 3.

220 Albemarle County Deed Book 53, p. 183; Albemarle County Deed Book 58, pp. 425–26. On November 14, 1854, Hartman also transferred the 30 acres to John L. Dawson.

221 "Trust Sale Of Valuable Real Estate And Personal Property," *Richmond Whig*, 26 December 1854, p. 4.

222 According to the Scottsville Museum website: "Although there is no extant official record of this house's ownership from 1830 to 1892, the Beal family said that the house was built by a builder/architect named William Magruder for James W. Mason president of the Bank of Scottsville and brought his bride to live there. Old Hall is often called the James W. Mason House after its first owner. After Mrs. Mason inherited Hatton Grange, they sold Old Hall to Joseph R. Beal in 1856." See: "Old Hall," Scottsville Museum website, accessed September 2017, http://scottsvillemuseum. com/homes/homeB253cd25.html; "Hatton Grange," Scottsville Museum website, accessed September 2017, http://scottsvillemuseum.com/homes/homeEE08cdEE01. html.

223 Albemarle County Deed Book 58, pp. 425–26; Albemarle County Deed Book 55, p. 501. In 1867, when the property was appraised in Peter Field Jefferson's estate, it was valued at $3,000. See Albemarle County Will Book 27, p. 418.

224 "Glimpse of the Past. A Very Attractive Picture of Scottsville in By-Gone Days," *Richmond Dispatch*, 9 November 1902, p. 1.

225 Ibid.

226 R. E. Hannum, "Jefferson Mills," 5 October 1937, Virginia Historical Inventory, Library of Virginia. Hannum's survey relates the oral tradition that the mills were established by a J. M. Moon; however, as is often the case with surveys for the Virginia Historical Inventory, the data recorded in "Jefferson Mills" is misleading. Hannum confuses the deed records for the property with those of Bleak Hill, which was adjacent the mills and also owned by Peter Field Jefferson. In "Jefferson Mills," Hannum states that Jefferson purchased the mill from Mahala Dawson rather than from the Masons. On January 28, 1857, Jefferson purchased Bleak Hill from Mahala Dawson. This plot of land containing 66 1/4 acres was "lying in Albemarle near Jefferson's Mill." See Albemarle County Deed Book 56, pp. 360–61.

227 Hannum, "Jefferson Mills."

228 Federal Population Census, Albemarle County, VA, 1860–1870. By 1880, Peter F. Jefferson was described as a laborer and as "idiotic." See Federal Population Census, Fluvanna County, VA, 1880.

229 Albemarle County Deed Book 56, pp. 360–61.

230 For a history of the property in the 20th century, see "Jefferson Mills," Scottsville Museum website, accessed September 2017, http://scottsvillemuseum.com/business/homeRM02cdRM01.html; "The William Thomas Moulton Family," Scottsville Museum website, accessed September 2017, http://scottsvillemuseum.com/portraits/homeRM18cdRM03.html; Steven G. Meeks, "Jefferson's Mill–A Unique Survivor," Albemarle Anecdotes, *Bulletin* (16 March 1988).

231 On November 25, 1875, Frances Ann Wade Jefferson married a carpenter named Hartwell Steven Moore in Albemarle County. Together they had ten children. In 1927, as Fannie A. Moore, she applied for a Confederate widow's pension. In 1930,

she lived with her daughter, Lula, and her husband, Everette L. Belew. She remained in Albemarle County until her death on February 3, 1937. See Marriage Record, Albemarle County, VA; Pension Application for a Widow of Confederate Soldier, Fannie A. Moore, Crozet, Albemarle County, VA, 17 September 1927; Death Record, Albemarle County, VA.

232 R. E. Hannum, "Bleak Hill," 23 September 1937, Virginia Historical Inventory, Library of Virginia. Peter F. Jefferson purchased Bleak Hill from Mahala Dawson, widow of Pleasant L. Dawson. By 1840, Mahala (a.k.a. Mahalia) Dawson was already a widow and responsible for twenty-three slaves. Ten years later, Mahala (age 55) and her son, George W. Dawson (farmer, age 23), were living together, possibly at Bleak Hill. Two millers, William W. Mayo (age 45) and Robert Roberts (age 50), lived adjacent the Dawsons. The Jefferson and Dawson families had a long, inter-twined history, beginning with the Martin Dawson, who rented Snowden from Peter Jefferson's estate in the mid-18th century. Rev. Martin Dawson had performed the wedding ceremonies for two of Peter Field Jefferson's siblings. Pleasant L. Dawson was the Reverend's nephew. See Yeck, *The Jefferson Brothers*; Federal Population Census, Albemarle County, VA, 1840, 1850; Sudie Rucker Wood, *Rucker Family Genealogy, with Their Ancestors, Descendants and Connections* (Richmond, VA: Old Dominion Press, 1932).

233 Hannum, "Bleak Hill."

234 Ibid.

235 Later, the effects of the accident would be argued in court. Peter F. Jefferson, Jr. and his heirs posited: "In 1856, Peter F. Jefferson, Sr, deceased, had a fall from a cherry tree in his garden which caused him great bodily injury his head being severely hurt and he being made a cripple for life. From this time his mind became seriously impaired, and growing more & more so continually. He had before or by 1858 become hopelessly imbecile, and utterly unfit to transact business." See Final Order, "Peter F. Jefferson & wife, etc. vs James Harris Executor, etc."

236 Peter Field Jefferson Estate Sale (1864), Albemarle County Will Book 27, p. 262; Jacob H. Briggs, deposition, "Peter F. Jefferson & wife, etc. vs James Harris Executor, etc.;" W. W. Hamner, deposition, ibid.; William D. Davis, deposition, "B. J. Harris, Executor, etc. vs Jefferson, etc." William Davis was Peter Field Jefferson's close neigh-bor in Scottsville, living within one hundred yards of his house. He was a cashier at a bank in Scottsville and the uncle of Jefferson's attorney, William M. Wade.

237 Joseph Walker, deposition, "Peter F. Jefferson & wife, etc. vs James Harris Executor, etc."

238 This is the only known reference to a middle name for Thomas Jefferson. The institu-tion opened in 1828, admitting both men and woman with a wide variety of mental disorders, both chronic and acute. When Thomas Jefferson was admitted, the hospi-tal was run by Dr. Francis T. Stribling, who was appointed to the job in 1840 and remained in charge until his death in 1874. Dr. Stribling practiced "Moral Therapy"

and was one of the thirteen founders of the American Psychiatric Association. See "Western State Hospital," accessed September 2017, http://www.wsh.dbhds.virginia.gov/history.htm.

239 Thomas Jefferson, Admissions Register, Western State Hospital, Library of Virginia.

240 Federal Census, Augusta County, VA, 1860.

241 "Heirs of Peter F. Jefferson vs Heirs of Peter F. Jefferson," Albemarle County Chancery Case, Original Case #766, 1867-016 CC, Library of Virginia.

242 In 1863, Elbridge G. Jefferson sold the five-acre property for $1,000. See "Wyatt Hare vs Heirs of Elbridge G. Jefferson, etc.," Nelson County Chancery Case 1871-054, Library of Virginia; John T. Noel, deposition, "Peter F. Jefferson & wife, etc. vs James Harris Executor, etc.;" W. W. Hamner, deposition, Ibid; Rev. John A. Doll, deposition, "A. W. Gantt & wife vs John T. Noel & others," Albemarle County Chancery Case 1882-045 Cc, Library of Virginia.

243 John T. Noel, deposition, "B. J. Harris Executor, etc. vs Jefferson, etc."

244 Ibid.; Joseph Walker, deposition, "Peter F. Jefferson & wife, etc. vs James Harris Executor, etc."

245 Following the accident, it became clear that Jane and Peter Field Jefferson, Sr. were unable to move to Buckingham County. Thomas Jefferson was committed in Staunton, never to be released. Peter Field Jefferson, Jr. and his wife were settled at the more manageable Bleak Hill.

246 *Richmond Whig*, 9 October 1857, p. 1. Peter F. Jefferson, Jr. brought suit against the James Harris estate, claiming that Winfrey's Tract was offered for sale under the fraudulent influence of William M. Wade, acting as Peter F. Jefferson, Sr.'s business advisor. Peter F. Jefferson, Jr., et al. asserted: "Wm. M. Wade moved by the selfish desire of controlling & using testator's money and being at that time particularly in need of several thousand dollars to discharge the debt he owed [the] bank, in the early part of 1858 concluded a contract on behalf of said Peter F. Jefferson senior for the sale to James Harris of Buckingham County Va, of the valuable Winfree tract mentioned in testator's will for the price of $18,000." The advertisements placed in the *Richmond Enquirer* were not exhibits in the suit nor were they explained by the plaintiffs. Unless William Wade "forged" Jefferson's name, in 1857, Jefferson was of sound mind and intended to sell the property for personal reasons. See Final Order, "Peter F. Jefferson & wife, etc. vs James Harris Executor, etc."

247 *Richmond Enquirer*, 22 September 1857, p. 2. According to Chronicling America: "*The Richmond Enquirer* remained strongly Democratic during the Civil War, ardently supporting the Confederacy and Jefferson Davis's administration." See "About Richmond enquirer. (Richmond, Va.) 1815-1867," Chronicling America, accessed October 2017, http://chroniclingamerica.loc.gov/lccn/sn84024735/.

248 John T. Noel, deposition, "B. J. Harris vs Jefferson, et al."

249 The deed transferring "Winfrey's Tract" from the Winfree Estate to Peter Field Jefferson was lost in Buckingham County's courthouse fire in 1869. Evidence of the payments for Winfrey's were recorded in Jefferson's estate accounts and in James Harris' personal papers. Peter Field Jefferson Estate Accounts; Albemarle County Deed Book 87, pp. 229–30.

250 In 1870, J. H. Briggs (age 45), boat inspector, lived in Scottsville adjacent Peter Field Jefferson's grandson, Peter V. Foland (age 25). See Federal Population Census, Albemarle County, VA, 1870.

251 J. H. Briggs, deposition, "Peter F. Jefferson & wife, etc. vs James Harris, Executor, etc."

252 Joseph Walker, deposition, ibid.; J. H. Briggs, deposition, ibid; Benjamin J. Harris, answer, ibid.

253 Samuel Allen Estate, Mss1 AL546 c 602-604, Section 24, Virginia Historical Society; Joanne L. Yeck, "*Locust Grove*: A Harris Plantation in Buckingham County and the People Who Lived There," Mss6:1 H2445:5, Virginia Historical Society. A suit and counter-suit were filed in the Buckingham County Court, with a final order recorded during the October 1875 term. In the chancery suits, Jefferson descendants complained that Nathan T. Payne was destroying the timber on the property. Ultimately, the Buckingham County Court upheld Payne's deed and his right to cut the lumber. See "Peter F. Jefferson & wife, etc. vs James Harris Executor, etc.;" Industrial Census, Buckingham County, VA, 1870; Buckingham County Deed Book 1, pp. 531–33.

254 After his accident, Peter Field Jefferson continued to transact real estate business. In 1857, he purchased part of lot #24 from the estate of James Brady. In 1858, Jefferson sold a lot #34 to William A. Woodward. See Albemarle County Deed Book 57, pp. 216–17; 220–21; John T. Noel, deposition, "A. W. Gantt & wife vs John T. Noel & others;" Rev. John A. Doll, deposition, ibid.

255 Peter Field Jefferson Estate Inventory (1859), Albemarle County Will Book 26, pp. 4–5; Peter Field Jefferson Estate Sale (1864), Albemarle County Will Book 27, pp. 262–63.

256 Jacob Briggs, deposition, "Peter F. Jefferson & wife, etc. vs James Harris Executor, etc.;" Ruben Lindsay, deposition, ibid.

257 "Committee appointed for Peter Field Jefferson," exhibit, "Peter F. Jefferson & wife, etc. vs James Harris Executor, etc.;" Peter Field Jefferson Estate Inventory (1859) Albemarle County Will Book 26, pp. 4–5. On December 2, 1859, Albemarle County Clerk Ira Garrett erroneously entered the inventory into the record as the "Estate of Peter F. Jefferson dec'd," creating persistent confusion as to the date of Jefferson's death. According to the 1859 inventory, he had $2,500 in Virginia State Bonds; however, the 1861 appraisal of his estate estimated that he owned $25,000 in Virginia State Bonds. A later appraisal, recorded in 1867, included $25,000 in Virginia State Bonds. [See Peter Field Jefferson Estate Appraisal (1861), Albemarle County

Will Book 26, pp. 330–33; Peter Field Jefferson Estate Appraisal (1867), Albemarle County Will Book 27, pp. 418–419.] Peter Field Jefferson's slave, Winston, may be Winston Jefferson who was born in Albemarle County and died on October 15, 1895 at Porter's Precinct, Albemarle. The cause of death was a "rupture." He was sixty-three years old. [See Death Record, Albemarle County, VA, 1895, p. 2, line 10.] Another Winston Jefferson died on April 16, 1892 at Porter's Precinct. The cause of death was consumption. Born in Albemarle County, he was thirteen years old. His mother was Mary Jefferson. His father, Winston Jefferson, reported his death. See Death Record, Albemarle County, VA, 1892, p. 2, line 27.

258 Albemarle County Will Book 26, pp. 4–5. The 1859 "tax ticket" shows that Peter Field Jefferson owned thirteen lots in Scottsville, including #43 and #44 which had once belonged to his brother, James Lilburne Jefferson. In this inventory, Jefferson's home was described as the "Homeplace at Scottsville supposed to be about 80 acres," valued at $3,500. In the 1861 inventory of his property, it was again referred to as "Homeplace at Scottsville"—yet another indication that the property may have been named after Jefferson's death. See Albemarle County Will Book 26, p. 332.

259 Albemarle County Will Book 26, pp. 4–5.

260 John T. Noel, bond, "Albert Gantt and wife vs John Noel, etc." George Walden Dillard, who lived at Mill House, owned various properties in Scottsville, including the old Eagle Hotel (later known as the Carleton House) on Valley Street. See "Dr. Benjamin Lewis Dillard," Scottsville Museum website, accessed September 2017, http://scottsvillemuseum.com/portraits/homeB114cdB17.html.

261 Federal Population Census, Albemarle County, VA, 1860. According to Rev. John A. Doll, "Jas. M. Noel lived some three or four hundred yards from P. F. Jefferson at that time, and Thos. Jefferson lived some half or three quarter of a mile from P. F. Jefferson. If either of them was engaged in any business during those years, I did not know it. They both seemed to be gentlemen of leisure." See Rev. John A. Doll, deposition, "Albert Gantt and wife vs John Noel, etc.;" Yeck, "Thomas Jefferson, Jr.," Lost Jeffersons.

262 Yeck, The Jefferson Brothers, 253–57.

263 Peter Field Jefferson Estate Appraisal (1861), Albemarle County Will Book 26, pp. 330–33.

264 Federal Slave Census, Albemarle County, VA, 1860; Peter Field Jefferson Estate Appraisal (1861). Adeline and her children, along with Wilson, appear on the inventory of Peter Field Jefferson's estate, and were later sold to Henry Newman, a Scottsville merchant, for $2,000. In 1870, Adeline lived with her husband and children in Albemarle County: Wilson Kenny (age 42, farm hand), Adeline (age 35), Betsy (age 18), Maria (age 16), Wilson (age 13), and Dorothy (age 8). Curiously, in 1860, Elbridge G. Jefferson owned one sixty-year-old female, living in Albemarle adjacent Thomas Jefferson, while the bulk of his slaves lived and worked in Buckingham County. See "Peter F. Jefferson in account with Thomas Jefferson, Commissioner," Jefferson vs

Jefferson Committee," Albemarle County, Original Case #648, 1861–002 CC, Library of Virginia; Slave Census, Albemarle County, VA, 1860; Federal Population Census, Albemarle County, VA, 1870.

265 Federal Slave Census, Albemarle County, VA, 1860. In 1860, only one male slave over fifty (presumably Winston) was reported by Peter Field Jefferson on the slave census. Yet, that year, he paid personal property tax on two slaves over sixteen and two slaves over twelve, three of whom were possibly purchased by his brother and hired out. Additionally, Thomas Jefferson paid personal property tax on three slaves over sixteen and three slaves over twelve. See Personal Property Tax, Albemarle County, VA, 1860.

266 Federal Population Census, Albemarle County, VA, 1860; Federal Slave Census, Albemarle County, VA, 1860. According to the Scottsville Museum, "Although there is no extant official record of this house's ownership from 1830 to 1892, the Beal family said that the house was built by a builder/architect named William Magruder for James W. Mason." See "Old Hall," Scottsville Museum website.

267 Federal Population Census, Albemarle County, VA, 1870. The relationship between the Singers and the Jeffersons is not noted on the census; however, in 1850, Cynthia and Maria Singer lived in Fluvanna County with Elizabeth (Wood) Jefferson's father, Thomas Wood. In *Scottsville on the James*, Virginia Moore makes reference to a story concerning Maria Singer: "It is not clear who Maria Singer was, the girl who eloped from Mount Walla by sliding down a sheet-rope from the little high east-side third-storey window." Indeed, on August 13, 1861, an underage Maria Singer married James B. Ellis, a photographer, in Albemarle County. Maria may actually have eloped from Bleak Hill. In 1870, the Ellis family lived in Fluvanna County, on Driver's Hill, adjacent Joseph Walker, Peter Field Jefferson's long-time associate. Maria's mother, Cynthia Singer, lived with them. Her husband, Mr. Singer is a bit of a mystery. He was either absent or dead by 1860. Richard L. Nicholas wrote, "According to a cavalryman of the 2nd Ohio (whose diary is held by the Cincinnati Historical Society), when he rode into Scottsville on March 9, 1865, he 'went into a house on the north side of the canal & began conversation with two ladies, one old, the other younger. I found the young lady, who by the way, seemed some 22 or 23 years of age claimed to be the neice [sic] of I. M. Singer, the inventor of the Singer Sewing machine.'" See Federal Population Census, Fluvanna County, VA, 1850, 1870; Virginia Moore, *Scottsville*, 97; William Norford, *Marriages of Albemarle County and Charlottesville, VA, 1781-1929* (Charlottesville, VA: Jarman Printing Company, 1956), 59; Richard L. Nicholas to Joanne Yeck, email, July 2010.

268 Bill of Complaint, "Jefferson vs Jefferson Committee." In 1860, lawyer Alexander A. Pollack (age 28) lived in Fluvanna County, on Drivers Hill above Scottsville, two doors from Joseph Walker. See Federal Population Census, Fluvanna County, VA, 1860.

269 Ibid. A copy of the Bill was delivered on December 21, 1860 to "Mrs. Jefferson, a white person over 16 years age the defendant not being found at the usual place of abode."

270 Ibid. Peter Field Jefferson, Sr. may have routinely provided his son with petty cash, the young man relying on his father's subsidy. Then, when his father lost his faculties, his uncle was disinclined to advance funds to him. Following his father's death, from 1862–1864, Peter Field, Jr.'s spending totaled $2,909.83. These accounts were kept by his trustee, Elbridge G. Jefferson. It is possible that some of these funds settled debts acquired from 1859–1862. See The Estate of Peter F. Jefferson, Sen, in account, "Heirs of Peter F. Jefferson vs Heirs of Peter F. Jefferson, etc." Albemarle County, VA, 1867-016 CC, Library of Virginia.

271 During the early 1860s, Robert A. Kent was the miller at Jefferson Mills. Peter Field Jefferson, Sr.'s slave, Winston, also worked there. See Federal Population Census, Albemarle County, VA, 1860; Rev. John A. Doll, deposition, "A. W. Gantt & wife vs John T. Noel & others."

272 *Memphis Daily Appeal*, 26 September 1861, p. 2.

273 Death Record, Albemarle County, VA.

274 Despite his overall lack of intelligence, Peter Field Jefferson, Jr. engaged attorneys to bring multiple chancery suits against his father's estate, including one against his cousin Elbridge G. Jefferson as Executor and one against Benjamin J. Harris, Executor of James Harris' Estate in Buckingham County. See "Peter Fields [sic] Jefferson vs Executor of Peter F. Jefferson, etc." Albemarle County Chancery Case 1866-049 CC, Library of Virginia; "Heirs of Peter F. Jefferson vs Heirs of Peter F. Jefferson," Albemarle County Chancery Case 1867-016 CC; "Jefferson's Administrators vs Woodward, etc.," Albemarle County Chancery Case 1870-8 CC, Library of Virginia; "Peter F. Jefferson & wife, etc. vs James Harris Executor, etc.," Buckingham County Chancery Case.

275 In 1863, Winston earned $52.50 for the estate. See "Heirs of Peter F. Jefferson vs Heirs of Peter F. Jefferson."

276 The Estate of Peter F. Jefferson, in account, ibid.

277 Jane W. Jefferson renunciation of Peter Field Jefferson Will, "Peter Fields [sic] Jefferson vs Executor of Peter F. Jefferson, etc.;" Albemarle County Deed Book 32, p. 260. It is probable that this action attempted to solve a major complication with Peter Field Jefferson's 1854 will. Between 1854 and 1861, the Buckingham County farm (which was to provide for both Jane and their son, Peter Field, Jr.) was sold and Jefferson purchased the significant properties of Albemarle Mills and Bleak Hill, just outside Scottsville, providing both a home and an income for Peter Field, Jr. and his family. Presumably, he intended them to inherit these properties, however, he did not amend his will. In 1854, Jefferson gave all the property situated within the town and immediately adjacent to the town of Scottsville to his grandson Peter V. Foland, ultimately leaving both Jane and Peter Field, Jr. without homes. Funds in

trust for son Thomas Jefferson were uncomplicated by these real estate transactions, still amply providing for his care in the Staunton asylum. Jane Jefferson died before Peter V. Foland was old enough to take possession of Mount Walla and remained in her home. Additionally, the renunciation of the will may have solved part of the problem of Peter Field, Jr.'s inheritance. On January 15, 1873, Peter "Fields" Jefferson requested that Rev. John A. Doll, who held his power of attorney, "take charge of all my interests; to manage and control my mill and its appurtenances. Also to manage and control my farm known as 'Bleak Hill' farm, and all other real and personal property." See Albemarle County Deed Book 66; pp. 7–8; Jane W. Jefferson Will, Albemarle County Will Book 27, pp. 259–60.

278 Peter Field Jefferson Estate Sale (1864), Albemarle County Will Book 27, pp. 262–63.

279 In 1864, the estate collected $1,368.15 for six months' rent for Jefferson Mills. After Peter Field, Jr.'s death, Rev. Doll transferred the "Albemarle Mills" tract and the "Bleak Hill" tract (by then known by the more appealing name of "Breezy Summit") to William N. Berkley on November 20, 1886. See Albemarle County Deed Book 87, pp. 229–30; Rev. John A. Doll, deposition, "A. W. Gantt & wife vs John T. Noel & others."

280 Federal Population Census, Albemarle County, VA, 1870; Marriage Record, Albemarle County, VA. Frances (Jefferson) Moore died in Crozet, VA on February 3, 1937. See Death Record, Albemarle County, VA.

281 Final decree, October Term 1875, "Peter F. Jefferson & wife, etc. vs James Harris Executor, etc.;" Answer of P. F. Jefferson, "Administer of Peter F. Jefferson, etc. vs Executor of William M. Wade, etc.," Albemarle County Chancery Case 1870-031 Cc, Library of Virginia.

282 Benjamin J. Harris Answer, 22 April 1875, "Peter F. Jefferson & wife, etc. vs James Harris Executor, etc."

283 Final decree, October Term 1875, ibid.; "Fields" Jefferson, Federal Population Census, Albemarle County, VA, 1880.

284 "Schedule of Defective, Dependent, and Delinquent Classes," Federal Census, Albemarle County, VA, 1880; Elizabeth Wong, "A Shameful History: Eugenics in Virginia," American Civil Liberties Union, accessed September 2017, https://acluva. org/10898/a-shameful-history-eugenics-in-virginia/.

285 Federal Population Census, Albemarle County, VA, 1880; Death Record, 1881, p. 3, line 21, Albemarle County, VA. Peter Field Jefferson, Jr.'s death record states that he was forty-four years old, though he was no doubt several years older. Erroneous reports of his death were recorded and oft repeated. In 1901, Rev. Edgar Woods wrote simply, "Peter Field Jefferson Jr., died in 1867." Virginia Moore reported, "Little Field," who busied himself at the big brick mill on the Hardware called Jefferson's Mill though someone else had built it, followed his father in 1867." The application for Mount Walla for the National Register of Historic Places repeated Peter Field Jefferson, Jr.'s dates as c.1830–1867. Today, Peter Field Jefferson, Jr. and his wife

are remembered in the Jefferson-Foland-Moulton cemetery at Mount Walla. Their prominent headstone reads: "In Memory of Peter F. Jefferson and his wife Elizabeth Wood." The marker appears to be a 20th-century addition to the cemetery. The couple may or may not be buried there. In 1940, Maria (Singer) Ellis was ninety-six years old and lived with her Foland cousins at Mount Walla, indicating a lasting relationship between the extended family of Peter Field Jefferson, Jr. and his nephew, Peter V. Foland. See Woods, 237; Virginia Moore, *Scottsville*, 97; "Mount Walla," NRHP Application, Section 8, p. 9; Federal Population Census, Scottsville, VA, 1940.

286 Federal Population Census, Albemarle County, VA, 1880; "Schedule of Defective, Dependent, and Delinquent Classes," Federal Population Census, Albemarle County, VA, 1880. In 1860, Thomas Jefferson Gantt, grandson of Robert Lewis Jefferson, was described as an idiot on the Federal Population Census. The enumerator first wrote "dumb," struck out the word dumb, and replaced it with "idiotic." In 1870, however, at age seventeen, Thomas Jefferson Gantt was described as a "farmer," living with his parents. No disabilities were noted. See Federal Population Census, Albemarle County, VA, 1870, 1880.

287 *Jeffersonian Republican*, 5 July 1882, p. 2. In May of 1919, William Thomas Moulton purchased Jefferson Mills and operated it with his son, John Adkins Moulton. In 1826, when W. T. Moulton married Harriet "Hattie" Foland, the mill was back in the family. It remained a working mill until 1945 when the last miller, William Williams, retired. William T. Moulton died on July 2, 1930, and was buried at Mount Walla. See "Jefferson Mills," Scottsville Museum website; "The William Thomas Moulton Family," Scottsville Museum website; "John Adkins Moulton and Innes Roberta (Harris) Moulton," Scottsville Museum website, accessed September 2017, http://scottsvillemuseum.com/portraits/homeRM13cdRM02.html.

288 Peter Field Jefferson Estate Appraisal (1867), Albemarle County Will Book 27, pp. 418–419. The Poplar Spring house was a lot with a brick building.

289 Peter V. Foland obituary, *Richmond Times-Dispatch*, 30 July 1915, p. 3.

290 Gift, Albemarle County Deed Book 64, pp. 280–281. In 1951, the sale of Mount Walla made news with the headline: "Jefferson Kin's Estate At Scottsville Is Sold." The article began, "An estate formerly owned by Thomas Jefferson's grand-nephew has changed hands for the first time in more than 100 years. The estate, located on a hill overlooking downtown Scottsville and the horseshoe bend of the James River, was sold to John A. Cristoffel of Warneck, Va. and Merrick, Long Island by Mrs. Hattie Foland Mounton [sic] and other heirs of the late Peter V. Foland." Again, Peter Field Jefferson, Sr. was misidentified as Thomas Jefferson's grandnephew. [See *Evening Star* (Washington, D.C.), 3 August 1951, B-22.] The "Gauge Dock" was located at lots #10, #11, and #12, just west of Ferry Street. See Richard L. Nicholas to Joanne Yeck, email, 28 March 2017.

291 Investments on the river were vulnerable to fire and flood. In 1873, the canal boat, Oceola, owned by Peter V. Foland's neighbor, J. H. Briggs, burned, about seventeen

miles above Lynchburg. The loss was estimated at $1,000. The cargo included 419 barrels of lime. See *Daily State Journal* (Alexandria, VA), 20 May 1873, p. 1.

292   *Scottsville Register*, 14 January 1871, clipping file, Scottsville Museum.

293   *Richmond Dispatch*, 23 December 1894, p. 6. In 1910, Frances (Moulton) Dunkum was married but had returned to Mount Walla to live with her parents. The Dunkums had no children and, during the early years of her marriage, Frances became ill. Her husband could not care for her and hold down a job, thus she returned to Scottsville. See Raymon Thacker interview with Joanne Yeck, 2010.

294   United States Civil Service Commission, *Official Register of the United States in the Civil, Military, and Naval Service, Volume 2* (Washington: Government Printing Office, 1889); Peter V. Foland obituary; "Mount Walla," National Register of Historic Places Registration Application, Section 8, pp. 9–10. Mount Walla remained in the Foland family until 1951–1952. In 1926, Hattie Foland married William T. Moulton, who joined her in the household at Mount Walla. In 1937, when R. E. Hannum surveyed the house for the Virginia Historical Inventory, he entitled the report, "Home of Mrs. Hattie F. Moulton." See Hannum, "Mount Walla."

295   Joseph R. Beal, deposition, "Jefferson and wife, etc. vs Harris Executor, etc."

Jefferson Gallery

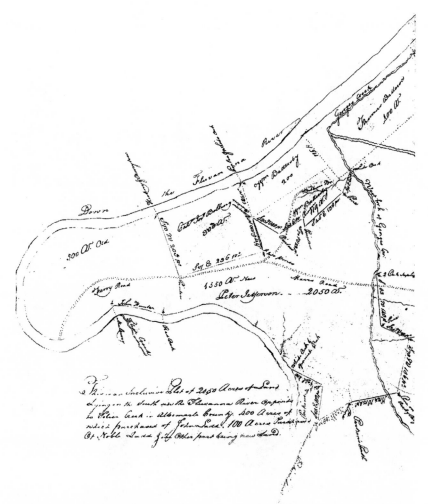

Survey of Peter Jefferson's Snowdon, 2050 acres, and neighbors at the Horseshoe Bend. (COURTESY RICHARD L. NICHOLAS.)

*"Three Slaves Steering a Bateau, watercolor, 1798, by Benjamin Latrobe. Prior to the coming of the canal, Peter Field Jefferson ran bateaux on the James River. Artist Latrobe noted inaccuracies in his illustration. The boat was "too short: they are from 60 to 75 feet long, & from 5 to 6 feet broad.... Each [bateau] is managed by 3 Men, who with great dexterity often carry them 30 miles against the stream in one day." (*COURTESY LIBRARY OF VIRGINIA*.)*

View of Richmond from the James River and Kanawha Canal, 1865. When the James River and Kanawha Canal reached Scottsville in 1840, it greatly increased commercial and tourist traffic downriver to Richmond, as well as adding significantly to Peter Field Jefferson's wealth. (COURTESY HARPER'S WEEKLY.)

Mount Walla, 1937, Virginia Historic Inventory. On October 8, 1836, Peter Field Jefferson paid $2,800 for the house and land that would be his home until his death in 1861. Restored and elaborated, in 2000, the house was placed on the National Register of Historic Places. It stands today, a preserved, 19th-century gem with a commanding view the Horseshoe Bend of the James River. (COURTESY LIBRARY OF VIRGINIA.)

Mount Walla, 2000. (COURTESY VIRGINIA DEPARTMENT OF HISTORIC RESOURCES.)

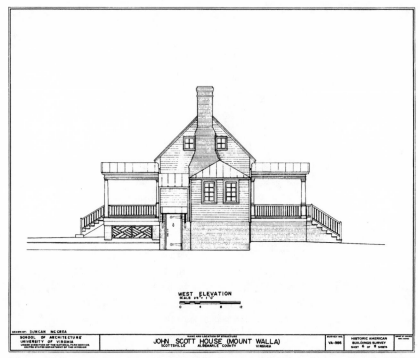

WEST ELEVATION
SCALE 1/4" 1'0"

DRAWN BY: DUNCAN MC CREA

| SCHOOL OF ARCHITECTURE | NAME AND LOCATION OF STRUCTURE | SURVEY NO. | HISTORIC AMERICAN |
| UNIVERSITY OF VIRGINIA | JOHN SCOTT HOUSE (MOUNT WALLA) | VA-906 | BUILDINGS SURVEY |

Mount Walla west elevation, 1974, Historic American Buildings Survey. For the HABS project, Mount Walla was misidentified as the "John Scott House." The builder of the original dwelling house on the property remains unclear. (Courtesy Library of Congress.)

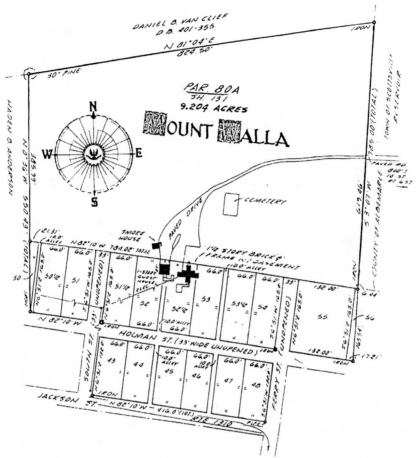

Mount Walla and surrounding lots in Scottsville, Virginia. (COURTESY RICHARD L. NICHOLAS.)

Jefferson Mills. In 1856, Peter Field Jefferson purchased the well-established Albemarle Mills, just outside Scottsville, Virginia. Soon it was known as Jefferson Mills and would provide income for Peter Field Jefferson, Jr. and his family. Surviving photographs taken c. 1940 capture the still-beautiful building, complete with a massive stone foundation and powerful waterfall. (COURTESY HARRIS MOULTON COLLECTION, SCOTTSVILLE MUSEUM.)

Jefferson Mills. (COURTESY HARRIS MOULTON COLLECTION, SCOTTSVILLE MUSEUM.)

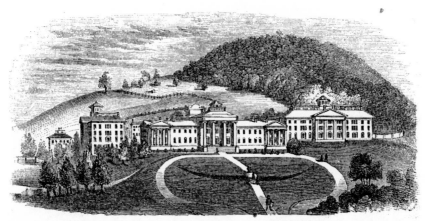

*"Hospital for the Insane" [Western Lunatic Asylum], by "Porte Crayon" [David Hunter Strother].
This engraving by Porte Crayon appeared in the February, 1855 issue of Harper's New Monthly
Magazine. In November of 1855, a fire totally destroyed the Female Ward. In 1857, Peter Field
Jefferson's son, Thomas, was committed to the Western Lunatic Asylum in Staunton, Virginia and
died there in 1863. Two decades earlier, his first cousin, Jefferson Madison Nevil, was refused
admittance to the institution due to lack of space.* (COURTESY HARPER'S NEW MONTHLY
MAGAZINE AND CHARLES CULBERTSON.)

*Bleak Hill, 1937, Virginia Historical Inventory. In 1857, Peter Field Jefferson purchased
Bleak Hill from Mahala Dawson, widow of Pleasant L. Dawson. It became the residence of
his son, Peter Field Jefferson, Jr.* (COURTESY LIBRARY OF VIRGINIA.)

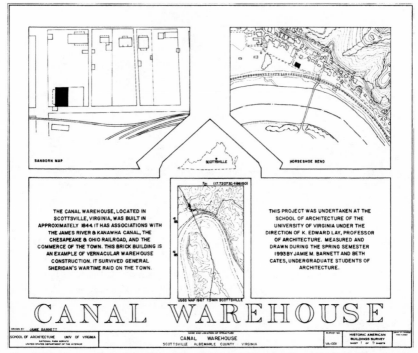

Canal Warehouse, situated at Scottsville, Virginia, Historic American Buildings Survey, 1993. The Scottsville Canal Warehouse has been misidentified as once the property of Peter Field Jefferson. While Jefferson owned another warehouse near the waterfront, the builder of Scottsville's iconic tobacco warehouse is unknown. According to architectural historian Ed Lay: "[It] is the only one of its kind remaining in the county. A two-story, five-course American bond brick building with two attics and huge wooden shear block mount atop its structural column, it is located on the James River and Kanawha Canal. The warehouse also was called a "lumber house," or a building for the storage of miscellaneous items including lumber." (COURTESY LIBRARY OF CONGRESS.)

Canal Warehouse, 1993, Historic American Buildings Survey. In 2017, the canal warehouse was undergoing restoration and preservation. (COURTESY LIBRARY OF CONGRESS.)

The Doll House. In 1854, Peter Field Jefferson purchased a group of buildings in Scottsville, including lot #36, which came complete with a one-story frame house. Inherited by Jefferson's son, Peter Field, Jr., the property was held in trust with Rev. John A. Doll, who co-founded Scottsville's Union Baptist Church in 1865 with the Rev. Henry Smith. Rev. Doll eventually purchased the house for his residence and the name, Doll House, stuck. (COURTESY RAMON THACKER.)

View of the Horseshoe Bend of the James River, 1911. This photo documents the new bridge at Scottsville. Completed in 1907, it crossed the James River from Scottsville on the north to Snowden on the south. The ferry, once owned by Peter Field Jefferson and inherited by his grandson, Peter Valentine Foland, ran approximately where the bridge was constructed. The train, which made the canal obsolete, is seen steaming into town from the west. (COURTESY LIBRARY OF CONGRESS.)

R. B. Moon Map of Scottsville, 1873. Note the Snowden Ferry House on the south side of the James River. (Courtesy Richard L. Nicholas.)

Scottsville Town Council, c.1900. (COURTESY RAMON THACKER.)

Front Row (L to R): Jacinto V. Pereira, Peter Foland, W. E. Moon.

Back Row (L to R): Dr. Joseph P. Blair, Tom Heath, Jackson Beal, Thomas A. Fox.

Peter Valentine Foland, pictured above, was a minor when he inherited significant property in Scottsville from his grandfather, Peter Field Jefferson. His assets included the ferry and grocery store, as well as Jefferson's home, Mount Walla. When this photo was taken, Foland was Mayor of Scottsville. Scottsville Museum provided the following identifications for Foland's peers and fellow councilmen:

Jacinto V. Pereira: President of Fidelity National Bank and builder of Travelers' Rest Hotel.

W. E. "Willie" Moon: owner of the Mercantile Store on Main Street.

Dr. Joseph P. Blair: dentist.

Tom Heath: operated Heath Mill and lived at the Old Tavern.

Jackson Beal: merchant and insurance agent for Shenandoah Life and New York Fire Company. Beal served as Mayor of Scottsville, 1905–1930.

Thomas A. Fox: plumbing contractor who installed the first water and sewer system in Scottsville.

Hattie (Foland) Moulton, great-granddaughter of Peter Field Jefferson.
(Courtesy Ramon Thacker.)

Elizabeth "Lizzie" Foland, great-granddaughter of Peter Field Jefferson.
(COURTESY RAMON THACKER.)

Bonair, Nelson County, Virginia. Originally owned by George Cabell, Jr., Bonair was purchased by Zachariah Nevil in 1826. His wife, Anna Scott (Jefferson) Nevil, was deceased and never enjoyed the beautiful house on the James River. Their four children inherited the property when Nevil died in 1830. In 1980, the house, "Bon Aire," was placed on the National Register of Historic Places. (COURTESY VIRGINIA DEPARTMENT OF HISTORIC RESOURCES.)

Millbrook, Buckingham County, Virginia. Millbrook was the home of Robert Lewis Jefferson, brother to Peter Field Jefferson, and later, his son, Elbridge Gerry Jefferson. When E. G. Jefferson died intestate in 1865, his two sons inherited the farm and the mill, which they eventually sold to M. L. A. "Matt" Moseley. (COURTESY JEREMY WINFREY.)

Drivers Hill, Fluvanna County, Virginia. Drivers Hill was home to Joseph Walker, life-long friend of Peter Field Jefferson. Located approximately one mile east of Scottsville, it sat atop a steep hill which flowed with wagons coming into Scottsville. Like the Jeffersons at Mount Walla, Walker enjoyed a beautiful view of the James River. In 1820, Peter Field's brother, James Lilburne Jefferson, lived two households from Walker at Drivers Hill. This photo was taken in 1937 for Virginia Historical Inventory. (COURTESY LIBRARY OF VIRGINIA.)

W. H. Ebeling,   ELKTON, KY.

Mary Ann (Jefferson) McLean (d. 1854), daughter of Isham Randolph Jefferson and Margaret Gwatkins Peyton. Photographer W. H. Ebeling, Elkton, Kentucky. (COURTESY JANE EATON.)

The sentiment on Mary Ann (Jefferson) McLean's grave stone reads:

Sister thou wast mild and lovely
Gentle as the summer breeze.
Pleasant as the air of evening
When it floats among the trees*

*From the song "Martha Jane."

Madora Elizabeth and Peyton Randolph McLean, great-grandson of Randolph Jefferson, grandson of Isham Randolph Jefferson, son of Mary Ann (Jefferson) McLean. Photographer W. H. Ebeling, Elkton, Kentucky. (COURTESY MARY BROACH.)

Peyton Randolph McLean (1844–1928) was a friendly and sociable man, who frequently visited his neighbors in Colorado where he lived with one of his daughters, Annie Linton. When physical infirmities confined him to his home, his friends and neighbors visited him. One obituary noted that he was frequently an honored guest at local gatherings, including the celebration of his eighty-fourth birthday. "His passing caused sorrow among his many friends and he will be sadly missed especially by his family and immediate circle of friends. The services were simple, sweet and comforting so befitting the occasion. Two of his favorite hymns "Nearer My God to Thee" and "Where He Leads Me I Will Follow" were sung by Mrs. Glenn Cheedle. The beautiful flowers attested to the high esteem in which he was held. The kindest wishes and tenderest sympathy is extended to the son and daughters and other relatives of this good man." *Daily Sentinel* (GRAND JUNCTION, COLORADO).

Part Two
LOST JEFFERSONS

If poetry is the little myth we make, history is the big myth we live.

ROBERT PENN WARREN, *Brother to Dragons*

Thomas Jefferson, Jr.:
The Enigmatic Jefferson

When Randolph Jefferson was married for the second time to the much younger Mitchie B. Pryor, his sons Thomas and Peter Field were openly disapproving. Jefferson described their conduct as "undutiful and disrespectful."[1] Like-minded in 1810, these two brothers may have remained close throughout their lives. Both men were financially competent and legally savvy.

Eventually, Thomas was made Peter Field's "Committee"—his legal guardian—when the latter became incompetent to handle his own affairs.

Randolph Jefferson may have found these two sons disloyal, however, there are indications that as young men they were also independent, energetic, and strong-minded; characteristics which fueled their later successes. Strong personalities often invite criticism and Thomas Jefferson, Jr. was no exception. He could be dogged in a court case and decisive in matters of money. In Thomas' case, his basic nature also led to remarkable longevity. He died in Fluvanna County, on July 8, 1876, at the advanced age of ninety-three. According to his death record, Thomas was born in 1784, however, he may have been born as early as 1781/82. His widow reported that he was the son of "R." and "Nancy" Jefferson. Born in Albemarle County, his mother likely went home to the Lewis plantation at Buck Island to give birth to her son.[2]

As a young man he was known as Thomas Jefferson, Jr. to distinguish him from his uncle President Thomas Jefferson. Late in life, he was known as Thomas Jefferson, Sr. to distinguish him from his nephew, Thomas, the elder son of Peter Field Jefferson.

He enjoyed a special connection with his uncle, President Jefferson, if only by virtue of his name. As a boy, he was singled out in the oldest surviving letter between his uncle and his father. Sent from Paris on January 11, 1789, Thomas Jefferson had been away from Virginia for five years and was not current with news of his brother's family. He wrote, "I suppose you are by this time the father of a numerous family, and that my namesake is big enough to begin the thraldom of education."[3]

Indeed, Thomas' education took him away from Snowden. During 1799–1800, he lived in Albemarle County, possibly studying with his Lewis cousins. His Uncle Thomas paid for six months of his nephew's schooling at Benjamin Sneed's "English School," as well as for dancing lessons from Thomas W. Vaughan. This time spent in Albemarle put young Thomas in close contact with his extended family, including his future wife, Polly Lewis, who was approximately his age.[4]

Married three times, Thomas Jefferson lived his exceptionally long life in the general vicinity of Snowden, Scottsville, and Buck Island, residing much of the time within Albemarle's boundaries, though he long owned land in Fluvanna County. While primarily a gentleman farmer and, until 1865, a slave owner, his interests were far flung, including business with various members of his extended Lewis family.

His first wife was his double first cousin, Mary Randolph "Polly" Lewis. Their marriage in October of 1808 may have been a long-assumed Jefferson-Lewis merger, cementing a complex and important relationship between the Randolph Jefferson and Charles Lilburne Lewis families. Polly's early life was one of style and plenty. Her father, Col. Charles Lilburne Lewis, succeeded both at farming and business. A trustee of the town of Milton, he was invested in a stage coach line and a tavern. President Thomas Jefferson proudly pointed out that his brother-in-law, Charles L. Lewis, was quickly "becoming one of our wealthiest people."[5]

∾

Jefferson–Lewis–Randolph

1. Peter Jefferson m. Jane Randolph	1. Charles Lewis, Jr. m. Mary Randolph

Jane and Mary Randolph were sisters

2. Randolph Jefferson m. Anne Lewis	2. Charles Lilburne Lewis m. Lucy Jefferson

Randolph and Lucy Jefferson were siblings.
Anne and Charles Lilburne Lewis were siblings.

3. Thomas Jefferson, Jr.	3. Mary Randolph "Polly" Lewis

∾

In 1785, Charles Lilburne Lewis was the proprietor of an impressive plantation, Monteagle, complete with numerous structures including: a new, two-story brick main house with a basement; the old house were the Lewises previously lived; three identical slave houses, plus fifteen other buildings. The new dwelling house, built about the time of Polly's birth, would be her home until her marriage. By 1803, however, following many financial setbacks, the house and this property belonged to Lewis' son-in-law, Craven Peyton (1775–1838), who had married Polly's sister, Jane.[6]

Clearly, Polly Lewis enjoyed the advantages of the Virginia gentry in her youth, however, she was not coming into her marriage with any significant property. In fact, the family was now destitute. The 1790s had been universally difficult for planters in central Virginia; weevils, drought, deluge, and overuse of the land all contributed to crop failure. In 1797, the wheat crop was a total loss. During 1799–1800, the bottom fell out of the tobacco market. Across the decade, most years brought losses to planters. When the Lewis family departed Virginia for Kentucky, they had long been financially "embarrassed."[7]

Polly was a middle child of ten. Isham, Elizabeth (called Betsy), Lucy, Martha Amanda Cary, and Ann Marks Lewis were younger. Randolph, Jane, Charles, and Lilburne Lewis were older. Siblings Charles and Elizabeth Lewis, both died in 1806.[8]

In 1807, when the majority of Polly's family moved westward to Kentucky, she remained at the Lewis home, Monteagle, with her sister Jane and Craven Peyton. The following year, she and Thomas Jefferson were wed by Baptist minister Martin Dawson. The bondsman was John Peyton, who affirmed that Polly was "upwards of twenty-one." Shadrick S. Lively testified that Thomas was "upwards of twenty-one," as well.[9]

By the time Thomas proposed marriage and she accepted, any family wounds caused by his sister Nancy Jefferson's broken engagement to Polly's brother, Charles Lewis, had healed.[10] As time passed, Thomas would become a surrogate son to her father, Charles L. Lewis, insinuating himself into the family's finances. Still, he would never achieve Craven Peyton's heroic position as a family benefactor. Much-loved by Lucy (Jefferson) Lewis, Peyton would sacrifice his own wealth and energy keeping the Lewis family afloat. On the contrary, later, some would paint son-in-law Thomas Jefferson as a villain.[11]

During 1807–1810, the Thomas Jeffersons began married life at Snowden, along with his brother-in-law Zachariah Nevil, his sister Anna Scott (Jefferson) Nevil, and his maturing, younger brothers. Thomas enjoyed a privileged relationship with his father. Prior to his marriage, Randolph Jefferson gave his eldest son property equivalent to £1,000, representing an advance against his eventual inheritance. He was the only one of Randolph Jefferson's sons known to receive such an advance. It may have been precisely this decision that moved Randolph to make his will in May of 1808, guaranteeing his other sons a fair share of a "hotchpot" upon his death. Now over fifty, Randolph could ease into retirement, putting Thomas and Zachariah Nevil "in charge" of farming at Snowden, as well as a business dubbed "Nevil & Jefferson."[12]

When Randolph married Mitchie Pryor, the interpersonal relationships at Snowden quickly became strained. By August of 1810, Thomas and Polly had removed to Albemarle County, where he succeeded financially, owning six slaves over the age of sixteen; another taxable slave above the age of twelve; six horses; and a gigg. His personal property tax obligation was a significant $4.66.[13]

From 1810–1812, the Thomas Jeffersons lived in Albemarle County, possibly at the old Lewis house at Buck Island or with the Peytons at Monteagle.[14] Then, on October 27, 1812, Thomas purchased roughly 200 acres on the Hardware River in Fluvanna County. In early December of 1813, he paid $1,000 for an additional adjoining 145 acres on the north side of the Hardware. His new farm lay about five miles east of Scott's Landing, convenient to commerce there. Thomas was well-established in Fluvanna when he witnessed the permission given by John Henderson for the marriage of his daughter, Mary Anne, to Thomas' younger brother, Isham "Randolph" Jefferson. Randolph and Mary Anne were married in Fluvanna County on December 20, 1813, eventually settled in Fluvanna, and named their first son Thomas.[15]

In addition to farming, Thomas conducted business, likely in or near Milton. Situated on the Rivanna River, the town was founded by a collection of Lewises and their relations, including the Henderson family; Martha Jefferson's husband, Thomas Mann Randolph; former President Thomas Jefferson and Craven Peyton.

In 1811, Thomas and his business partner, Joseph Brand, hired a slave belonging to future President James Monroe, who took the men to court, accusing them of assaulting the laborer. Defendants Brand and Jefferson sent an attorney to court to plead "not guilty." After two years, the charges were withdrawn.[16] In early 1812, Jefferson had more labor troubles, advertising that his slave, Gary, a skilled cooper, had run away, noting that he had "eloped" from Albemarle County, near Milton. Jefferson offered ten dollars for his return.[17]

Thomas Jefferson's new sister-in-law, Mary Anne (Henderson) Jefferson, was the granddaughter of Bennett Henderson, who had married Charles L. and Lucy (Jefferson) Lewis' daughter Elizabeth and established what would become Milton. In 1780, he built a mill at Mountain Falls and, in 1789, he established Henderson's Tobacco Warehouse, situated at The Shallows on the Rivanna River. In 1799, his son, John Henderson, insured a valuable dwelling house ($1,400), a mill ($3,750), and a cluster of five warehouses ($1,510), for the legatees of Bennett Henderson.[18]

The town of Milton grew rapidly, filled with thriving businesses. Until the War of 1812, Milton was Albemarle County's "chief commercial center." Rev. Edgar Woods observed in his history of the county, published in 1901: "Its business gradually declined as Charlottesville grew; and when the town of Scottsville was established . . . its prestige was completely broken, and it quietly subsided into the straggling hamlet which now crowns the river hill."[19]

As Milton spiraled down, so did the long and troubled financial story of Craven Peyton and the Lewis family. By 1814, Charles Lilburne Lewis and his remaining family in Kentucky were once again in desperate straits, both financially and emotionally. Contriving a bizarre (and fundamentally deceitful) solution to their insolvency, Lewis, in collaboration with his daughters Lucy, Martha, and Anna devised a plan to sue their sister Jane and her husband, Craven Peyton, for the land in Albemarle County that had once belonged to Charles Lewis, Jr., who sold it to Craven Peyton in 1804 for $5,000.[20]

The suit was based on the claim that Charles Lewis, Jr. did not hold a clear deed to the land. His parents had transferred the land to him on the condition that, should he die without legitimate heirs (which he did in 1806), the whole of the six hundred and fifty acres would be inherited by the "Daughters of the said Charles L. Lewis and Lucy his wife as may then be living or their lawfull (sic) issue of them as may be dead."[21]

In an attempt to challenge Craven Peyton's ownership of the Buck Island property, the Lewis sisters in Livingston County, Kentucky enlisted the help of their first cousin and brother-in-law, Thomas Jefferson, Jr., to act as their agent in Virginia. Implicitly, his wife and their sister, Polly Jefferson, also stood to gain if the Lewis women were awarded the land. The document read in part:

Know all men by these presents that we Washington A. Griffin, and Lucy His wife, formerly Lucy Lewis, Martha C. Lewis, Ann M. Lewis of the state of Kentucky have constituted and by these presents do constitute Thomas Jefferson junior esq. of the state of Virginia our attorney to prosecute for us any suit . . . to recover any lands to which we may be legally entitled . . . and especially to reduce to possession for us our interest respectively in an estate of Buck Island containing 650 acres of land situated in the county of Albemarle in the state of Virginia aforesaid now in the occupancy of a certain Craven Peyton and claimed by us by virtue of a deed executed by Charles L. Lewis and Lucy his wife bearing date of 30th July 1802 and duly recorded in the court of the county aforesaid.[22]

Ultimately, the Lewis women wanted cash, not land, and had no intention of returning to Virginia to live at Buck Island.[23]

There had never been a more accommodating son-in-law than Craven Peyton. As Lucy (Jefferson) Lewis wrote to her brother Thomas: "Mr. Peyton has been . . . to my daughters as long as they were undar [sic] his guidance, as the most just and affectionate farthar [sic]."[24] Now that the Lewises were once again destitute, the long-generous Craven Peyton was targeted to play the patsy in what former President Thomas Jefferson called "fraudulent silence" on the part of Charles L. Lewis. If there was not a clear title to the land when it was first sold to Peyton, the Lewises had not disclosed this fact.[25]

In May of 1815, Thomas Jefferson, Jr. initiated a complaint against Craven Peyton in the Augusta County Superior Court. Peyton's response was lengthy, yet to the point: "For there is no man in his senses that would have given $5000 for the life estate of a departed [?] young man & and an officer in the army or 1/4 thereof in the land in question. Your orator avers that he never did know or believe that any estate was limited upon the sale."[26]

A hearing was set for June of 1816, however, depositions continued to be taken into 1817 and a final decree was not handed down until June of 1818.[27]

In 1815, Thomas Jefferson, Jr. made the arduous trip to Livingston County, Kentucky, bringing his father-in-law, Charles Lilburne Lewis, home to Virginia. It is probable that Jane Woodson Lewis, Peter Field Jefferson's future wife, traveled with them. Living with the Thomas Jeffersons, the Lewises were provided with a comfortable home in Fluvanna County, valued at $800. Jefferson owned seven slaves above sixteen years of age to work the farm, as well as four horses, and five head of cattle. In the fall of 1819, Jane married Peter Field Jefferson, moving to Scott's Landing. Her grandfather, Charles Lilburne Lewis, likely stayed on with the Thomas Jeffersons.[28]

By September of 1827, when Thomas Jefferson offered his farm or lease for sale, his property had increased to include fourteen or fifteen "uncommonly healthy, likely young negroes." His advertisement in the *Virginia Advocate* read:

SALE AND LEASE

The subscriber residing within five miles east of Scottsville, will offer for sale to the highest bidder, on the premises, on Wednesday the 14th of November next, (if fair if not the next fair day.) on 12 months credit, the purchasers giving bond with approved and satisfactory security, for all sums above ten dollars. . . . The following property . . . 14 to 15 uncommonly healthy, likely young negroes; consisting of men, women, boys and girls; about 15 head of cattle, among which are, two yoke of well broke oxen, stock of hogs, crop of corn, tobacco, and fodder; all the plantation tools, and a cart.

If the land on which the subscriber resides should not be leased or rented before the day of sale, it will be offered for lease for a term of years, and the terms made known on the day of sale.

THOS. JEFFERSON.
Fluvanna County, Sep 17, 1827.[29]

Initially, the Jeffersons leased the farm, later selling 245 acres in 1836 and another 255 acres in 1838.[30]

By 1830, the Thomas Jeffersons lived on Buck Island Creek in Albemarle County, fifteen miles southeast of the courthouse at Charlottesville. There they owned 425 3/4 acres worked by seven slaves, five males and two females. About half the farm was developed, producing wheat, oats and corn, but not tobacco. They kept typical livestock, including five dairy cows.[31] Throughout their long marriage, the Jeffersons remained childless and, when Polly Jefferson died at Buck Island on June 3, 1855, the middle-aged Thomas Jefferson was alone to contemplate a new life.[32]

On January 4, 1857, about eighteen months after the death of his wife, Thomas Jefferson, Jr. sold his Albemarle farm to Benjamin J. Haden of Fluvanna County for $3,000. Within months, on October 5, 1857, Jefferson purchased a house in Scottsville from George W. Dillard and his wife, Lucy Jane, paying $2,400 for the property, which adjoined the lands of prominent local citizens: John O. Lewis, Mrs. Mary E. Brokenbrough, Thomas J. Johnson, and Zachariah Lewis. The house sat on about five acres. Approaching seventy, the conveniences of Scottsville likely appealed to Jefferson. An even stronger motive to move to town may have been the prospect of a second and considerably younger wife.[33]

On January 4, 1858, Thomas Jefferson married a widow, Mrs. W. S. Barker, in Albemarle County. Rev. Jacob Manning of the Methodist Episcopal Church performed the ceremony. In the marriage record, the Jeffersons were described as: Thomas, age seventy, widower, born Albemarle County, and Eliz. W. Barker, age "thirty-two," widow, born Prussia. Thomas gave his occupation as farmer.[34]

Born in Germany, on June 21, 1822, Elizabeth Wilhelmina Siegfried, called "Willie," was the daughter of Henry D. and Anna C. (Blaettermann) Siegfried and the niece of Dr. George W. Blaettermann, a professor of Modern Languages at the University of Virginia. Edgar Allan Poe was one of his students. The cultivated Dr. Blaettermann had previously taught in London and was the first Professor to sign a contract with President Thomas Jefferson's new university. Once in the United States, Elizabeth Wilhelmina Siegfried migrated to St. Louis, Missouri, where she married Levi Barker on October 3, 1847.[35]

In August of 1859, when Thomas took over the management of Peter Field Jefferson's property as "Committee," he and Willie were well-settled in Scottsville, in a house not far from Mount Walla. He had had the opportunity to closely observe his brother's decline during 1858–1859. The mentally impaired Peter Field was suffering from dementia and, in short order, Thomas made many changes in his brother's investments.

By July of 1860, the Thomas Jeffersons owned real estate valued at $4,680 and personal property valued at $15,750, including six slaves. On September 3, 1860, he added to his real estate, purchasing two tracks of land from George W. Coleman and his wife, Mary Ann, which had recently been surveyed at 72 1/3 acres and described as "in the vicinity of the town of Scottsville near the site of the Old Concord Church." The price was $5.00. Perhaps, the Colemans were indebted to Jefferson, who was willing to take the land to settle accounts.[36]

After Peter Field Jefferson's death in August of 1861, Thomas Jefferson rather quickly drifted out of the protracted arguments over his brother's estate, as he was neither an executor nor a legatee. The Thomas Jeffersons remained in Scottsville; then, after only six years of marriage, on April 24, 1864, Willie Jefferson died of dropsy (swelling of tissues). She was forty-three years old and was buried at Limestone Farm in Albemarle County, the home of her uncle, Dr. G. W. Blaettermann, and her mother, Anna C. (Blaettermann) Siegfried.[37]

A year later, in March of 1865, Thomas Jefferson was once again alone as the Civil War drew to a close. When General Philip Sheridan raided Scottsville, his headquarters were in Jefferson's "back yard." If he was in Scottsville that week, Jefferson witnessed shocking events, as reported in the *Richmond Dispatch*:

SHERIDAN'S RAIDERS AT SCOTTSVILLE.

A private letter from Scottsville gives a sad account of the action of Sheridan and his raiders:

The enemy were in two columns:—one from North Garden, commanded by Sheridan in person, passed towards Howardsville and New Market; the remainder, from Charlottesville, supposed to have been about four thousand, went to Scottsville. They entered the town on Monday, about 1 o'clock in the afternoon. The citizens were in the streets at the time of the entry of the advanced guard, who were somewhat disguised, and were not sure that they were Yankees until they began to fire promiscuously upon the citizens. They immediately broke open the bank, and were greatly disappointed at not finding anything, as all the effects had been removed the week previous. None of the people were hurt, but some were made prisoners, and carried away some distance from town, and then released. The stores were broken open and their contents appropriated and indiscriminately distributed by the Yankees to the negroes and low class of whites, who led the robbers from place to place and pointed out property to be robbed. This was done nearly all together by the white people; and the loss in this way is very heavy. On Monday evening they burned Brady's candle factory and the stable of Mr. J. O. Lewis. On Tuesday morning, they burned the mill, factory, company's shop, foundry and many other buildings, which caught fire from the burning of these. Twenty-five dwelling-houses were destroyed, and people are in a state of destitution.

On Thursday, Sheridan's force came down the canal, and on Friday pillaged everything they could find in town, and then left for Columbia [Fluvanna County].

Some persons were treated in a most shameful manner, and some with inhumanity. The Yankees entered the room of the young lady who was very ill, and cursed her and other ladies of the family. A drunken party went to the house of Mr. Charles Scott, who lives about six miles from Scottsville, insulted his wife, pushed her out of the house, and fired it. Mr. Scott had gone to the woods to secrete some valuables, and returning, saw his house in flames; he fell dead, and was found so the next day. When Sheridan found himself in town, those with whom the officers were quartered, and also those who applied for a guard, were not molested.

We learn that the Yankees took Mr. Turner, the President of the Bank of Howardsville, and whipped him in the presence of his family in order to compel him to tell the whereabouts of the specie. It had been removed. The damage done to the canal is, of course, very great, but can be repaired so as to be somewhat available in three weeks. The aqueduct at Columbia was not injured. The Yankees made a deep cut through the embankment, and thus drew off the water from the canal; otherwise, the aqueduct is uninjured. The locks are all injured to some extent, but can soon be repaired. About a thousand negroes went off with the raiders.—Among them, women with small children. On the second day, some of them tired of their burdens, and the Yankees not caring to help them, as many as sixteen threw their babies into the canal. The men were taken off whether they were willing to go or not, and forthwith mounted and armed. Wherever Sheridan's raiders went, they took whatever they wanted, and did as they pleased.[38]

Once again a widower, and no longer involved in his brother's estate, Thomas Jefferson had no reason to remain in a town that had been devastated by the Yankees. In December of 1865, he sold his Scottsville property back to G. W. Dillard, including the house and five acres. Jefferson received "thirty hundred and eighteen dollars" for the property.[39]

In 1868, Thomas married for a third time in Fluvanna County. The wedding took place on November 30th and the bride was Ann "Nancy" W. Pollard, a spinster and the daughter of Zachariah Pollard. The marriage record stated that her age was fifty. Thomas gave his age as eighty-three. In fact, she may have been a bit older. On the 1870 census, she aged to sixty-five, while Thomas was enumerated at eighty-seven. By 1880, Nancy's age had jumped to eighty-two![40]

Following his marriage, on August 23, 1869, Jefferson paid $990 for a tract of land in Fluvanna County. The 112 acres included a "mansion home" and other buildings. By the end of the following month, he had composed his last will, dated September 26, 1869, requesting that after his debts were met, the whole of his estate was to go to his "beloved wife," Nancy. Upon her death, the remainder was to be equally divided between Elizabeth and Robert Ligon, naming Robert as his Executor. No particulars of his property were described.[41]

The Ligons were Nancy's niece and nephew. Before her marriage, she shared a home with them. They had not only cared for her but also for her brother, Robert Pollard, who was idiotic and illiterate, a dependent without occupation.[42]

By 1870, Thomas Jefferson took his ease on his modest Fluvanna County farm, where no active cultivation took place. Nancy kept the house. His real estate was valued at $555, indicating truly reduced circumstances for the elderly Jefferson who had enjoyed the comforts of affluence for most of his life. Twenty years earlier, one Scottsville native observed that Thomas Jefferson was a gentleman, a man "at his leisure."[43]

In July of 1873, Jefferson decided to give his farm outright to Elizabeth and Robert Ligon, in exchange for "comfortable support and maintenance" for himself and his wife. He died of old age on July 8, 1876, outliving his brothers and sister, two wives, and several sisters-in-law. Oddly, Fluvanna County listed the informant of his death as "Elizabeth Jefferson, wife." Yet, Nancy was his widow and survived him by at least four years. Following Thomas' death, in 1880, she was enumerated in Fluvanna, once again living with Robert Ligon; his sister, Elizabeth; and her brother, Robert Pollard.[44]

In 1901, Rev. Edgar Woods, in his history of Albemarle County, errone- ously identified Thomas' brothers—Peter Field Jefferson (d. 1861) and Robert L. Jefferson (d. 1858)—as his children, beginning an oft-repeated confusion of Randolph Jefferson's descendants. Woods wrote:

> [Thomas Jefferson's] children were Peter Field and Robert L. Peter
> Field lived in Scottsville, and by his shrewdness and frugality amassed

a large fortune. He died in 1861, leaving a son bearing his own name, a daughter, the wife of Peter Foland [sic]. Peter Field Jr., died in 1867 [sic]. Robert L. married Elizabeth, daughter of Robert Moorman, lived near Porter's Precinct, and died in 1858. His children were Eldridge [sic], who lived in the same section of the county till after the war, and Mary, the wife of Albert W. Gantt.[45]

This error was particularly ironic since Thomas Jefferson had no known children, his Jefferson line ending with his death in 1876.

Isham Randolph Jefferson:
"A Striking Resemblance"

The death of one of Thomas Jefferson's nephews always held the potential to become national news. Isham Randolph Jefferson, known to the family in his youth as "Randolph, Jr.," was no exception. On August 9, 1862, the *Buffalo Evening Post* printed the following:

> Isham Randolph Jefferson, a nephew and adopted son of the immortal Thomas Jefferson, died on the 6th of July, at his residence in Todd county, Kentucky, in the seventy-first year of his age. The personal resemblance which he bore to the author the Declaration of Independence is said to be striking.[1]

Not to be outdone, the following week, Buffalo's *Evening Courier and Republic* put the same announcement on their front page, adding another glowing remark: "nor was he deficient in those great mental and moral attributes which distinguished that illustrious statesman."[2]

This exaggeration that Randolph Jefferson, Jr. was an "adopted son" of President Thomas Jefferson persisted through the next generation. A brief biography of one of Isham Randolph's sons reinforced and elaborated this "fact":

> Dr. Walter B. Jefferson is a son of Isham R. and Sarah A. (Mansfield) Jefferson, who came separately to Todd County in 1833, from [Albemarle] County, Va. The father was a native of that county, and was there reared by his uncle, Thomas Jefferson, the famous author of the Declaration of Independence, and third Chief Executive of the United States, Isham's father, Randolph Jefferson, being the youngest brother of the President.[3]

Having removed to Todd County, Kentucky in the early 1830s, there were few, if any, relations around to contest the claim that Isham Randolph Jefferson was closely associated with his uncle. By the time of his death in 1862, who could challenge the nature of his connection to President Jefferson? Was there even a shred of truth to this claim?

President Thomas Jefferson did show interest in his brother's children, particularly Thomas and James Lilburne, and their sister, Nancy. Virtually nothing
is known, however, about his relationship with Randolph, Jr. It was not until
Jefferson's retirement in 1809 and his return to Monticello that he was home long
enough to get to know any of the Randolph Jefferson family. By then, Randolph,
Jr. was far beyond "rearing" whether his birth was as early as 1784 or as late as
1791. That noted, he did not marry until December of 1813 and could have spent
time at Monticello between 1810 and 1813.[4]

Currently, the only certain document connecting Randolph, Jr. to his uncle
is Thomas Jefferson's 1815 deposition concerning his brother's first will:

> [O]n Saturday the 5th Randolph Jefferson, son of the testator, came
> to this deponent, informed him of the extreme danger of his father's
> situation, that he had expressed to him his uneasiness as to a will he had
> signed, which he did not understand, that his former will in possession
> of this deponent was the one he wished to stand, and his anxiety to see
> this deponent and have this effected: that this deponent assured the [said]
> Randolph the younger that he would go to see his brother the moment
> his horses returned from carrying mrs Marks [Thomas Jefferson's sister,
> Anna Scott], who had gone that day to see him but that he would imme-
> diately prepare a short instrument for revoking the will recently made, and
> reestablishing the former one, which if his brother chose to sign it would
> effect what was said to be his wish whi[ch] instrument he did prepare
> and deliver to the said Randolph the young[er]. . . .[5]

That Randolph, Jr. was sent to Monticello in the emergency of his father's
dying hours indicates a comfortable relationship with his uncle. It is unknown
whether he rode from his father's home at Snowden in Buckingham County,
across the James River, and north to his uncle's hilltop plantation or from
Fluvanna County, where he lived in the summer of 1815. In either case, he was
confident in making the day-long trip to Monticello.

～

Isham Randolph Jefferson was over twenty-one years old when he married
on December 20, 1813. His bride was Mary Anne L. Henderson, born sometime
after December of 1794. As she was not yet twenty-one years old, her father

John Henderson, of Fluvanna County, was required to give his consent for her marriage.[6]

> Sir,
>
> Mr Isham R Jefferson requests to me to notify you of his wish to obtain a License to marry my daughter Mary Anne L Henderson & of my approbation thereto
>
> I am respectfully
Jno Henderson
Dec 16th 1813
>
> Witness
> Thomas Jefferson, Jr.
> John Winn[7]

Mary Anne Henderson was Randolph Jefferson, Jr.'s Lewis cousin, who grew up at the town of Milton, where her father maintained a mill and a residence on her grandfather's estate.

~

Lewis-Henderson-Jefferson

1. Elizabeth Lewis m. Bennett Henderson	1. Anne Lewis m. Randolph Jefferson

Elizabeth and Anne Lewis were sisters.

2. John Henderson m. Ann "Nancy" Hudson	2. Isham Randolph Jefferson
3. Mary Anne Henderson	

~

During 1815 and 1816, brothers Thomas, Isham Randolph, and Peter Field Jefferson all paid personal property tax in Fluvanna County. It is possible the Jefferson men were living together on Thomas' farm, until they could acquire property of their own. The wait for distributions from their father's estate would prove lengthy.

Early in their marriage, Mary Anne and Isham Randolph Jefferson moved frequently—from Albemarle County (possibly the town of Milton) to Fluvanna County to Buckingham County (probably at Snowden) and back to Fluvanna, where they purchased land in 1818. Located nine miles west of the county courthouse, the farm was on Shepards Creek, which flowed into the Hardware River. The couple had been married over five years when, on March 1, 1819, Mary Anne gave birth to her only known surviving child, yet another Thomas Jefferson. Before Thomas' third birthday, Mary Anne died on December 3, 1821. Significantly, in an era in which few obituaries appeared in newspapers, a notice of her death was printed in Virginia's *Central Gazette*.[8]

With a small son to rear and in immediate need of a wife, Isham Randolph Jefferson did not wait long before marrying another Lewis cousin—Margaret Gwatkins Peyton, the daughter of Jane Jefferson Lewis and Craven Peyton. The couple wed on July 2, 1822. Methodist Episcopal minister John Goodman officiated. The bondsman was James M. Eskridge, who affirmed that Margaret was over twenty-one. Albemarle County Clerk Ira Garrett was the witness.[9]

～

Jefferson–Lewis–Randolph

1. Peter Jefferson m. Jane Randolph	1. Charles Lewis, Jr. m. Mary Randolph

Jane and Mary Randolph were sisters

2. Randolph Jefferson m. Anne Lewis	2. Charles Lilburne Lewis m. Lucy Jefferson

Randolph and Lucy Jefferson were siblings.
Anne and Charles Lilburne Lewis were siblings.

3. Isham Randolph Jefferson	3. Jane J. Lewis m. Craven Peyton
	4. Margaret Gwatkins Peyton

～

In 1830, the Jeffersons lived in Fluvanna County; three boys and two girls were living with the couple. Young Thomas Jefferson was one of the boys. Their daughters, Mary Ann (b. abt. 1823) and Louisiana "Luiza" Jane (b. 1826–1829), were the two girls. The other two boys remain unidentified.[10]

Isham Randolph's 296-acre farm lay adjacent Daniel Stone; structures were valued at a modest $200; and he paid $1.52 in land tax. Contrasted with the Fluvanna County holdings of his brother Thomas, Isham Randolph's property was modest. Thomas owned three tracks of land, including structures valued at $1,600 on which he paid $3.26 tax.[11]

In 1832, the Isham Randolph Jeffersons had been married ten years when they sold their farm in Fluvanna to neighbor Daniel Stone. Subsequently, on September 30, 1833, Isham Randolph Jefferson granted lot #1 in the town of Scottsville to the trustees of the Methodist Church for the price of $1.00. The deed stated that, "Whereas the aforesaid Trustees have erected a House (in the Town of Scottsville Albemarle) for religious worship and the said Isham R. Jefferson is desirous to aid in defraying the expense incurred in the erection of said House. . . ."[12]

Soon, Isham Randolph and his children removed to Kentucky. It is unknown if Margaret lived to travel with them or died in Virginia. Far from wealthy when he arrived in Todd County, Kentucky, as late as 1995, stories repeated that he brought 100 slaves with him from Virginia. In 1826, Isham Randolph Jefferson owned five slaves and two horses. By 1830, after he received his distribution from his father's estate, he owned seventeen slaves and his Fluvanna farm. Ten years later, living in Todd County, he still owned only seventeen slaves.[13]

Once again a widower and settled in Kentucky's beautiful Pennyroyal Region, on October 28, 1834, Isham Randolph Jefferson married for a third time. His new wife, Sarah Ann Mansfield, was also a Virginian, however, they met and married in Todd County. Together, they had at least six children—William A., James M., Walter Bolling, Susan M., Nancy (a.k.a. Nannie), and Wirt (possibly named for Jefferson family friend and attorney, William Wirt, who represented the children of Randolph Jefferson's first marriage in the contest over his estate).[14]

At the time of his third marriage Isham Randolph was a middle-aged man. His bride was in her early twenties. Unlike his father's May–December union, Isham Randolph lived to rear most of his third family, dying when his youngest son was ten years old.[15]

Isham Randolph Jefferson's removal to Kentucky geographically separated him and his children from Virginia, the concentration of Jeffersons living around Scottsville, and the family tensions surrounding Peter Field Jefferson's estate. In Todd County, he prospered as a gentleman planter. In 1860, he owned $20,000 in real estate and $30,000 in personal property, including twenty-seven slaves.

On July 6, 1862, Isham Randolph Jefferson died, leaving his property, real and personal, to be managed by his widow, Sarah Ann, and their children. They would face the postwar transition without him. Only months after his death, Isham Randolph Jefferson was used as an example of the brutality of Abolitionists and their cause of freedom. In December of 1862, the *Cincinnati Enquirer* printed a lengthy, pro-Southern article entitled, "How the Abolitionists Treated a Member of Thomas Jefferson's Family." Authored by "An Illinois Democrat," it used Isham Randolph as an example of Abolitionist abuses against "innocent" slaveholders who had inherited their human property from American patriots such as Thomas Jefferson, or in this case, Randolph Jefferson, who had inherited his slaves from his father, Peter Jefferson. It read in part:

> The following is a well authenticated instance, among many others, to establish this painful truth: The venerable Isham Randolph Jefferson, a nephew and adopted son of the immortal Thomas Jefferson, and one of the most useful and honored citizens of Kentucky, was most wantonly and shamefully insulted and abused by these disciples of the "irrepressible conflict" and "higher law," for no other reason than that he demanded his negroes, whom they had seduced away and harbored in their camp. The life, the person, the property of this good, innocent old gentleman were brutally menaced because he humbly asked to be possessed of his property, guaranteed to him by the Constitution of his country, which he loves, and to which he had ever been loyal. No! The deeds of Jefferson, the name of Jefferson could not exempt him from the monstrous outrages of these men, because abolitionism slanders the noble acts and glorious memory of the patriot beyond the grave.[16]

Despite the fact that his first two wives were Lewis cousins, Isham Randolph's descendants apparently escaped the genetic decline that plagued other branches of the family. His children and grandchildren were well-educated and successful in their own right, making their way in a New South without slave labor.

His oldest son, Thomas, married a Kentuckian, Fredonia E. Banner, and spent his life as a farmer.[17]

His two daughters with Margaret G. Peyton, Mary Ann and Louisiana "Luiza" Jane, were remembered in Craven Peyton's will dated September 23, 1836, with a codicil, dated December 12, 1836, pertaining to the Jefferson legatees. Their grandfather wrote: "I give to the two daughters of Isham R. Jefferson by his second wife Margaret one thousand dollars each either in property or money." Later he added, "The legacies of the two daughters of Isham R. Jefferson is to be paid at any time my two [Executors] may deem it best to do so without [interest]."[18]

Mary Ann Jefferson married widower Andrew "Jackson" McLean on March 23, 1843 in Todd County, Kentucky. McLean was a member of the Cumberland Presbyterian Church, a prosperous farmer, and a slaveholder. The McLeans named their oldest son Peyton Randolph, remembering Mary Ann's families. She died in 1854 at the age of thirty-two, leaving three young children to be reared by McLean's third wife.[19]

Her sister, Luiza Jane Jefferson, married Paul Hampton Salmon, a merchant, minister, and farmer. His biography is included in the *History of Todd County, Kentucky*:

> PAUL H. SALMON was born September 25, 1814, in South Carolina. His parents are George and Elizabeth (West) Salmon, the father a native of Virginia, the mother of Maryland. The father was a teacher, merchant and farmer. He died in Marshall County, Miss., in 1865, aged eighty-seven. The mother died in South Carolina in 1829. Paul H. came to this county in 1844. Six years previous he had been engaged in the cotton mills. He sold goods in Elkton six years, and in 1850 he came to the farm on which he now resides.
>
> After the death of his father-in-law, he bought the farm. It is known as the "Jefferson farm"; it contains 360 acres, about half of which is improved. He has a good liberal education; he has the finest library in this neighborhood, and is very fond of reading; consequently is well informed. He is an ordained minister of the Methodist Episcopal Church South, and has been preaching the past ten years.
>
> He was married in 1859 [sic] to Miss L. J. Jefferson, born in 1828 in Virginia. She is the daughter of I. Randolph Jefferson and Louisa J. [sic] (Peyton) Jefferson, old Virginia stock. Mr. and Mrs. Salmon have six living children, viz.: George Randolph, who was married to Miss Ellen Stokes, now deceased; Evaline, the wife of Harlan Lucaus (John H. is their only child); Lewis Jackson, married to Miss Rosa Montlow (William H. and America A.—deceased—were their children); Martha J., Paul H. and Mary Ann.[20]

In 1902, Rev. Paul H. Salmon died at the advanced age of eighty-eight. His wife preceded him by several years. In his obituary, which appeared on the front page of the *Hopkinsville Kentuckian*, the newspaper erroneously stated that his wife was "a direct descendant of Thomas Jefferson." Was this a reporter's error or, as the decades passed, had the community come to believe that she was President Jefferson's descendant rather than the granddaughter of Randolph Jefferson?[21]

Isham Randolph Jefferson's daughter, Nannie, whose mother was Sarah Ann Mansfield, married into a family with Virginia roots when she wed Frank M. Byars on December 24, 1869. According to the *History of Todd County, Kentucky*:

F. M. BYARS was born in Todd County, Ky., January 18, 1847, and is a son of T. A. and Harriet (Eddington) Byars; the former born May 5, 1816, the latter born September 10, 1828, and died in 1854. They were both natives of Todd County, Ky. T. A. Byars was reared and educated in Todd County, Ky. His father emigrated from Albemarle County, Va., to Kentucky; about the time of the organization of Christian County, he settled in what is now Todd County, near Hadensville. T. A. Byars was married about 1840. Four children were added to this union, of whom F. M. was the second. Both he and wife were devoted members of the Methodist Episcopal Church South. F. M. Byars, the subject of our sketch, received a good education in his youth; he remained with his parents until December 28, 1869, when he was married to Miss Nannie, daughter of I. R. and S. A. Jefferson and sister of the Honorable Dr. Jefferson. She is a native of Todd County, born October 3, 1847; her parents and grandparents were natives of Virginia. Six children bless their union: Jennie, born November 13, 1871; Alexander T., born October 28, 1873; Wirt, born May 22, 1876; died September 10, 1876; Nannie, born April 17, 1877; Marie, born March 20, 1879; Frank M., born August 15, 1881. Mr. Byars follows the quiet but industrious life of a farmer; in 1870 he settled on the farm on which he now lives; it consists of 300 acres, 250 of which are under a high state of cultivation. It is located one and one-half miles from Elkton, on the Trenton road. Mr. Byars and lady are consistent members of the Methodist Episcopal Church South, and one of the leading families of the county.[22]

In 1893, the Byars family left Todd County for Hopkinsville where he became the local tobacco inspector. Popular among merchants—tobacco buyers, sellers and warehousemen—Byars was a thorough tobacconist. He died there in 1905. Nannie proved to be yet another long-lived Jefferson, dying of consumption at the ripe old age of eighty-seven. At the time of her death, she was living with her daughter, Mrs. Manie Brawner, in St. Louis, Missouri. Her obituary identified her as the great-great-grand-niece of Thomas Jefferson, adding two extra generations. Not so far removed from the great man, Nannie was Randolph Jefferson's granddaughter and Thomas Jefferson's grand-niece.[23]

Isham Randolph's sons William A. Jefferson and James M. Jefferson, were trained as attorneys. Their brother, Walter Bolling Jefferson, first attended the University of Virginia (1860–1861), where he was enrolled in Chemistry; Medicine; Physiology and Surgery; and Anatomy, demonstrating that the family had maintained ties with Virginia. In 1862, he graduated from the University of Nashville's Medical Department.[24]

The *History of Todd County, Kentucky* also includes a fulsome biography of Walter Bolling Jefferson:

DR. WALTER B. JEFFERSON is a son of Isham R. and Sarah A. (Mansfield) Jefferson, who came separately to Todd County in 1833, from Albemarle County, Va. The father was a native of that county, and was there reared by his uncle, Thomas Jefferson, the famous author of the Declaration of Independence, and third Chief Executive of the United States, Isham's father, Randolph Jefferson, being the youngest brother of the President. The father of our subject married first a Miss Henderson, and afterward a Miss Peyton. He located, on coming to Todd County, upon a farm in Jesup's Grove, removing afterward to within a mile south of Elkton, where he died in 1862. His third marriage occurred in this county. He wedded Miss Mansfield, and the union was blessed with the following children: William A., James M., Walter B., Susan M. (deceased), Nannie, wife of F. M. Byars, and Wirt, who died in 1875, in early manhood. Dr. W. B., the subject of these lines, obtained his early schooling in Elkton, and began the study of medicine under Drs. James A. and John O. McReynolds. He attended the University of Virginia, and afterward the University of Nashville, graduating from the latter institution in 1862, since which date he has practiced his profession in Todd and Logan Counties and in Paducah, Ky. He married, in 1863, Miss Mamie, daughter of Judge Ben. T. Perkins. She died in 1877, leaving one child, Anna M. His second marriage was with Mrs. Evelyn A. Taylor, a daughter of Edwin Johnson, of Montgomery County, Tenn. Dr. Jefferson is a man of ability, and of high standing with the community. His sunny nature and high social worth attract to him a large circle of acquaintances. He was elected to the Legislature of 1883, and is now serving in that body, and was elected a delegate to represent the Third District in the Democratic National Convention held at Chicago.[25]

What the biography does not reveal is that Walter Bolling and Mamie (Perkins) Jefferson had a son named Randolph Jefferson, who was born on July 21, 1872 and died soon after on August 5th. A second son, Marion, was born in May of 1877 and died that August. Mamie died following Marion's birth.[26]

Later in life, Dr. Jefferson entered politics and, as a result, his name appeared in numerous newspaper articles.

Dr. W. B. Jefferson, the accomplished representative from Todd county, is a candidate for delegate from his district to the Chicago convention. Several counties have warmly indorsed him, and the indications are that he will be chosen. He will make a good representative to the National Council.

Courier-Journal, 30 April 1884

Dr. W. B. Jefferson, of Elkton, Todd county, is stopping at the Willard on his way to Frankfurt. The doctor is a great nephew of Thomas Jefferson, the father of democracy. His father was Isham Randolph Jefferson, son of Randolph Jefferson, who was the youngest brother of Thomas Jefferson. The grandmother of Dr. Jefferson was a Randolph, cousin of John Randolph, of Roanoke. Isham Randolph Jefferson moved from Albemarle county, Va., to Todd county in 1833, where he lived the remainder of his life. Dr. Jefferson bears a striking resemblance to his great uncle, and has many of the qualities which distinguish his family. He was a leading member of the Legislature during the memorable Blackburn–Williams contest, and also delegate to the Democratic national convention of 1884, which nominated Mr. Cleveland. He is an applicant for the place of Pension Agent for Kentucky.

Courier-Journal, 14 January 1893

In Letter From Thomas Jefferson's Grand-Nephew
FOR CAUSE OF DEMOCRACY.
Frankfort, KY., Jan. 20.–[Special.]–
A Jefferson Compliments Campbell

A grandnephew of Thomas Jefferson, who learned his democracy at the fountain source, almost directly from the founder of Democracy himself, Dr. W. B. Jefferson, of Elkton, has written to Senator J. Wheeler Campbell, commending him on the position he has taken in the senatorial race. Dr. Jefferson's father studied with Thomas Jefferson and was taught Democracy by Jefferson himself. He handed down these principles of Democracy to his son, Dr. Jefferson. The letter from Dr. Jefferson to Senator Campbell is as follows:

Elkton and Guthrie, Todd County—Hon. J. Wheeler Campbell, Frankfurt—

My Dear Sir: I knew your grandfather, Dr. James Wheeler, and Judge James Campbell, your father, and I have met your accomplished mother. I was a roommate of your uncle, Dr. W. G. Wheeler, when we were students at the University of Virginia, all of whom you should be and doubtless are, proud: I venture to say, if all were living, would be proud of you for the service you are rendering your State and party in this hour of humiliation and shame.

I am a life-long Democrat. I heard my lessons of democracy from a father who learned his from the father of the Democratic Party, who was his uncle, and by whom he was practically raised. I do not speak of this, except to emphasize the fact that I am a Democrat, and could not be otherwise if I would, and would not if I could.

Your efforts, with the other good and true men who are associated with you, will save the party. If you are successful. If you fail it means Republicans or machine rule in Kentucky for years to come.

I believe in saying this that I voice the sentiments and opinions of 49,000[?] Democrats in Kentucky, and I will say, taken as a whole, composing the best elements in the State. We simply will not indorse the methods of the gang that has run rough-shod over anybody and thing that happens to fall in their way, and who intend to be political orphans until the last vestige of the machine is destroyed and entirely eliminated. I write this from a sickbed, because I cannot resist the temptation to express my admiration of your superb courage and lofty patriotism. I wish I was able to write to each one who is aiding you.

With best wishes for your success, I am, sincerely,

Dr. W. B. JEFFERSON.

Courier-Journal, 21 January 1908

∿

Even Dr. Jefferson persisted in disseminating the notion that his father was "practically raised" by President Thomas Jefferson.

In many ways, Dr. Walter B. Jefferson was the ideal great-nephew of President Thomas Jefferson. Unlike the sons of Peter Field Jefferson, he had a fine intellect, treating the ill and advocating for hospitals, rather than being committed to one. In 1884, he served on a committee to investigate conditions at Kentucky's Central Lunatic Asylum. Like his father, it was said that he bore a "striking" resemblance to President Jefferson. He attended his great-uncle's university and his sunny nature brought him a wide acquaintance. What a pity he spent his life in Kentucky rather than Albemarle County, Virginia where he would have conspicuously honored the "healthy and productive" side of the Jefferson–Lewis–Randolph alliance.[27]

Walter Bolling Jefferson died on March 26, 1928 of bronchial pneumonia complicated by influenza. He was survived by his second wife, Evelyn A. (Johnson) Jefferson; his son, Edwin Randolph Jefferson; and grandchildren. Dr. Jefferson was eighty-two years old and a credit to his family.[28]

In 1943, Edwin Jefferson attended the dedication of the Jefferson Memorial in Washington, D.C. His presence at the event was national news and his likeness to President Thomas Jefferson was noted. A childless widower, Edwin was believed to be the last of Randolph Jefferson's descendants to bear the Jefferson name.[29]

James Lilburne Jefferson:
A Young Man Adrift

James Lilburne Jefferson (born abt. 1797), known as Lilburne to his family, was the youngest son of Randolph and Anne (Lewis) Jefferson. Born when Randolph was about forty-two years old, Lilburne had a rocky start in life beginning with his mother's death (c. 1800), his father's unpopular second marriage to Mitchie B. Pryor (c. 1810), the family discord that ensued, and his father's death while he was still a minor.[1]

In 1813, Lilburne joined the Virginia Volunteers and fought against the British, declining an opportunity to study at Monticello with his uncle, Thomas Jefferson. Entering as a Private under Capt. Boaz Ford of Buckingham County, Lilburne served in the Light Infantry, 7th Regiment, Virginia Militia. Stationed at Camp Carter near Richmond, he was credited with five months, twenty-eight days of service on Capt. Ford's pay roll from August 29, 1814 to February 22, 1815. These were significant months of the war, especially in eastern Virginia. During August 24–25, 1814, the British burned Washington, D.C., and President James Madison fled the White House.[2]

Lilburne was home only a few months when his father died in August of 1815. The Buckingham County Court assigned him a guardian, indicating he was not yet twenty-one. Again, he hesitated to stay at Monticello, writing to his uncle of his restlessness:

Scott's Ferry Feb 18th 1816
Dear uncle

I received your letter by Guilley you advice in respect to my situation. I thank you kindly for your advice. I went to Buckingham CH on monday last and spoke to the Curator in respect to my situation and he refused to let me have money out of the estate. I then appealed to the Court for justice. The court would not authorize the curator to let me have money out of the estate unless I would shoose [sic] a guardian. I then choosed a guardian and he will no doubt do justice by me. I have not been in want of clothing but I thought that I was entitled to funds out of the estate I should be very happy to come and live with you but I have rented the ferry and the man that I rented it of wont I am affraid compromise with me but if he will I will come over. My anxiety is to travel and that Westardly. The plantation snowden is to be rented out next week and I had a thought of renting a part of it. The widow has moved to her mothers. She had not moved there more than two days before the house caught on fire and bournt everything into ashes. I will let you know in a few days is as I can see Mr. Thomas the gentleman that I rented the ferry of he is gone to Richmond.

I am Sir your affectionate nephew

James L. Jefferson [3]

Lilburne's "anxiety" to travel "westward" is intriguing. With his home at Snowden burnt, his father dead, and his family fighting over the estate, leaving Buckingham County no doubt had a great appeal. Having served during the War of 1812, Lilburne was hardly a boy, yet without funds or a livelihood of his own, he was tied to the area around Scott's Landing while his father's estate was contested. How far west did Lilburne imagine going? His Lewis cousins had relocated to western Kentucky (though by 1816 they were dispersed from there) and he had witnessed at least two of Mitchie Jefferson's brothers remove to Tennessee. Lynchburg, however, may be as far west as he ever traveled.

Indications are that Lilburne remained near Scottsville. Throughout 1816 and 1817, he stayed in contact with his uncle, Thomas Jefferson, who noted in his memorandum book: "Gave James Lilburne Jefferson 10. D." (13 June 1816) and "shoes for J. Lilburne Jefferson 2.75." (20 January 1817).[4]

In 1818, Lilburne became one the earliest investors in Scottsville, purchasing lots #42 and #43 from John Scott. He paid $296 for the two undeveloped lots, a typical price. That year he also purchased 1/4 acre located in the Coles Division from Samuel Dyer. He served as postmaster at Scott's Landing, 1817–1819. By 1818, he had turned twenty-one and paid personal property tax on himself, a horse, and two slaves. He settled in adjacent Fluvanna County and, that autumn, joined the Fluvanna County Militia.[5]

Fluvanna Cy To Wit

James L. Jefferson this day came Before me a Justice of the Peace for the said county and Qualified to a Commission as Ensign of the 12th Reg. 3rd B.G. [?] and 2nd Division of Virginia Militia by taking the several oaths prescribed by Law—Given under my hand the 2nd October 1819—[signature illegible].[6]

In 1820, Lilburne still lived in Fluvanna County, a short distance from what was quickly becoming the town of Scottsville. His home was two households from Joseph Walker, who became a close friend and associate of Lilburne's brother, Peter Field Jefferson. That year, Lilburne was living with another man between sixteen and twenty-six years old, whose identity is unknown. Four slaves were enumerated with them; Lilburne paid personal property tax on two.[7]

Prior to 1821, Lilburne purchased another half-acre lot in Scottsville's Fluvanna addition from Randolph Turner. On April 3, 1821, he still lived in Fluvanna when he sold it to Martin B. Tutwiler. The price was $700, cash in hand. During 1822, after selling to Tutwiller, Lilburne was taxed in Nelson County, where he may have stayed with his older brother, Robert Lewis Jefferson. During 1823–1825, they both lived in Buckingham County, likely managing or renting Snowden before it was sold to Capt. John Harris.[8]

Lilburne continued to invest in Scottsville. On June 7, 1823, he purchased lot #44 from Susan and John Scott. His four lots remained undeveloped, valued at $240. By comparison, at that time, his older brother Peter Field's property was worth only $120.[9]

From 1826 until his death in 1836, Lilburne Jefferson lived in Lynchburg, southwest of Scottsville and Snowden, and not far from Thomas Jefferson's Bedford County plantation, Poplar Forest. By 1830, the thirty-three year-old Lilburne lived in town with another man who was between twenty and thirty. No slaves lived with them. In 1835, he wrote to Peter Field Jefferson about his plans to go into the tobacco business—which undoubtedly meant buying and selling, not growing tobacco.[10]

His death, on October 22, 1836, was a long time coming. A chronic alcoholic, the demise of James Lilburne Jefferson was called a "casualty" rather than an accident. The *Lynchburg Virginian* lamented the loss of a man who might have been a useful citizen, but for his weakness for whiskey. Northern newspapers printed the scandalous news of one of President Jefferson's nephews—a warning not to give in to the temptation of drink.[11]

His death continued to be reported into 1837, when the *Republican Farmer and Democratic Journal* of Wilkes-Barre, Pennsylvania printed this lament:

FAMILY SCRAPS.

The Lynchburg Virginian mentions the death of James L. Jefferson, a nephew of the late Thomas Jefferson. According to the verdict of the coroner's Jury, he died from the effect of intemperance. "He possessed fine talents, learning, and friends."

"O: thou invisible spirit of wine!" How many more must you rob of Godlike dignity, and transform them to beasts; how many more must you poison to death in high and low places, before the world will be convinced that you are, and ever have been, and will be, a murderer, and banish you from the earth?[12]

Anna Scott Jefferson:
The Rise and Fall of the Nevils of Nelson County

Anna Scott Jefferson (b. 1781–1785) may have been Randolph and Anne (Lewis) Jefferson's first child. She was called "Nancy," as was her mother. Following naming practices of the day, the Jeffersons favored family names. Anna Scott's namesake was her father's twin, Anna Scott (Jefferson) Marks, named for her aunt, Anne (Randolph) Scott. Anna Scott Marks must have been well-loved for Randolph and Anne Jefferson to forego honoring their mothers. Since Anna Scott was the Jefferson's only daughter, neither her paternal grandmother, Jane (Randolph) Jefferson, nor her maternal grandmother, Mary (Randolph) Lewis, would be remembered in this Jefferson line.[1]

The details of Nancy Jefferson's early life are unknown. The first significant event is her engagement in 1801 to her double first cousin, Charles Lewis, son of Charles Lilburne Lewis and Lucy Jefferson. Charles Lilburne Lewis was Nancy's mother's brother; Lucy Jefferson was her father's sister. Young Charles Lewis was also, of course, Thomas Jefferson's nephew and Jefferson took an interest in the couple's plans. Despite the fact that he had just been inaugurated President of the United States, he took time to share a bit of family news. In a letter to his son-in-law, John W. Eppes, dated April 8, 1801, Jefferson commented, "Nancy Jefferson is said to be about marrying Charles Lewis."[2]

That spring, Thomas Jefferson contributed to Nancy's trousseau, paying several accounts for his niece, including 21 shillings, on April 20, 1801, for "things furnished Nancy Jefferson." Another notation on May 19, was for an account "against my brother for Thos. & Nancy." It totaled a significant £15/3/0.[3]

Through the summer months, Nancy Jefferson's future welfare continued to be on her uncle's mind. On August 16, 1801, she was inoculated against small pox at Monticello, along with her younger cousins, Ellen and Cornelia Randolph.[4]

While Nancy anticipated her wedding, the Lewis family faced deepening financial troubles. During the 1790s, their substantial fortune had significantly declined. They were not alone. The decade was disastrous for many Virginia planters, their crops ruined by weather and infestations. The "Panic of 1792" created an unstable financial market and, by 1796, when sixteen-year-old Charles joined his older brother, Lilburne, and their father in business, the Lewises were worth a fraction of their previous wealth, which had once included a tavern, investments in a stagecoach line, as well as a large and prosperous plantation.[5]

In July of 1802, Charles and Lucy Lewis deeded one-half of their 1,300-acre tract to young Charles. The gift did not include the dwelling house at Monteagle, but did contain 200 acres of fertile bottom land on Buck Island Creek and the Rivanna River, as well as 450 acres of upland timber.[6]

Was this gift timed to nudge the Lewis-Jefferson engagement toward a wedding? The young couple had been engaged since at least early April of 1801. Charles was about twenty-one, had five years business experience, and now owned 650 acres of land—an attractive package, if not for his father's financial losses. Randolph Jefferson may have hesitated to tie his only daughter to this sinking ship, despite the family's preference for marrying close cousins.[7]

It was one thing for his sons to marry impoverished Lewis cousins (which four eventually did), but quite another for his daughter to be dependent on a young man whose father faced bankruptcy. Randolph Jefferson, who did not feel comfortable with debt and never overextended himself with credit, had survived the economically tumultuous 1790s with most of his property intact.[8]

Eventually, the Lewis-Jefferson engagement was broken, though the precise timing of the rupture is not known, nor is its cause, which has been the subject of speculation. There was gossip the Charles Lewis had fathered an illegitimate, "yellow" child called Matilda, who was the property of Charles' older brother Randolph Lewis. The precise date of Matilda's birth is unclear, though she was likely born about 1801. In the end, Charles Lewis was not a good match for Nancy Jefferson, on several counts.[9]

In 1811, when Randolph Lewis died in Livingston County, Kentucky, Matilda was one of seven slaves in his estate. Valued at $300, she was reportedly ten years old. Initially, Matilda was hired out, for $10.00, to Patrick Calhoun, then, when Robert Lewis' slaves were sold in January of 1815, she (along with "Old Sarah") was purchased by a man named Aaron Threlkeld. In Matilda's recollections, printed in *The Crittenden Press* on December 22, 1880, she identified her father as Charles Lewis. Known as "Aunt" Matilda Threlkeld, the elderly woman then lived in a log cabin in Crittenden County, Kentucky. The Marion Woman's Club had contributed the story to the newspaper, noting that Matilda was the "niece of Thos. Jefferson."[10]

Ultimately, Nancy's situation was a fortunate turn of events. Over the next few years, young Charles proved fiscally irresponsible, though he recovered his composure and, in 1806, apologized to his uncle, Thomas Jefferson, for his past indiscretions. That year, Jefferson facilitated a commission for his nephew as a lieutenant in the army. Later that fall, Charles died at a camp in Louisiana of inflammation of the head. He was unmarried and without legitimate heirs.[11]

The Nevils of Amherst and Nelson Counties

In late 1802, Nancy Jefferson married Zachariah Nevil of Nelson County. They were listed, along with eighteen other couples, on Baptist minister Martin Dawson's "minister's return," dated January 1, 1803 and recorded in Albemarle County, Virginia.[12]

A marked contrast to Nancy Jefferson's youthful and irresponsible Lewis cousin, Zachariah Nevil was old enough to be her father. Stable, responsible, and a veteran of the American Revolution, Nevil must have been a great comfort to Randolph Jefferson. They may have long been friends.

The Jefferson and Nevil families had been associated for generations, particularly through their involvement in politics, public service, and the Virginia Militia. A pioneering family in Henrico-Goochland-Albemarle-Amherst-Nelson counties, a series of James Nevils acquired extensive land patents from 1662–1780. Zachariah's grandfather, James Nevil, and Nancy's grandfather, Peter Jefferson, served together as Magistrates of Albemarle County. In 1750, Nevil patented over 2,500 acres on the branches of the south fork of the Rockfish River, adjoining William Cabell and others. He died in 1752, leaving a son, James Nevil, Jr., Zachariah Nevil's father.[13]

When James Nevil, Jr.'s will was proved in Amherst County on February 7, 1785, Zachariah was over twenty-one years old and, along with his elder brothers, took responsibility for his widowed mother and his youngest siblings, Cornelius and Esther, who were minors and in need of guardians. In his will, their father lent the dwelling house, a portion of the land, slaves, etc., to his widow Mary. At her death, the homeplace was bequeathed to her son Cornelius, however, Zachariah ultimately purchased it.[14]

Zachariah Nevil was appropriately educated to fulfill his role as a gentleman planter. He may have attended William Fontaine's school at Union Hill or a similar plantation school. According to Alexander Brown, author of *The Cabells and Their Kin*:

> In the spring of 1774, William Fontaine, the son of Col. Peter Fontaine, commenced teaching at "Union Hill," and taught Col. Cabell's children, his brother, James Fontaine, John Nicholas, Jr., and one of Col. James Nevil's sons.
>
> It seems well to say here that the custom with the landed gentry of this region with their minor children, before the Revolution, was this: First one and then another of a circle of friends would employ a tutor, and take the young sons of the others as boarders. . . .
>
> There were also teachers of music, of dancing, of fencing, etc., who gave lessons by the month or by the quarter. Most of the sons of the wealthier class received a classical and polite education, and the daughters were not neglected.[15]

Following his school days, Private Zachariah Nevil joined the 3rd Regiment of Light Dragoons during the Revolution, serving for 29 months, 27 days, beginning on May 20, 1781. A loyal cavalry man, he was paid $80.00 gratuity for staying until the end of the war. During June and July of 1781, the 3rd Regiment of Light Dragoons camped at Randolph Jefferson's Snowden, providing an opportunity for Nevil and Jefferson to become acquainted.[16]

As a son-in-law, Zachariah Nevil was warmly embraced by the Randolph Jefferson family, and the newlyweds spent at least part of their early married life at Snowden. Their first two children, James Lilburne and Louisa Nevil, were likely born there.[17] During 1805–1809, a business called "Nevil and Jefferson" operated at Snowden. When Randolph Jefferson married Mitchie B. Pryor, the Nevils returned to Nelson County.[18]

There, the Nevils owned twenty-four slaves to serve the family and work the fields. Zachariah proved to be an excellent provider for Nancy Jefferson. Their plantation was located twelve miles southeast of Nelson County's courthouse (at Lovingston) and six to seven miles from "New Market," where Zachariah long served as Tobacco Inspector at the Warehouse on the Tye River, a position he held for roughly two decades.[19]

In 1812, he purchased an insurance policy, protecting his property from fire. The plantation structures were valued as follows: the dwelling house (one story high, 28x18 feet), $1,000; the kitchen, $170; and a smoke house, $100.[20]

In 1815, Randolph Jefferson died at Snowden. Nancy was not mentioned in his will, drafted in 1808. This is particularly odd considering that the Nevils were probably living at Snowden when the will was written. Perhaps, Jefferson believed that Nancy was now his son-in-law's responsibility.[21]

While many early Virginians divided their property equally between their sons and daughters, many others did not. Col. Charles Lewis, Jr., Randolph Jefferson's father-in-law, was an example of the latter. He gave his daughter, Anne Jefferson, and most of her sisters, a single, personal slave. His land went to his sons. Peter Jefferson was of the same disposition. His plantations were bequeathed to his two sons, his daughters were given domestic servants. Randolph Jefferson may have given Nancy a servant or two at the time of her marriage and considered that a sufficient inheritance.[22]

Immediately upon his death, Randolph Jefferson's 1808 will was challenged in the Buckingham County Court and Zachariah Nevil was appointed Administrator of what became a long-contested estate. As Administrator, Zachariah naturally dealt closely with his brothers-in-law, particularly Robert Lewis Jefferson, who maintained an intimate relationship with the Nevil family, and Peter Field Jefferson, who helped facilitate the sale of Snowden.[23]

~

As a gentleman, Zachariah Nevil not only valued higher education for his own children, but for other Virginians. In July of 1818, he was among the "subscribers, contributors and founders of the establishment of Central College," spearheaded by Thomas Jefferson and many other leaders of Albemarle, Nelson, and Buckingham counties. Central College provided the foundation of what would become the University of Virginia.[24]

Zachariah maintained a personal library, containing a broad selection of volumes concerning religion, literature, drama, biography, history, government, science, and geography. While most of the volumes in the Nevil family library were not "school books" per se, Oliver Goldsmith, author of *The Vicar of Wakefield*, compiled the histories of England, Greece and Rome for use in schools. *Pleasing Instruction* certainly may have been designed for teachers. The presence of *Enfield Speaker* in the library indicates a value of poise and elocution in the Nevil home. Eventually, Zachariah served as a representative to Virginia's General Assembly. Son Lafayette chose to study the law, benefiting from training in oratory. Patrick Gass' *Journal of the Lewis and Clark Expedition* was of current interest; while Shakespeare represented the classics. The collection certainly influenced son Madison, who eventually became a member of the Literary Society at Washington College.

Youth's Friend was a compilation of simple Sunday School texts. The two volumes of the life of George Washington hint at a family hero, whose grandeur was passed down to the Nevil children. The biography by Parson Weems, the original Washington myth maker, was augmented with Dr. David Ramsay's version of Washington's life (published in 1807). The library also reveals that Zachariah was likely a Freemason, as he owned a copy of *Freemason's Monitor or Illustrations of Free Masonry*. Nancy Nevil's household concerns were addressed with volumes such as *Domestic Cookery* and *Ewell's Medical Companion Or Family Physician*.

∽

2 vols American Revolution	$ 1.50
12 vols Encyclopedia & Goldsmith's Greece and Rome	$10.00
1 map of United States	$12.00
2 vols Youth's Friend	$ .75
Ewell's Medical Companion	$ .75
Thompson's Late War	$ .50
Freemason's Monitor	$ .50
Richard Preston	$ .25
Ramsay's Life of Washington	$ .50
Weem's Ditto	$ .25
Goldsmith's England	$ .25
2 vols Guardian	$ .50
Pleasing Instruction	$ .25
Scott's [illegiable]	$ .25
Gass's Journal	$ .25
Doctrinal Tracts	$ .25
English Reader	$ .37
Molier's Works in 4 vols	$ .50
[Rev. David ?] Bogues Essay [on the New Testament ?]	$ .50
New Testament	$ .50

Enfield's Speaker	$ .25
Constitution of the United States	$ .50
1 vol of Shakespeare's works	$ .25
Domestic Cookery	$ .12
3 old books damaged	
	$16.00[25]

~

By 1820, Zachariah and Nancy Nevil, along with their three sons and one daughter, enjoyed a comfortable lifestyle in southeastern Nelson County. Their possessions included wine glasses, imported Liverpool dishware, and silver flatware. That year, forty-four slaves served the family and labored in the fields. Zachariah rose to the rank of Colonel in the Virginia Militia.[26]

Nancy (Jefferson) Nevil was roughly forty years old when she died sometime before September 1, 1825. That day her first cousin Martha (Jefferson) Randolph wrote to her daughter, Ellen (Randolph) Coolidge, informing her that "Mrs. Nevill" was dead, sarcastically referring to her as "Nanny Dish." Martha, who also spoke unkindly of her own aunt, Anna Scott "Nancy" (Jefferson) Marks, maligned Randolph Jefferson's widow Mitchie (Mrs. Johnson), in the same letter:

> ...Mrs. Judge Johnson (Mrs R–Jefferson) and Mrs Nevill (your old friend Nanny Dish) are both dead the poor clergymen who pronounced their funeral orations must have been considerably embarrassed for a subject for the accustomed eulegium on such occasions.[27]

Given the relative affluence of the Nevils, Martha Randolph's comments were potentially tinged with jealousy. In 1825, her Nevil cousins were still on the rise in Nelson County. Importantly, Zachariah Nevil did not carry significant debt. By contrast, in Albemarle County, Martha Randolph's branch of the Jefferson family struggled under the weight of her father's overwhelming debt at Monticello.

By 1826, Zachariah Nevil was at the height of his powers. A Gentleman Justice in Nelson County, he also established Zachariah Nevil and Co., in association with Robert Rives and Alexander Brown. They were granted the right to stem and manufacture tobacco, agreeing in court not to "buy or receive any tobacco from any Negro, Mulatto or Indian, bond or free."[28]

Zachariah significantly expanded his real estate holdings, buying the impressive farm, Bonair, from Dr. George Cabell, which cost him $7,500 and consisted of 940 acres. The plantation bordered the James River, near Wingina. Its majestic Palladian-style home had been insured by the Mutual Assurance Society in 1812. Four buildings were protected by the policy, including the dwelling house, valued at $5,000; two offices, valued at $400 each; and a combination meat house, well, and dairy, valued at $450. The out buildings were brick, covered with wood.[29]

Tradition attributes the design of the house to Thomas Jefferson, however, it has been said that if Jefferson planned every house attributed to him, he would never have had time to be President. Yet, Bonair's tri-part design, with a two-story center and single-story wings, certainly reflected Jefferson's architectural preferences. A 20th-century sales brochure detailed some of the home's fine points:

> The house was built of local kiln dried brick, walls 16 to 18 inches thick, including not only the exterior walls but the walls between the different rooms, thus substantially reducing general fire hazard. The roof is of slate, and the woodwork was built with "shop" or homemade nails, and in certain vital points with wooden pegs made of alleged indestructible red pine.[30]

In 1829, Zachariah Nevil represented Nelson County in the Virginia House of Delegates.[31] It was a fervent time in Virginia politics, especially The Constitutional Convention of 1829–30. Then, on April 8, 1830, Nevil died suddenly, throwing the family into chaos. Still full of energy, he had many irons in the fire. His competency would be sorely missed by his community. The absence of his paternal love would prove devastating to his children. This sterling gentleman who was Randolph Jefferson's friend, his son-in-law, his business partner, and, ultimately, the Administrator of his estate was memorialized in the *Richmond Enquirer*:

> Departed this life on the 8th inst. at his residence, in the county of Nelson, Col. Zachariah Nevil, a man whose character [enfolded] the higher virtues. Col. Nevil was a member of the last Legislature. In that body he gave evidences of a vigorous and discriminating mind, of a firm and independent spirit. He was a magistrate of the county of Nelson. In this station he was capable—he was faithful. Whether in his public or private relations, he manifested a correctness of demeanor, a loftiness of sentiment, which secured to him the approbation of the virtuous—the commendation of the wise. The softer touches of our nature were happily

blended with the masculine traits of his mind. He was benevolent—he was affectionate. He was a devoted parent, and a devoted friend. In this bereavement his children have sustained a loss truly afflicting—they made the strongest ties which were severed by his death—his consort having some years ago preceded him in the awful journey to eternity. The county responds to their grief, and joins them in their mourning.[32]

Zachariah Nevil left no will. His son, James Lilburne Nevil, and his associate, Jesse Jopling, were appointed his administrators and took over Zachariah's responsibility for his mother's estate. The division of the estate came in November of 1834 and property was distributed equally among the four Nevil children: James Lilburne, Lafayette, Jefferson Madison (called Madison), and Louisa, who was by then married to Jesse Mundy.[33]

∾

Following Nancy Nevil's death in the mid-1820s, her four children remained in contact with the larger Jefferson family. Records in Nelson and Albemarle County, including guardianship papers, deeds, and chancery cases link Nancy's children especially to their uncle, Robert Lewis Jefferson.

James Lilburne Nevil, the first-born of Nancy's children, was named for her youngest brother, James Lilburne Jefferson. Born on May 24, 1806, he grew up in Nelson County and, on October 3, 1831, married Dorothy S. "Dolly" Moorman, the sister-in-law of his uncle Robert Lewis Jefferson. Beginning in January of 1832, they rented Bonair for four years. Later, they removed to Tuscaloosa, Alabama, where James Lilburne died sometime between 1842 and December of 1844. Jefferson administered James Lilburne's Virginia estate in Nelson and Albemarle counties.[34]

Louisa Ann Nevil (a.k.a. Louisanna) was about twenty-two years old when she married Jessie Mundy, on August 22, 1831, in Nelson County. Her brother, James Lilburne Nevil, was their bondsman. The Mundys lived in Amherst County, apart from her brothers, farming, rearing their children, and stirring up constant conflict with the larger Nevil family. Within a few months of their marriage, in November of 1831, "Jesse Mundy and wife" initiated a chancery suit against Zachariah Nevil's Administrators which did not conclude until 1872.[35]

∾

When Zachariah Nevil died in 1830, his two youngest sons, Lafayette and Madison, required guardians. In July, Lafayette (born about 1810) chose Jesse Jopling as his guardian, though he would soon be twenty-one years old. Lafayette's name was significant to both his father and his mother. Nancy no doubt grew up hearing stories of Lafayette's heroics in the vicinity of Snowden during 1781 and Zachariah's war experience likely led him to admire the Frenchman.[36]

During 1829–1830, Lafayette Nevil studied at the University of Virginia. A letter from Joseph C. Cabell to Zachariah Nevil, written from Edgewood on October 19, 1829, offered advice concerning Lafayette's course of study. He also enclosed, as a "present" to Zachariah, copies of the "Laws of the University" and the "Constitution of the State." Cabell recommended a two to three-year course of study, which would have resulted in a well-rounded gentleman and scholar. Lafayette did not follow the advice, however, and enrolled in courses that interested him—Chemistry, Moral Philosophy, and Law. He did not return to the university for the academic year 1830–1831, probably due to his father's death in the spring of 1830.[37]

From the time of Zachariah Nevil's death, the lives of Lafayette and his unfortunate younger brother, Madison, became permanently entwined. Born in about 1815, Zachariah's death left Madison's immediate future in the hands of the Nelson County Court. On November 22, 1830, Madison appeared in court and chose his uncle, Robert Lewis Jefferson, as his guardian.[38]

When Jefferson took responsibility for his nephew, he was well-established on his farm in Buckingham County on Sharps Creek, where he lived with his second wife, Elizabeth Ann "Bettie" Moorman, sister to James Lilburne Nevil's wife, Dolly. Beginning in 1831, Jefferson kept Madison's accounts, paid some of his bills, and rented out his slaves to Sharps Creek neighbors, creating income to cover Madison's expenses. That year Elvira, a slave distributed to Madison from his father's estate, was sold, raising $750.[39]

In late 1830, Madison attended Major Charles Yancey's school. Under his uncle's guidance, his education continued with various tutors, apparently uninterrupted.[40]

In 1832, Madison decided to attend classes at Washington College in Lexington, Virginia. The college offered accommodations for fifty to sixty students and an impressive library containing 1,500 volumes. A comparatively affordable and intimate school, in 1833, there were forty-six scholars enrolled.[41]

Beginning in the early 1830s, Washington College had begun expanding, adding a new Federal-style Lyceum on the crest of College Hill, situated between the older Centre Building and Union Hall. The expansion was, in part, to house the school's growing commitment to the physical sciences.[42] In 1835, author Charles Fenno Hoffman included this evocative description of Lexington and the college in his travel memoir, *Winter in the West*:

> About noon I found myself on the meadowy bank of a clear rushing stream, whose opposite shore rose in precipitous cliffs from the water. Here the rifted hemlock and cedar, flinging their branches far over the current, contrasting vividly in their dusky green with the light foliage of the willows and sycamores that skirted the water's edge where the highway approached the brink. The Collegiate institution of the little town of Lexington with its rather pretty but formal looking pleasure grounds, first met my eye after fording the stream: it stands on an eminence back from the road, and forms the first object of attention on entering the village. I paused merely long enough to observe that there were indications of wealth and style about the place which were seldom met in the country towns of west Virginia.[43]

Madison Nevil matriculated in the Winter Session 1832–1833 and was well on his way to becoming a polished gentleman. Despite the fact that Robert Lewis Jefferson remained his legal guardian, the college recorded Lafayette Nevil as his "Parent or Guardian," and their residence as at "Tye river warehouse, Nelson." During Madison's tenure at Washington College, kinsmen Cornelius and Samuel J. Thomas were engaged to accompany him on the fifty-mile ride to and from Lexington, settle accounts at the school, etc.[44]

In addition to his studies, Madison joined the Washington Literary Society, which debated philosophical questions and, among other missions, oversaw the purchasing and lending of books for the school's library. In January of 1832, Madison was one of a three-man Librarian's Committee reporting on back-ordered books. Members were frequently fined 12½–25 cents for disorderly conduct during a meeting or for interrupting fellow speakers. The gentleman debated such topics as "Is the crime of seduction more criminal than that of murder?" Madison voted "negative" on that particular issue.[45]

Examination results from March of 1833 indicate that Madison Nevil had adjusted well to college life, earning "distinguished" marks in "Justin" (Latin) and "approved" marks in mathematics.[46]

~

Beginning in January of 1832, Lafayette Nevil rented the old family plantation, Locust Grove, from his father's estate for four years. In 1833, he presented a certificate to the Nelson County Court concerning his authority to practice law in several courts in the Commonwealth. Among other civic duties, he served the county as an overseer for the poor and as a Captain in the County Militia.[47]

As the records at Washington College suggest, when Madison Nevil was not in school, he lived in Nelson County with his unmarried brother, Lafayette, not with his official legal guardian, Robert Lewis Jefferson, in Buckingham County. Madison much preferred Lafayette to his other siblings and, naturally, felt at home at Locust Grove where he had grown up.

While Robert Lewis Jefferson kept Madison's accounts and managed his slaves, he did not regularly provide the young man with spending money. His living expenses were provided by Lafayette, who even paid some of Madison's debts while his estate was still under their uncle's control. Some family members and friends questioned Jefferson's handling of Madison's money. Years later, John W. Thomas stated to Lafayette:

> Madison told me, when he was in his [right] mind, that he owed a good deal of money and had consulted his uncle Lewis Jefferson whether it would not be advisable to sell a Negro for the purpose of paying his debts . . . [H]is uncle advised him to sell and pay his debts [and] that the hire of his Negroes was not sufficient to pay his debts, but the Negro was not sold.[48]

In 1835, the Nevil heirs decided to sell both Bonair and Locust Grove, placing an advertisement in the *Richmond Whig*:

> VALUABLE LANDS FOR SALE–Will be offered [?] for sale, on Thursday, the 28th day of August, at the town of New Market, in the county of Nelson, Va., 2 very valuable tracts of land lying in the said county, belonging to the estate of Zachariah Nevil, deceased. One tract, "Bonair," the former residence of Dr. Geo. Cabell, jr. deceased, lying on James River, about one

mile from the town of Warminster, containing 910 acres, a large proportion of which is low grounds of first and second quality, well adapted to
the culture of tobacco, corn and wheat: about one half of this tract is still
in woods, and well timbered. The other tract, "Locust Grove," the former
residence of the late Zachariah Nevil, deceased, lying on the main road
leading from Thomas' Ford, on Rockfish River, to Lovingston, about
nine miles from the latter place, five miles Northwest of Warminster, and
about the same distance from New Market and Variety Mills. This tract
contains 666 acres, about 300 acres of which are cleared; a large portion
of the balance is fine tobacco land, and well timbered.

About one-third of the purchase money will probably be required,
and the balance made to accommodate the purchasers; but the terms will
be more particularly made known on the day of the sale. Those inclined
to purchase will of course view the premises previous to the day of sale,
(and are respectively invited to do so.) They, or either of the above tracts
of Land, will be shown at any time by Jas. L. Nevil, residing on the
"Bonair" estate. Possession will be given to the purchaser or purchasers
immediately after the sale, for the purpose of seeding a crop of "wheat
in good time," and full possession of the whole premises on or before the
first of January next.

BY THE LEGATEES.
August 4.[49]

Lafayette stayed on at Locust Grove, eventually buying out his siblings on
May 22, 1837, becoming the plantation's sole owner.[50]

∾

On October 7, 1835, Lafayette Nevil married Mary J. Labby in Lynchburg,
Virginia. She was the daughter of Pleasant Labby, a pioneer of the city's tobacco
industry, an Apostle of the Universalist Church, and future Mayor of Lynchburg
(1836). The couple resided in Lynchburg. Locust Grove, where Lafayette maintained five slaves, three horses, and a carriage valued at $200, was managed by
his overseer.[51]

Within a few months of Lafayette's marriage, Madison's mind began to
"wane," his behavior becoming increasingly erratic. He fought with his brother,
James Lilburne, and, as a result, Madison was ordered out of his house and told

him not to "pester" him again. Adrift, Madison went to Amherst County to visit his sister, Louisa Mundy, for a couple of months. Shortly after his arrival, "he was attacked with a severe spate of sickness" and "required much nursing and attention." Deranged, Madison threatened to "wring his sister's head off" and Jesse Mundy reacted by "cowhiding" his unstable brother-in-law. Mr. Mundy said he would not keep Madison in his house if he were paid $1,000 a year. Indignant at this treatment, Madison returned to Lynchburg, seeking Lafayette's care and protection. The newly wed Mrs. Nevil was uneasy with Madison in her home. As a result, Lafayette took his brother to live with their uncle, Robert Lewis Jefferson.[52]

It is unknown if Madison went to Buckingham or Albemarle County. By 1835, Robert Lewis Jefferson had moved from his farm in Buckingham to his wife's homeplace, Rock Island, in southern Albemarle. His son, Elbridge Gerry Jefferson, was about twenty-two and his daughter, Mary Elizabeth, was just five or six years old. Mrs. Jefferson may have hesitated to include Madison in her household. At that time, Jefferson still maintained his farm in Buckingham, which Madison knew and, perhaps, had an affection for. Whichever farm Madison visited to rest and recuperate in hopes of calming his mind, both Jefferson plantations offered more space and quiet than Lynchburg. His stay with the Jeffersons, however, proved temporary.[53]

Still ill, Madison returned to Lynchburg and the Lafayette Nevils. During 1835–1836, John W. Thomas visited the city, boarding in the same house. There, he observed Madison closely and recalled: "His situation while in Lynchburg was as bad as it possibly could be. He was perfectly deranged nearly the whole time."[54]

By the fall of 1836, Madison needed constant care and his physician, Dr. Irving, suggested that the young man's only hope of recovery was in the countryside. As a result, Lafayette broke up his residence in Lynchburg and moved back to Locust Grove. Years later, Lafayette told the Nelson County Court that it was always his hope to restore Madison's mind and "to retrieve [him] from a condition so calamitous and distressing." No expense was spared. Every treatment was tried, in vain. For nearly three years, Lafayette sacrificed his profession, other pursuits, and domestic comfort, including long separations from his wife, living at Locust Grove. He gave of his time and his resources out of devotion beyond duty.[55]

During these three years, from late 1835 to December of 1838, not only was Madison "out of his mind," but he was also often gravely ill. Lafayette had to keep someone with him from the winter of 1836 onward, hiring servants to attend to his brother, as well as enlisting James Powell and members of the Thomas family to help him. Madison's unpredictable insanity terrified Lafayette's wife, Mary, who was afraid to be alone with her brother-in-law. When Lafayette was away from Locust Grove on business, Mary stayed with neighbors; the Thomas family or Mrs. Murphy.[56]

At one point, the family decided that Madison should be placed in Western Lunatic Asylum in Staunton, Virginia, which had opened in 1828. "The hospital" (as the Nevils called it) was designed on the compassionate philosophy of "moral therapy." Surrounding gardens provided a parklike, tranquil atmosphere. Patients were encouraged to work and exercise outdoors. Doubtless the family believed that life there would be not unlike Locust Grove, with medical professionals in residence to help and, perhaps, cure Madison of his mental illness. Additionally, if Madison were committed, Lafayette and his wife could return to a normal married life.[57]

Lafayette hired a barouche, asking Cornelius Thomas to take his brother to Staunton. Once there, he was denied admittance, no room being available. The men returned to Locust Grove, at which point Mrs. Nevil refused to stay on with Madison in the house, forcing her husband to choose between her and his insane brother. Lafayette argued that he could not turn his brother out of his house. Good to her word, Mrs. Nevil and her mother, Mrs. Labby, returned to Lynchburg and her father's protection. John W. Thomas accompanied Mrs. Nevil on her return to Lynchburg and believed she should leave Locust Grove. He later told Lafayette, "It was not prudent for her to stay where [Madison] was. Your brother at times was dangerous."[58]

By early 1838, Madison had not improved and the Nelson County Court appointed a Curator to manage his estate. His property was appraised. Nine slaves and a $4,000 bond were valued at $9,400.[59]

Nelson County, February Court, 1838.
On the motion of Lafayette Nevil It is ordered that Martin Brown, Nelson Anderson, Norborne Thomas, John Ligon, and David Thomas or any three others be appointed commissioners to ascertain the value of the estate of Jefferson M. Neville a person of insane mind. . . .[60]

On May 25, 1838, Lafayette Nevil was appointed Curator for his brother's estate, charged to "safely keep" his brother's property "without waste or destruction and shall competently support and maintain him with the profits of the same, if the said profits shall be sufficient for that purpose." Allowance was made for the possibility that he might again "become of sound mind."[61]

> At a Court held for Nelson County, the 28th day of May, 1838.
> The court doth appoint Lafayette Neville [sic] curator of the person and estate of Jefferson M. Neville a person of unsound mind, and thereupon, the said Lafayette Neville together with James L. Neville, John W. Mosby and H. B. Scott his securities entered into and acknowledged a bond in the penalty of $18,000, conditioned according to law which bond is ordered to be recorded.[62]*

*Following Zachariah Nevil's death, the spelling of the family's name drifted to Neville, written that way in both public and private documents.

~

On August 21, 1838, Lafayette wrote to his sister, Louisa Mundy, from Locust Grove. He opened with a teasing tone: "On taking up my pen [I] was smartly at a loss to know whom to address, you, or Mr. Mundy;—but as you seem to wear the pants, I halted (not long) between two opinions." He followed with the news that "Mr. Smith has (owing to the times I suppose) been rather tardy in his payments [for Bonair]," and continued with an optimistic assessment of their brother's condition:

> Madison has improved very much since I took him home, and might be reinstated under proper management I think. His mind is better at this time, than it has ever been since he has been thus afflicted. He is very thin however, and has been complaining for a week or ten days of bodily indisposition. The rest of us are as ever.[63]

Months passed and the Mundys did not visit the ailing Madison. On November 18, 1838, Lafayette wrote to his sister again. His servant Jeffery carried a more pessimistic letter.

> Madison is as low as he well can be, and has been so, for two months at least. He may linger for some time,—but can never recover his health. He curses you among others very frequently, being under the impression

that you pester him. His mind is variable; it is not however so bad as it has been.

Mary has been sick, but is now well and in Lynchburg. We had the misfortune to loose [sic] our last child which was quite a promising little girl, about 4 weeks old. We do not know with what complaint. . . .

Give my Respects to Mr. Mundy, and tell him I should be glad to see [him],—if he will come down I will give him a <u>new calico petty coat</u>. I would send you an <u>old pair</u> of breeches, but weather is waning cold & I am forced to give them to my negroes.

I shall start to the North about the first of the week and take Mary with me—Suppose you & Mr. Mundy go also.

In Haste.

Yrs &c.

L. Neville[64]

Again, Lafayette teased his sister about her dominance over her husband. Offering a petticoat to Jessie Mundy likely vexed his brother-in-law, and, with Madison cursing the Mundys, why would they want to visit Locust Grove? Unsurprisingly, they did not.

One final letter, written Christmas Day and addressed to Jesse Mundy, reported Madison's demise.

Dear Sir.

Mr. Brown does me the fav.ʳ while on a visit to Amherst, to be the bearer of a few lines to you.

You no doubt have heard ere this, of the death of my brother which happened on Tuesday—the 11th Inst. About 1.oclk: in the morning. After my letter by Jeffery, we were expecting yourself and Louisa daily.—time will not allow of my mentioning the particulars of his death.

In as much as a New Year is beginning I deem it proper to divide his Estate, that is the Slave portions. I have had commissioners appointed, and have [signed] on Monday the 31st of the present month for that purpose. I shall therefore certainly expect you down before, or about that time.

Write me particularly on this subject, by Mr. Brown.

Present my compliments to Louisa. In Haste.

With Much Esteem I am Yrs &c.

L. Neville[65]

Because Lafayette wrote in haste, no particulars of Madison's death are known. He had died intestate and a "lunatic."

Jefferson Madison Nevil was one of several descendants of Randolph Jefferson to suffer from a deranged mind. His decline began with an extended illness. However, it is entirely possible that the inbreeding of Virginia gentry was at the root of his decline. Like his first cousins, Thomas Jefferson (who died in Western State Asylum) and Peter Field Jefferson, Jr. (whose limited intelligence dissolved into idiocy), Madison Nevil was a product of Lewis-Jefferson-Randolph inter-marriages. Like his mother's first cousin, Lilburne Lewis, who carried the same genes, violence and erratic behavior accompanied Madison's unsound mind.

Sadly for Robert Lewis Jefferson, Madison's guardian, defective traits lurked in his line, as well. In 1860, his grandson, Thomas Jefferson Gantt, was described as "idiotic."[66]

~

As Curator of his brother's estate, Lafayette had pressing business at Nelson County courthouse. Madison's personal property would have to be divided as his Curator saw fit. In the past, Madison told many people that he did not wish the Mundys or his brother, James Lilburne, to get one penny of his estate. Lafayette, however, took family politics into consideration, as well as his brother's wishes.[67]

On the motion of Lafayette Neville, Curator of the person and estate of Jefferson M. Neville dec. It is ordered, that Martin Brown, David C. Thomas, Nelson Anderson, Norborne Thomas and John W. Thomas or any three of them, be appointed [commissioners] to divide and allot in equal portions, among the legal heirs and representatives of the said Jefferson M. Neville, who is now dead, the slaves of which he died seized and possessed, and make a report.[68]

In 1842, John W. Thomas expanded on the relationship between Lafayette and the Mundys:

I was at your house after the death of your Brother. Mr. Mundy was there and stated that he had come at the solicitation of his wife, for her portion of Madison's Negroes but for the wish of his wife he would not of asked for any portion of Madison's Estate. You stated that rather than have any difficulty and to preserve peace in the family you would divide the Negroes, accordingly: on the next day David Thomas, Martin Brown & myself went to New Market and valued and divided the Negroes; and delivered Mr. Mundy his portion which he hired out the same day. Mr. Mundy got Dandridge, Eloy [sic] & George. Valued as well as I recollect to about twenty two hundred dollars.[69]

~

In January of 1842, Jesse and Louisa Mundy filed a Bill in the Nelson County Court against "Lafayette Neville, Administrator of the Estate of Madison Neville." It should be remembered that the Mundys liked to go to court and, in November of 1831, had filed a Bill against the Administrators of Zachariah Nevil's Estate. Though their case against Lafayette was discontinued "by consent" on September 29, 1845, Lafayette went to a great deal of time and expense to defend himself against their claims for more of Madison's estate.[70]

Lafayette stated that he was "mortified" when he was presented with the Mundys' allegation, could find "no apology for it." He maintained that he had ever been "tender and mindful" of the duties which he owed his brother, who was "divested of his reason . . . incapable of taking care of himself."[71]

While supporting Madison, Lafayette's financial situation became increasingly strained and, on August 31, 1842, in Amherst County, he signed a deed of trust to John Thompson, Jr., Sterling Claiborne, Charles Perrow, and other sundry creditors and securities. It included 655 acres (Locust Grove) and slaves named Spencer, Fields, Cary, Kesiah, Balinda [sic], and Eliza, with the future increase of the women. Lafayette's creditors included his brother-in-law, Jesse Mundy ($2,500), and his father-in-law, Pleasant Labby (about $100).[72]

On the same day, in Amherst County, Lafayette entered into a separate agreement with Sterling Claiborne, to hold in trust for his wife, Mary, the following personal property: a "negro woman" named Ellen and her children, Flora, Maria, Henry, Albert and an infant; a "negro boy" named Richard; one bed, bedstead, furniture, and a rocking chair.[73]

These indentures suggest that Lafayette, once he sold his property to cover debts, would be much reduced in wealth. What remained was transferred to his wife, perhaps protecting it from additional creditors.

To raise monies for his debts, his 555-acre plantation was to be sold and was advertised under the name "Mount Lebanon," not generally used by the family since his father insured the dwelling in 1812. This advertisement appeared in the *Richmond Enquirer*.

> MOUNT LEBANON FOR SALE—Having determined to reassume the practice of my profession, I offer for sale this very desirable residence and valuable Farm, in Nelson county, containing by recent survey, 655 acres. Its location is within 4 miles of the James River and Kanawha Improvement, 6 miles of Tye River Warehouse, (a flourishing village, with a tobacco inspection.) And within four miles of Variety (manufacturing) Mills. I deem it altogether unnecessary to enter into minute detail here of this plantation, so well known in this section of country—suffice it to say, that it is well watered, the South Fork of Rockfish river running immediately through it, with many small tributaries passing through the different shifts. The wooded timber is superabundant, and the best quality. The improvements consist of a good framed dwelling house, with nine rooms, a framed barn and stable, good tobacco houses, spring house and ice house, together with all other buildings which attach to farms generally. Those who may desire to purchase are hereby invited to come and view the premises, and judge for themselves.
>
> Terms—One third of the purchase money in cash—the residue two equal annual instalments.
>
> LAFAYETTE NEVILLE.[74]

~

In 1849, Lafayette died of paralysis from an unknown illness. About forty years old, the last decade of his life had been filled with struggle and tragedy. His death was announced in the *Lynchburg Virginian*, a touching tribute to Nancy Jefferson's refined and accomplished son.[75]

> DIED, on the night of 29th Jan., 1849, after an illness of but few days, Lafayette Neville Esq., of this place, (formerly of Nelson county, Va.) The writer of this can truly say, that he was a gentleman, who possessed, in a

very distinguished degree, all those propensities of benignity, which adorn and dignify the human nature. His charity and exemplary benevolence cannot be equaled: he was urbane in his manners, and possessed, in an eminent degree, all the facilities of intellect for which [he] was distinguished. He died to the inexpressible grief of many relations and friends.

> "Shed not for him the bitter tear,
> 'Nor give the heart to vain regret;
> 'Tis but the casket that lies here,
> The gem that filled it sparkles yet!"
> J. B. C.

Elbridge Gerry Jefferson:
Surrogate Son of Peter Field Jefferson

Elbridge Gerry "E. G." Jefferson was the son of Peter Field Jefferson's brother, Robert Lewis Jefferson. As an adult, he assumed the role of a competent surrogate son to Peter Field Jefferson, whose own sons, Thomas (born about 1825) and Peter Field Jefferson, Jr. (born about 1829), proved to be incompetent and mentally ill. Born in about 1814, Elbridge Gerry Jefferson was significantly older than his Scottsville cousins. This intelligent, vital man would become a successful planter and a Baptist minister, founding a church in Buckingham County. He helped Peter Field manage at least two properties and, eventually, became an executor of his uncle's estate. These kinsmen were not only compatible in business but also personally as uncle and nephew. Given Peter Field Jefferson's eccentric personality that says a great deal about Elbridge's nature.

In his will, Peter Field Jefferson left Elbridge significant property and, at the estate sale, he purchased some of his uncle's personal property, including the family Bible. As an executor, Elbridge paid a high price for his filial piety. Peter Field Jefferson's long-contested estate would not only complicate E. G. Jefferson's life, but also the lives of his sons, Elbridge "Gerry" and Lindsay "Bolling" Jefferson.[1]

~

Elbridge Gerry Jefferson's father, Robert Lewis Jefferson (called Lewis), was born at Snowden in about 1786 and was one of Randolph Jefferson's younger sons. Lewis Jefferson's life fell into several distinct phases: his early years at Snowden, his marriage and association with his first wife's extended family in southern Nelson County, his return to Buckingham County and the establishment of his own farm on Sharps Creek, and his second marriage to Elizabeth Ann "Bettie" Moorman, during which he reestablished himself on her family farm in southern Albemarle County.[2]

Lewis Jefferson was especially close to his father—in temperament and in sensibility. They both played the violin. They both enjoyed, and succeeded at, life as a planter. He was the only one of Randolph Jefferson's sons to be named as an executor in his 1808 will, about twenty-one years old at the time.[3]

Compared to his brothers, Lewis Jefferson was a relaxed, apparently unambitious man. In an advertisement for a runaway slave, published in 1811, his language was colloquial. He referred to his slave David, who was in the habit of altering his name, sometimes using "Billy Logan," as a "fellow" who was "tolerably void of hair."[4]

In about 1812, Lewis left the Scottsville area, moving to Nelson County, where his married sister, Anna Scott (Jefferson) Nevil, lived with her husband and family. There, on October 10, 1812, he wed a Miss M. Jordan. She is nearly a complete mystery, even her first name is unknown. They were likely married at the home of her father, William Jordan, who owned land on Elk Island Creek, located about eighteen miles south of the Nelson County courthouse. In the spring of 1814, the young couple acquired farmland near Elk Island Creek as it flowed into adjacent Amherst County. About this time, their only child was born—Elbridge Gerry Jefferson, named for the statesman who served as Vice President under James Madison. Elbridge remained deeply connected to Nelson County and his mother's family. This was Cabell country and Miss Jordan had ties to the Cabells, as well as the influential Horsley family. Before 1820, Mrs. Robert Lewis Jefferson died from unknown causes.[5]

Following his wife's death, Lewis Jefferson was slow to remarry, which was atypical in those days for a man left alone with a young child. Rather, he remained close to his wife's family and his married sister, Anna Scott Nevil, and either family may have helped care for Elbridge. In 1820, Lewis Jefferson and his son were living in Nelson County. By 1823, they relocated to Buckingham County, likely overseeing Snowden until Randolph Jefferson's estate was distributed beginning in 1826. Shortly afterwards, Lewis Jefferson took possession of his future farm on Buckingham's Sharps Creek, located fifteen miles northeast of the courthouse. A 531-acre plantation known as Millbrook, the farm was modest compared to Snowden's 2,000 acres on the James River, but it was Lewis Jefferson's own to develop as he pleased.[6]

In the fall of 1828, a new union invigorated Lewis Jefferson's prospects yet again—both personally and professionally. About forty years old, Jefferson married after at least ten years as a widower. His bride, Elizabeth Ann "Bettie" Moorman, was at least twenty years his junior. Unlike Randolph Jefferson's ill-fated marriage to Mitchie B. Pryor, Lewis Jefferson's second marriage lasted for thirty years—a good match and a financially sound one. Soon, Lewis Jefferson was the new owner of the Moorman homeplace in Albemarle County, known as Rock Island.[7]

Despite the acquisition of Rock Island and other land in Albemarle County, Jefferson and his family did not immediately leave Buckingham, continuing to live on and expand the Sharps Creek plantation. There, their daughter, Mary Elizabeth Jefferson, was born in about 1830.[8]

The dwelling house at Millbrook was likely constructed at least in part by Lewis Jefferson, possibly elaborated by his son, Elbridge, and later expanded by the subsequent owner, Matt Moseley. A cryptic note survives on a photocopy showing two views of the house. Neither signed nor dated, the note identifies the house as the Moseley home near Tucker, Virginia, and goes on to claim it was "built by Thomas Jefferson for a nephew—Monticello his home in Charlottesville is about 30 miles from here." Given that Lewis Jefferson did not establish himself on this farm until between 1826 and 1828, and that President Thomas Jefferson died in 1826, his architectural advice was not available for his nephew.[9]

Architectural historian S. Allen Chambers, an expert on Thomas Jefferson's dwelling at Poplar Forest, evaluated the Jefferson-Moseley house, drawing the following conclusions:

> The only thing at all Jeffersonian about the house is the lunette in the pediment of the portico. This makes me think the portico may be a bit older than it appears; i.e. the scroll-sawn trim may have been added later. The lunette in a portico pediment (which can be seen in the facade of Poplar Forest) is something Jefferson apparently devised out of whole cloth, and became, if not a standard feature, at least an often-used one in area houses of the mid-19th century. I would date this dwelling as no earlier than 1830, and think it may well have been built by or for Robert Lewis Jefferson when he moved to the property. The shallow-gabled roof is much more Greek than Roman (i.e. Jeffersonian), and could be as late as 1850.[10]

∼

By 1834, Lewis Jefferson moved to Albemarle County and, before 1842, he legally conveyed Millbrook, now 666 ½ acres, to his bachelor son. Elbridge G. Jefferson was over thirty years old when, on October 27, 1845, he married Mary Cabell Horsley in Nelson County. It is likely that Elbridge had known Mary all his life, having grown up among relations that involved several prominent Amherst/Nelson County families, some of whom were his father's business partners.[11]

In 1846, Elbridge Jefferson's grandfather, the well-to-do William Jordan, died in Nelson County. His son, William C. Jordan; J. M. Loving (daughter Sarah Jordan's husband); and Elbridge witnessed Jordan's will, in which he was left a substantial bequest.

> Fourthly, I give and bequeath unto my grandson Elbridge Jefferson the following Slaves, Armistead, Phillis, Dick, John, Louisanna, William and Nancy, with the increase of the Females. But for his life only. And at his death to pass to the lawful issue of his body, should he have any, and in default of having such issue, then to be sold, and the proceeds of the said property to be divided equally between William C. Jordan and Sarah W. Loving, or their respective heirs. I also direct that such sums of money as I have lent to the said Eldridge [sic] Jefferson as will appear by reference to his notes and bonds in my possession. Should he the said Eldridge Jefferson die without lawful issue, shall also be collected from his the said Eldridge Jeffersons Estate, and the amount divided equally between the said William and the said Sarah, or their heirs, precisely as directed with the slave property aforesaid.[12]

～

Over the next two decades, Elbridge's wealth steadily grew. By 1860, the forty-six-year-old planter owned $7,000 in real estate in Buckingham County and $35,000 in personal property, which included thirty-three slaves, some of whom worked his 300 improved acres. His dairy cattle provided enough butter for the neighborhood and, like his uncle, Peter Field Jefferson, Elbridge kept bees.[13]

In 1860, an overseer named Richard Robertson (age 26), lived with the Jeffersons, freeing Elbridge for pursuits other than tending his crops and super-vising the agricultural slaves. Mary (age 38) was the mother of three surviving children: "Sallie A." (age 11), Elbridge Gerry, Jr., called "Gary" (age 7), and Lindsay Bolling, called "Bolling" (age 5). On June 28, 1861, Sallie died of "dropsy"—a condition characterized by tissue swelling and edema. She was twelve years, three months, and twenty-five days old. Mary Jefferson died the next year, on December 2, 1862, of "dropsy of the heart." Married seventeen years, she was forty years old.[14]

~

As Elbridge G. Jefferson matured, he took on broader responsibilities in his community. During the 1840s, he rose to the rank of Captain in the 24th Regiment of the Buckingham Militia, as his grandfather, Randolph Jefferson, had before him. His duties included acting as superintendent of elections for the company, which he did in October of 1848 and April of 1849, reporting by letter to the Governor of Virginia in Richmond. On May 5, 1849, Elbridge was promoted to Major in the place of William W. Newton, who was promoted to Lt. Colonel.[15]

In addition to being a significant planter in the county, Elbridge was a member of Sharon Baptist Church and became one of Buckingham County's spiritual leaders. Since the early 1830s, the congregation had held services at Pine Grove Meeting House. In 1854, they voted to build a new church. E. G. Jefferson and William P. Snead were appointed to raise funds, with Jefferson as the Foreman of the Building Committee. By 1855, he was licensed to preach by Sharon Baptist Church and was ordained in 1857. The following year, he and Rev. J. H. Fox established Gooseberry Baptist Church in Buckingham.[16]

Lewis Jefferson may have influenced his son's interest in the Baptist Church or possibly the other way around. In 1851, Lewis and Elizabeth Ann Jefferson donated an acre of land in Albemarle County to the Ballinger Creek Regular Baptist Church, where Rev. Martin Dawson preached. It was described as being "on the South side of the Road leading to Warren & bounded by the Road on the North East side on which lot now stands a house built for a Church."[17]

On March 13, 1858, Robert Lewis Jefferson died of cancer at his home near Porter's Precinct in southern Albemarle. He was seventy-two years old. In his will, Lewis left half of "Porter's Precinct" (a 26-acre development) to Elbridge in "fee simple." The other half went to his sister. Lewis provided amply for his wife Elizabeth Ann, leaving their home, Rock Island, its contents, numerous slaves, and farmland, for her use during her lifetime, on the condition that she not remarry. She remained single, long outliving both her husband and her stepson. As a result, Elbridge never received his bequest of two slaves, Leanne and Daniel, who were left to him by his father, following the death of his widow Elizabeth Ann.[18]

In 1860, Mary Elizabeth (Jefferson) Gantt, was the mother of five children. Elizabeth Ann Jefferson and the Gantt family managed two plantations, Rock Castle and Porter's. Mental deficiency manifested again in this Jefferson line.

That year, seven-year-old Thomas Jefferson Gantt was enumerated on the federal population census as "idiotic."[19]

~

During the 1850s and 1860s, Elbridge G. Jefferson took on a series of duties in the larger Jefferson family. Trusted and respected by his wealthy uncle, Elbridge was named as one of the executors in Peter Field Jefferson's 1854 will. He was also designated as trustee for Jefferson's dependent adult sons, Thomas Jefferson and Peter Field Jefferson, Jr. On April 15, 1864, he purchased many items at his uncle's estate sale, an indication he envisioned an expanding future.[20]

In August of 1865, when most of Buckingham County was struggling in the immediate post-war months, Elbridge Jefferson, in partnership with James M. Dunkum and John P. Jones, purchased Diana Mills for $5,000. Before the Civil War, when the mill was still owned by William J. Fontaine, it was valued at $6,000. Fontaine reported that his water-powered grist mill ground wheat and corn, employing one man, whom he paid $30 per month.[21]

Powered by the Slate River and located on today's Route 671, five miles east of Highway 20, Diana Mills had been in existence since about 1835. In addition to the mill, the site once included a post office, three stores, and several dwellings.[22] In 1867, when the mill was advertised for sale again, it was described as follows:

> ... situated on Slate River, in the county of Buckingham, together with the dwellings, store-houses and land thereto attached, or belonging.
>
> The MILL is in good order, having been recently refitted for manufacturing flour—has two pairs of burrs, a never-failing supply of water, and is located in a fine wheat and corn section, being one of the best and most profitable mills in the country. This is also a good location for a county store—formerly sustained two—both of which store-houses are in good repair.
>
> There are also two neat and comfortable dwellings on the premises.[23]

Then, within a few months of the purchase, Elbridge G. Jefferson, who was fully engaged in his work and community, died suddenly on September 10, 1865. About fifty years old, he left no will and Capt. John Clark Turner was appointed guardian to his two sons. For a time, his brother-in-law, Albert W. Gantt, was named Administrator of the substantial estate. The estate remained open for many years, while assets were liquidated and chancery cases were initiated;

Gantt and Turner represented the boys. In at least two cases, suits languished, undetermined.[24]

Capt. Turner preserved at least some of the Jefferson boys' wealth in the financially challenging, immediate post-Civil War environment. In 1870, when many in Buckingham County were destitute, mature scholars Elbridge Gerry, Jr. (age 17), and Bolling (age 15), owned real estate valued at $3,000 and personal property valued at $7,000. In the post-war era, given that slaves had been emancipated, this is an exceptional amount of personal property for anyone in Buckingham County, particularly for orphaned minors.[25]

In 1880, these Jefferson brothers were still boarding with John C. Turner: "Gerry" (age 27) was a trader and Bolling (age 25) was a laborer, suggesting he may have had limited skills or intellect. Their father's estate remained unsettled, and their former home, Millbrook Farm, was not sold until 1882–1885.[26]

These Jefferson males did not fulfill their early promise and their lines ended with their deaths. In 1910, both men were living in Buckingham County and, oddly, both were enumerated as fifty-six years old. Gary was single, a farmer, renting his farm and living alone. Bolling was also single, a farm laborer, boarding with the merchant Joseph K. Irving and his family. Bolling died on July 26, 1916 of acute nephritis. His brother, Gary, followed two years later on March 20, 1918, dying at University Hospital in Charlottesville of heart failure, complicated by chronic intestinal nephritis.[27]

It is particularly unusual that these Jefferson brothers did not marry, especially considering the lack of available men in the county following the Civil War. Reasons for this and for their financial decline are unknown.

Lilburne Lewis:
Virginia Gentry Gone Wrong

L ilburne Lewis, first cousin to Peter Field Jefferson, was also the father-in-law he never knew. By the time Peter Field married Lewis' daughter, Jane Woodson Lewis, in 1819, Lilburne Lewis had been dead for over seven years. His horrible legacy of murder and suicide, however, lived on well into the 20th century, haunting members of the Lewis and Jefferson families.

In *Jefferson's Nephews*, Boynton Merrill, Jr. wrote the definitive version of Lilburne Lewis's life and violent death, detailing the murder of his slave George, a killing so heinous it would become legend and serve as a cautionary tale against the evils of slavery. In addition to the material held in the court archives of Livingston County, Kentucky (where the crime took place), Merrill compares four versions of the story, "None . . . are at the same time, both detailed and of unquestionable reliability."[1]

Importantly, the only witnesses to the murder were Lilburne, his brother Isham, and possibly other slaves. At that time in Kentucky, a black man could not testify in court against a white man and there are no records of what the slaves might have seen. Lilburne died and Isham escaped without making a full confession. Yet, this did not stop journalists from imagining elaborate details of what took place during George's murder and the suicide pact between the two brothers at the Rocky Hill graveyard, which ended in only Lilburne's death.

Beginning in late April of 1812, the Lewis brothers' crime was told and retold, damning this branch of the Lewis family to generations of condemnation. The story grew far beyond "news," becoming part of the national consciousness, the gossip persisting beyond the life of Lilburne's children, his grandchildren, and even his great-grandchildren. The resulting shame was undoubtedly a shaping influence in the life of Jane Woodson Lewis, Lilburne Lewis' oldest child and the wife of Peter Field Jefferson. What follows are several versions of the tale, which, like a game of telephone, compound errors from one telling to the next.[2]

∼

During the era of Reconstruction and beyond, newspapers across the nation printed stories of the days of slavery so recently passed. By then, Peter Field and Jane W. (Lewis) Jefferson were both dead, however, the descendants of Lilburne Lewis, which included the children of Peter Field Jefferson, still bore the brunt of both whispered and published judgements against their family. The personal narrative which follows was originally printed in the *Banner*, published in Princeton, Kentucky and was reprinted in Louisville, Kentucky's *Courier-Journal* on December 24, 1873. The *Chicago Daily Tribune* ran the story on December 28, 1873 and, on January 1, 1874, the article was published in Rochester, New York's *Democrat and Chronicle*.

It appeared in Frederick Douglass' *New National Era and Citizen*, running as a front-page story entitled, "An Elevating (?) Institution. Some frightful Reminiscences of Slavery." The author's name was not printed, nor were the names of the "two other persons now living, who were then very young" at the time of George's death.[3]

The article contains minor errors too numerous to point out. One of the most glaring includes identifying Jane W. (Lewis) Jefferson's grandfather, Charles Lewis, as a doctor. He was not one in Virginia, nor did he practice medicine in Kentucky. He was, however, a Colonel in the Virginia Militia and used that title. He was also a business man, a developer, invested in a stage coach line and owned a tavern, as well as being a planter. It was Lilburne Lewis, not his father Charles, who established the farm called Rocky Hill near Smithland, Kentucky.[4]

In this article, several of the Lewis children are unaccounted for. Another is mistakenly present. Lilburne's brother, Charles Lewis, Jr., was not at the scene of the crime, nor could he have shot his brother. Charles died of inflammation of the head in Louisiana, in the autumn of 1806. If anyone cried out "Oh, brothers, the judgment of God is upon us!", it was Isham Lewis, who committed more than one crime during 1811–1812.[5]

"Mr. Samuel McCanly," who received a cryptic note from Lilburne Lewis, was actually "James McCawley," a tavern owner, justice of the peace, and one of Lilburne Lewis' executors.[6]

In spite of its many errors, the article is fascinating. Like all oral history, the details reveal a great deal about the values of the teller, as well as the community and time in which he lived. What follows is the narrative in its entirety as it appeared in the *New National Era and Citizen*.

An Elevating (?) Institution.
Some frightful Reminiscences of Slavery.

In presenting the following narrative, I have to depend upon my memory for the facts detailed to me more than fifty years ago by persons who were fully informed on the subject, aided at present by two other persons now living, who were then very young, and indistinct as to their recollections of the strange occurrences. In addition, the records of Livingston Circuit and County Courts furnish some further light.

Some time between the years of 1805 and 1807 a gentleman by the name of Dr. Chas. Lewis with his family, moved from Virginia and settled on a military tract of land on the Ohio River, some five or six miles above the town Smithland, in Livingston county. His family consisted of his wife, three sons—Lilburne, Charles, and Isham—two daughters and some ten or more slaves. That part of the county was then wild, and its population sparse. The Doctor selected the place to build, cleared away the forest, and erected log cabins for the whites and blacks of the family, opened up a farm, put it in cultivation, and gave his residence the name of Rocky Hill. His eldest son, Lilburne, was also a married man, he and his wife residing in his father's family at Rocky Hill. In 1807 the Doctor's lady died; soon after her death Mrs. Lilburne Lewis also died. They were buried at Rocky Hill. Their graves were enclosed by a post-and-rail fence. The whole of the white family in their intercourse with the inhabitants had made the impression that, in point of literary attainments, elegance of manners, and accomplished demeanor, they had no equals in the county, and had occupied as high a position and as great social advantages as any in their native State. It was, however noticed, that the slaves were treated with cruel severity.

In 1809 Lilburne was married to a young lady of the county, Miss L. Rutter, her family of high standing, and herself faultless in form and beauty and pre-possessing accomplishments. The Doctor about that time left Rocky Hill with his daughter, and went to Salem, or that neighborhood, leaving the farm and most of the slaves to his three sons, Lilburne having taken his bride there. It was soon reported that the marriage turned out to be an unhappy one. Mrs. Lewis from some cause becoming extremely unhappy, it was supposed on account of the

BARBAROUS TREATMENT OF THE SLAVES.

In the year 1811 she gave birth to a son. On the 16th day of December of that year she noticed unusual deportment and private consultations between her husband and his two brothers. George, a half-grown boy, a waiter about the house, who had repeatedly run away when whipped, that evening was waiting on the table at supper, and let some articles of furniture fall and break. Isham Lewis looked at the other two brothers across the table with a significant nod and said, "That will do." This was noticed by Mrs. Lewis.

Immediately after the meal was over, it being dark, the brothers left the house, repaired to one of the negro cabins, had a large hickory log fire made, and summoned George and all the rest of the slaves to that cabin. When all were in the object was explained to them by Lilburne Lewis, to the effect that their disobedient conduct had been such that it had become

NECESSARY TO KILL ONE OF THEM

that the rest might know their fate unless they acted better in the future; told what George had done, and that they were going to kill and burn him up. An axe was brought in, George tied and laid on the floor, and one of the negro men directed and forced to chop off each hand and each foot, then each arm and leg half way to the elbow and knee, and so on until the body was reached. The brothers stood around with pistols in hand to shoot the negro with the axe if he failed to obey. The horror commenced when the first blow severed a hand, and the shrieks of the victim reached the ears of Mrs. Lewis. She became panic-stricken with terror, until her cries were heard by all in the house where the murderous butchery was going on. The amputation proceeded as directed; each piece as severed was caught up and thrown on the fire. Before life was extinguished the head was chopped from the body: then it and the body committed to flames. All remained in the cabin until the entire mass appeared to be consumed effectually. The door was then opened, and the servants admonished that if any of them should ever whisper what had taken place, they should be served in the same way.

About 2 o'clock the three brothers left the cabin and started to the dwelling. On their way they were startled by what appeared to them to be the heavy sound of distant thunder. In an instant the earth beneath their feet heaved and swelled, and shook with such violence that the parties could with difficulty keep from falling. Charles cried out, "Oh, brothers, the judgment of God is upon us!" This is the first shock of the great earthquakes of 1811 and 1812 in the valley of the Mississippi. They hurried to the house, and found Mrs. Lewis on the floor stupefied with terror.

George, being a house-boy, was soon missed by the persons in the habit of visiting the family. Answers to inquiries about him were not satisfactory. The other servants when interrogated expressed by looks that were interpreted to mean that they knew something that they would not tell. Eventually, in a month or so after, a dog was found gnawing

A HALF-CONSUMED HUMAN FOOT

near the premises. A gentleman by the name of Josiah Hibbs, with others of the neighbors, in the absence of the three brothers, searched the cabin where the tragedy was committed, and found the burnt bones of the human frame. The Lewises were arrested, and gave bail for their appearance at the ensuing term of the March Circuit Court, at which Lilburne and Isham were indicted for the murder of George. In the mean time the relations of Mrs. Lewis learning that she was in great fear for her safety, went after her, and took her and child to her father. The two Lewises indicted were again allowed bail by the Court. It seems shortly after Lilburne and Charles agreed to commit suicide within the enclosure surrounding the graves of their mother and Lilburne's first wife. On the 9th of April following, Lilburne made his will, and, after disposing of his property, he made at the end of it the two following requests:

ROCKY HILL, April 9, 1812.
Mr. Samuel McCanly:

I have fallen a victim to my beloved but cruel Letitia. I die in the hope of being united with my other wife in heaven. Take care of this [will] and come here, that we may be decently buried. Adieu.

G. H. & L. L.[7]

Within this enclosure myself and brother request to be interred in the same coffin.

ROCKY HILL, April 10, 1812.

MY BELOVED BUT CRUEL LETITIA: Receive this as a pledge of my forgiveness to your connection. The day of judgment is to come. I owe you no malice; but die on account of your absence and my dear little son James. Adieu, my love.

LILBURNE LEWIS.

A servant was immediately dispatched with this to Smithland, and delivered it to Squire McCanly, who on its reception and reading the request to him, hastened with others of his friends to the place designated, and found Lilburne dead within the enclosure,

SHOT THROUGH THE HEART,

surrounded by a pool of blood, and Charles on the outside with two rifles. He said Lilburne had accidentally shot himself while making preparation for the fulfillment of their purpose for both to die at the same time. That the sight of his brother struggling in death had deterred him from his purpose. Lilburne was buried beside his first wife. Isham was never heard of after; Charles but once, then among the troops at the battle of New Orleans.

Their father, Dr. Charles Lewis, had a public sale, sold all his personal property and went back to Virginia and died. He and his family when they came back to Kentucky claimed to be descendants of the Indian Princess Pocahontas. The doctor had been at one time very wealthy, entertaining a great deal of company, surrounded by the gay trappings of opulence and luxury, and associating with the most distinguished families and personages in that refined State. Having met a reversal of fortune, and lost his property and his former position in the society in which he moved, he estranged himself from all he held so dear, and

SOUGHT OBSCURITY

in the dark and gloomy haunts of the then-lonely backwoods of Kentucky. It is difficult to philosophize upon the events narrated as to the death of George, and the more than savage feeling that prompted the act. No people of any clime are more justly proud of and devoted to the land of their nativity than the Virginians are. None, when away, cherish more fond and vivid memory of the pleasing scenery and happy days they have enjoyed. In no land or country have the better feelings of the human heart and the nobler qualities of our nature been more assiduously cultivated and refined than in Virginia; how such departure could have happened with three of her well-educated sons, is an unaccountable mystery. It may be possible that their losses and reversed fortune and estrangement from all they deemed so desirable in the land they so much loved, with Lilburne's domestic troubles, so wrought upon them that they became reckless and desperate to such an extent as to be regardless of their own lives and that of their servants.

It will not detract from the interest of this narrative when the reader is informed that Mrs. Dr. Charles Lewis was the sister of President Thomas Jefferson. The old farm at Rocky Hill is waste and overgrown with brush-wood, brambles, and other wild forest growth, with nothing to point to the place of the dead. It stands to-day a melancholy monument of an unfortunate family in times long ago.[8]

~

A few days later on January 6, 1874, the same story was printed in the *Indiana State Sentinel*. Entitled, "A BLOODY EPISODE. A DIREFUL HISTORY. A BACKWOODS FAMILY OF THE OLDEN TIME—THE LEWISES OF LIVINGSTON COUNTY, KY.,—WORSE THAN THE BENDERS," it began: "A writer to the Princeton (Ky.,) Banner gives the following wonderful history. . . ."[9] Interestingly, this version was incomplete and did not include the sympathetic explanation for Lilburne Lewis' madness nor did it mention the connection to Lucy Lewis and President Thomas Jefferson.

~

The gruesome story, revived again about twenty years later, in late 1892 and early 1893, was published in Hartford, Kentucky's *Hartford Weekly Herald* and Marion, Kentucky's *Crittenden Press*, reprinted from the *Paducah Standard*. Commemorating eighty years since the crime's occurrence, the story had taken on mythic proportions, the passage of time compounding errors in the tale.

Significant errors include: Charles Lilburne Lewis married Lucy Jefferson, not Mary H. Jefferson, in Virginia, not in Kentucky. They lived near Birdsville, not Birdsall, Kentucky, where Lilburne Lewis' first wife, Elizabeth Jane Woodson (Lewis) Lewis, died on April 25, 1809. Lucy (Jefferson) Lewis died in 1810, not in 1807, and her son, Randolph, who died early in 1811, could not have witnessed the murder of the slave George. Isham Lewis, not Randolph, was Lilburne's partner in crime. Implicit in these errors, the memory of the innocent Randolph Lewis was maligned and slandered. What went through the minds of his descendants when he was wrongly attached to George's murder we shall likely never know.[10]

As for where and how George was murdered, versions of the story vary. The county coroner reported that a deep wound in the slave's skull caused his death.[11]

Filled with errors and assumptions, this version strived to get into the twisted minds of the Lewis brothers, providing a vivid, if inaccurate, version of the crime. It also acts as a cautionary tale—complete, à la the brothers Grimm, with ghosts and frightened children, who should stay out of the woods, day or night.

The article's headline promised, and delivered, a sensational story.

A TRUE STORY,
Of an Ancient Tragedy in Livingston County.
A Negro Boy's Feet and Hands Cut Off
—Retribution Swift and Sure—
The Wrath of God of Heaven
(Paducah Standard.)

The old town of Smithland—old when Paducah was in swaddling clothes—once the seat of power of Western Kentucky—and the place from which sprung many of our own leading and most prosperous citizens—this old town is rich in reminiscence and a startling story. Her musty and time-worn records are burdened with cold and crystallized facts; but behind many of these facts which alone have been preserved, and leading up to them have been enacted the most thrilling and

BLOOD-CURDLING TRAGEDIES.

We are prone to discourse upon the prevalence of crime in these modern times, and to deplore the total depravity and horrible fiendishness which often characterize their commission. But we have never heard of any tragedy, either in ancient or modern times, in the old world or in the new, in the north or in the south, in the east or on the extreme borders of Western civilization, committed by christian, by pagan, or by savage, more intensely and thrillingly terrible than the one of which we shall write in the paragraphs that follow. Every statement is authentic, as all that we say is matter of record at the county seat of Livingston county, and can easily be verified. But to

THE STORY.

In the year 1811 a man named Charles Lewis married Miss Mary H. Jefferson in Livingston county. Their bones now rest in the tomb at Rocky Hill, near Birdsall. Their issue was two sons, one of whom was named Randolph and the other Lilburn. Lilburn, who had already buried one wife, married Miss Letitia Rutter, to console him for his loss. Among their possessions was a little Negro boy, who, by some active carelessness, had mortally offended Lilburn Lewis. Now comes one of the horrors. It is related that he, assisted by his brother Randolph, took the little trembling wretch to an out-of-the-way place, and

CUT HIS HANDS OFF

One by one at the wrists. The piteous wails and the heart-rending screams of the sufferer were unheeded. While yet the mangled wrists dripped with blood, the inhuman torturers chopped off both of his feet at the ankles. The air was split right and left again and again, by the wild shrieks of the mutilated lad, and yet these fiends in human form heeded them not. On the contrary, they seemed to take a devilish delight in his writhing and contortions as they gathered

FAGGOTS.

What were faggots used for in the days of the martyrs of old? "But you do not say that these brutes burned the boy alive?" The reader inquires, with a countenance aghast. That is exactly what they did. Slowly, surrounded by scorching flames, the poor wretch's skin shriveled, his flesh sizzled and fried until amidst the most frightful bodily contortions his soul took flight. And in a short time the flames flickered and went out, and nothing was left of what was once one of God's creatures but a handful of charred and crumbling bones. But

RETRIBUTION

Was certain, and swift! As soon as the deed became known, the greatest indignation prevailed in the neighborhood; and no one was more horrified than Letitia, Lilburn's wife, and her parents, the Rutters. The former at once deserted her husband, and her father threatened to prosecute these worse than savages. The result was that both Randolph and Lilburn Lewis began to feel very uncomfortable. They were not only afraid of prosecution and punishment of the courts, but they dreaded the social ostracism which would be sure to follow. Then conscience, which My Lord Hamlet says makes cowards of us all, began to work, if such wretches can be said to have consciences, and they were continually haunted with remorse. While in this frame of mind, the earth along the Ohio and Cumberland rivers was severely shaken by an earthquake. With blanched faces and frightened mien these brothers looked at each other in silence for a moment when one exclaimed, "The

WRATH OF GOD OF HEAVEN

Is descending upon us!" The other acquiesced.

They could not sleep, for every time they closed their eyes the distorted countenance and burning body of the footless and handless little negro boy danced in hideous delusion before them!

They could not sleep, because every time they courted Morpheus he was driven away by the dying shrieks of their victim as they again and again pierced their ears.

They could not sleep, because Remorse, that implacable foe to crime, occupied the couch with them, prodding them into wakefulness every time they began to sink into oblivion.

They could not sleep, because the wrath of God was indeed upon them, and the fear of hell and eternal damnation was in their blackened hearts.

When sleep is impossible, what?

INSANITY OR DEATH!

These men could not sleep, and they concluded to die. It is hard to make up one's mind to die, but having done so, death comes easy. Having concluded to shuffle off, they chose shotguns as the weapons, and the grave of Lilburn's first wife was selected as the place. All arrangements being completed, they repaired thither and proceeded to business. It was arranged that each should kill himself, the guns to be discharged simultaneously at the given signal. The handkerchief was dropped—(we will suppose that to have been the signal), and—bang! Were both guns discharged? No, only one, and Randolph Lewis

GAZED DOWN IN HORROR

Upon the mangled corpse of his only brother. Could Retribution go further? He stood there paralyzed, frightened, frenzied, but riveted to the spot. He pulled the trigger, but the priming had failed to ignite. Was this the work of Omnipotence that he might be further punished upon earth for his heinous and unparalleled crime? Be that as it may, he was so completely unnerved in the lonely presence of death with another sleeping beneath the sod upon which

THE BLEEDING CORPSE

Of her suicide husband then lay, that he had not either the will nor the physical power to again attempt to carry out his part in the terrible fraternal dual agreement. As soon as he was able to comprehend the situation, he slowly and sadly turned away, but he went to his home no more. He walked on, and on, and on, until far beyond the confines of his country and his State. It was known that he afterwards enlisted in the war then raging, but he never returned, and his fate is to this day

A MYSTERY.

There is little more to tell. The next day the body of Lilburn Lewis was found lying across his first wife's grave, and in spite of his wicked and unpardonable course on earth, kind hands tenderly laid him beside her in the ground, in accordance with the written request which was embodied in the note to his second wife, Letitia, found upon his person after he was dead. In this note he upbraided Letitia, and charged her with having driven him to the awful crime of

SELF-DESTRUCTION.

The actors in this tragedy are all long ago dead. But their descendants still live in the neighborhood where these thrilling scenes were enacted. The Rutters, descendants of Letitia's parents, now reside near Hampton, in Livingston county, and are very wealthy. On April 9, 1812, Lilburn Lewis made his will, which is still on record and throws a great deal of light on this affair. The graves of

THE MURDERER SUICIDE

And of his first wife are on an elevation, and are unmarked by stone or epitaph. For years, world-wide stories have been afloat, regarding certain shrieks that are heard on stormy nights, accompanied by the booming of a gun. None, even of mature years, who have heard this story, pass that way after nightfall, fearful that the dead will stalk and gibber in their pathway. And little children on their way to school, hurry swiftly by with dreaded glances toward the spot, and while their breath comes quick and short, they say not a word. The subject is too awful to mention among them.[12]

～

It is perplexing that neither account of that terrible night mentions the Lewis children. Jane, the eldest, was thirteen. Lucy, Lilburne, Elizabeth, and Robert were all younger and James Rutter Lewis was not yet born.[13]

If the children of Livingston County dreaded this gruesome story and eschewed the spot of Lilburne Lewis' suicide for decades after the event, what did his daughter Jane suffer? Was she there the night the George was murdered? Did she hear the slave boy's screams? Did the horror and the shame of her father's crimes haunt her until her death?

～

Following the murder, Charles Lilburne Lewis and his remaining family were in dire circumstances. His wife Lucy was dead; sons Charles, Jr., Randolph, and Lilburne were dead; son Isham had escaped charges as an accessory to George's murder and fled Kentucky; daughters Lucy, Martha, and Nancy were unmarried dependents. Additionally, Charles Lilburne Lewis had the sudden burden of Lilburne's minor children. In desperation, he wrote to his brother-in-law, Thomas Jefferson, asking for a loan.

5 August 1813

Dear Sir

myself & daughters being in reduced circomstances have been constrained to ask of several of our friends in Virginia if conveniant the friendly assistance of a few dollars I take the liberty to ask the same of you I can ashure you my dear Sir nothing short of rail want would or could induce me to make such an application to my relations and friends my Friend mr Woods will be the barer of this letter should you be inclin'd to assist us he will be a safe hand to send by I hope you will excuse me for asking this favour. want alone is the rail cause my daughters Joins me in Love & respect

Chas L. Lewis[14]

～

In Kentucky, time covered the physical tracks of the crime and the last imprints of the Lilburne Lewis family and their home at Rocky Hill. This description was published in 1894:

> ... The Lewis home, together with the fences inclosing it and the little graveyard on Rocky Point [sic], were long ago swept away by a forest fire. Noble specimens of oak, hickory, beech and walnut remain unscathed by fire, the years, and the sad fortunes of the family they sheltered, over three-quarters of a century ago. A cellar marks the site of the house, and several piles of rough stone attest their former service in chimneys. In the extreme rear of the home grounds is a pile of stone that is supposed to have constituted the chimney of the cabin where the negro George met his horrible fate.
>
> Bushes and tangled vines run wildly together over the three graves. The rough, uninscribed stones that once marked them have fallen to earth, and the spot itself is only to be found by the aid of a guide. Hope Cowper, an ancient colored man who has lived in the neighborhood all his life, acts in this capacity to the few whose interest is sufficient to carry them over a rocky, shrub-grown, winding and well night [sic] inaccessible way to behold the grave of Thomas Jefferson's sister and that of her unfortunate son and his wife. The property now belongs to a youth of eighteen or nineteen years named Carson Nelson. Mr. W. C. Watts and Hon. John K. Hendrick, of Smithland, who recently visited the site of the Lewis home and the old graveyard, say that not only is the river valley portion of the Lewis land quite fertile, but the limestone plateau is remarkably rich, and that there is on the property a deposit of oolite stone that will someday render it highly valuable.

ATLANTA H. TAYLOR POOL[15]

In 1874, one member of the Lewis family tried to correct at least one of the persistent myths about the murder/suicide. Charles L. Peyton, grandson of Charles Lilburne Lewis and nephew of Lilburne Lewis, wrote a letter to the Editor of the *Paducah Kentuckian*, published in Louisville, concerning an article reprinted in the *Christian Observer* and the *Atlanta Constitution*. He deftly cleared his grandfather's name without mentioning his uncle as the murderer:

JEFFERSON'S SISTER.
She Was Not the Wife of a Kentucky Murderer.

The following paragraph printed a short time since in the Paducah Kentuckian, elicited a letter of explanation from one of Jefferson's sister's descendants, a copy of which is also appended:

"It is not generally known that a sister of Thomas Jefferson, author of the Declaration of Independence, is buried at Rocky Hill, two miles back of Birdsville, on the Ohio river, in Livingston county, Kentucky. She was the wife of Dr. Charles Lewis, who had the reputation of being a cruel and bad man, and who was killed on the Illinois shore by a mob, after being arrested on the charge of murder."

"NEAR LEWISBURG, GREENBRIER Co.

West Virginia, Nov. 20, 1874

Editor *Kentuckian*: I was shocked to find some weeks ago the inclosed publication in the *Christian Observer*, published in Louisville, Ky. The 'sister of Thomas Jefferson' referred to was Lucy Jefferson, and was married to Col. Chas. Lilburn Lewis, an officer in the revolutionary war, and lived and died respected by all who knew him.

"In about 1816 [sic], he and his two married sons sold a large landed estate in Albemarle county, Va., and emigrated to Livingston county, Ky., with their families, with the exception of two daughters, one of whom (my mother) then married to Craven Peyton, and the other to Thomas Jefferson, Jr., son of Randolph Jefferson, only brother of President Jefferson, who is still living in the county of Fluvanna, Va., at the advanced age of ninety-two.

"Some years after the death of Mrs. Lewis (my grandmother) his son-in-law, Thomas Jefferson, Jr., went to Livingston county, Kentucky, and brought his father-in-law, Col. Charles Lilburn Lewis, back to Albemarle county, Virginia, and he died at my father's, in Albemarle, in 1828, in the eighty-fourth year of his age an honored member of a christian church.

"As a grandson who knew and revered his grandfather, I give you the above unvarnished facts; how far they correspond with your statement, I leave you to judge.

"CHARLES L. PEYTON."[16]

∾

Sixty years after Charles L. Peyton strove to correct the misconceptions about the Lewis murder, noted local historian Otto A. Rothert presented a paper to the Filson Club, Louisville's historical society, dedicated to preserving the history of Kentucky and the Ohio Valley Region. The content of his presentation was reported in Louisville's *Courier-Journal* under the headline, "Acts of Jefferson's Nephews In Horrible Crime Recalled":

> How nephews of Thomas Jefferson were the leading actors of a crime of particular atrocity was related before the Filson Club Monday night by Otto A. Rothert, secretary of the Filson Club, in a paper on "The tragedy of the Lewis Brothers," a Western Kentucky tragedy "of the olden days."
>
> "This tragedy has not only never been recounted with historical accuracy, but it has never before been fully told by any single writer," Mr. Rothert said. "Such being the case, I am quoting from and paraphrasing the four chief now-known sources and hope of presenting the story both fully and accurately for the first time, also in the hope of checking the distorted tales now extent."[17]

While Mr. Rothert repeated some minor errors, his version of the tragic story was far more accurate than the accounts appearing in newspapers for over a century. Significantly, he noted that nothing was known about the fate of Letitia Rutter Lewis and her son. The newspaper reported that Rothert spent fifteen years collecting material concerning the Lewis family and that his work would be printed in the club's quarterly magazine.[18]

It would be nearly another four decades before Boynton Merrill published the definitive version of George's murder. His book, *The Jefferson Nephews*, still in print, preserves both the lives and the context of this Lewis family in rich detail. Combined with Robert Penn Warren's more imaginative prose poem, *Brother to Dragons*, posterity is left with a complex, and still fascinating, portrait of the extended Lewis-Randolph-Jefferson family.[19]

Jefferson Myths

Virginia Moore's highly readable history, *Scottsville on the James*, originally published in 1969 for the town's 250th anniversary, is a blend of documentable facts and a significant amount of oral tradition. Sometimes historic events are compressed or even rearranged to facilitate her narrative. Her anecdotes include several intriguing comments about Peter Field Jefferson and his family. One of her sources, George W. Foland, a descendant of Jefferson's daughter, Frances A. (Jefferson) Foland, apparently based his accounts on an article that ran in the *Richmond Dispatch* on February 25, 1900, for which there is no attributed author. Both the newspaper and George W. Foland make the perplexing mistake of calling President Thomas Jefferson's brother Bushrod, instead of Randolph, Jefferson.[1]

The *Dispatch* article is packed with errors, misconceptions, and fantasies about the Jefferson family at Snowden and Peter Field Jefferson's life in Scottsville. Virginia Moore borrowed many details from the newspaper article, including her description of Peter Field Jefferson, calling him "an eccentric genius"—which, indeed, he was.

The article, transcribed here in its entirety, is followed by corrections, comments, and a more accurate version of Thomas Jefferson's "Escape from Monticello."

A BIT OF HISTORY.
"Snowden" and Its Owner—Jefferson's Escape
(Correspondence of the Dispatch.)

SCOTTSVILLE, VA., February 23.—On one of the most commanding hills surrounding our town the grandest view that is to be had of the noble James River for three miles above and five miles below the town, stands on a beautiful plateau a quaint old mansion of one and a half stories and basement, built about one hundred years ago, and which for nearly three-quarters of a century was the home of an eccentric genius and quite a remarkable man, Peter Fields Jefferson, an own nephew of the immortal statesman, Thomas Jefferson, of Monticello. His father, Bushrod Jefferson, owned the beautiful estate called "Snowden," just across the river, which occupies the area of land almost enclosed by horseshoe bend of river, the town of Scottsville being opposite the toe of the horseshoe. This Bushrod Jefferson was a brother of President Jefferson. He came into possession of "Snowden" under peculiar circumstances. At that early day the lands along the James, especially the lowlands, were considered very unhealthy, and were consequently rated at very low prices, much lower than those in the mountain districts. A man named Lucid (called Ladd) was the owner of Snowden, and becoming involved in debt to the amount of $500, and unable to pay, his creditor threw him into jail, under the debtor law, which was then in force. After lingering some time in jail, which, with Albemarle Courthouse, was at that time located one mile above our town, on what is now the beautiful farm "Velmont," Laird [sic] was told by a friend that Mr. Jefferson was a man with plenty of ready money, and he might be able to manage with him to get him out of jail. So he immediately sent for him, and after a good deal of parlaying over the matter he proposed to Mr. Jefferson if he would pay the $500 for him and give him a barrel of rum he could take "Snowden." This proposition was accepted by Mr. Jefferson, and Snowden became his property.

His two sons, Peter Fields and Thomas Jefferson, were among the early settlers of Scottsville; Fields as he was called, engaged in merchandising, and owned a good many batteau freight-boats, that navigated the James from Richmond to Lynchburg, from which he made considerable money, but during the building of the James river and Kanawha canal the operatives were paid off mostly in State "scrip," instead of money, and Mr. Jefferson bought up all of this he could get, and turned it into State bonds, from which he realized a good profit. Being an uncommonly shrewd and close businessman, he had, it is thought, when the war between the States broke out, accumulated from $75,000 to $100,000. When in order to close up the matters of the estate, "Snowden" had to be sold at auction, Fields Jefferson intended to buy it; but another bidder, Mr. John L. Harris, offered him $1,000 not to bid against him, which Mr. Jefferson accepted, and Mr. Harris became the purchaser.

Soon after that, when the Winfrey place, a fine farm four miles below, was offered for sale, Mr. Jefferson bought it, and paid $20,000 cash down for it. During the war his estate became very much depleted, mainly on account of having made large loans to men who failed. He lost $35,000 by the failure of one man.

Mr. Jefferson toward the close of the war died at the home of his close friend, Mr. James Madison Noel, at the age of 77 years.

His grandson, Mr. Peter V. Foland, one of our most substantial citizens, who inherited a large portion of his estate, now owns and occupies the old home of this remarkable man.

Old citizens here say that when Thomas Jefferson made his escape from the hands of Tarleton, from Monticello, he came around to the mountains by blind pass until he struck the Rockfish river, which for a considerable distance is the boundary line between Albemarle and Nelson counties, and which he followed until he arrived at the ford, near Mount Alto. Crossing the river to the Nelson side he stopped at a man's house, who lived there, and after explaining to him the circumstances that brought him there he asked him to let him stay a while with him. But the man told him that Tarleton's men would certainly pass down that road, as it was the only road open to that section, and they would be sure to capture him if he stayed there but he could take him to a place of safety, about two miles up the river. This Mr. Jefferson readily agreed to, and he was conducted to the home of Mr. Thomas Farrar, where he stayed two weeks, and then came to Scottsville, and lived in a cave, under a large rock in the bluff, one mile below town, and was daily furnished with food from "Snowden" by his brother.

When the canal was built the celebrated rock and cave was destroyed, as they were just in the course of the canal.[2]

~

Within the article, the original owner of the property that became Snowden is compressed, confused, and conflated with the origins of Peter Jefferson's Shadwell, the Jefferson homeplace in Albemarle County near Thomas Jefferson's Monticello.[3]

More accurately, Peter Jefferson, father of President Thomas Jefferson, acquired the land at the Horseshoe Bend by both patent and purchase, eventually amassing a valuable plantation of 2,050 acres. Sections were purchased from Amos Ladd and two of his sons, John and Noble Ladd. No man named Lucid or Laird was involved in landownership at the Horseshoe Bend, however, Ladd was sometimes spelled "Lad." Importantly, it was Peter Jefferson who named Snowden after the Jefferson ancestral home in Wales, not Amos Ladd. He originally patented several hundred acres, which were then in Goochland County, described as lying opposite "Totero" Town, which referred to a long abandoned Native American village at the mouth of Totier Creek.

That any of the Ladd men were debtors is unlikely and has yet to be confirmed. This part of the story, as printed in Richmond's *Dispatch*, doubtless refers to a 225 acre parcel that was transferred to Peter Jefferson. It was originally surveyed for a man named David Watkins, who was proclaimed insolvent on June 30, 1747. The spicy addition of the "barrel of rum" as part of Peter Jefferson's payment for Snowden is borrowed from his more famous acquisition—the land that eventually became Shadwell. In 1736, Jefferson purchased that tract from his friend William Randolph. The payment included "Henry Weatherbourn's biggest bowl of Arrack punch."[4]

While Peter Field Jefferson was indeed a founding father and eager investor in Scottsville, his youngest brother, James Lilburne, initially owned more lots than either of his brothers, Thomas Jefferson, Jr. or Isham Randolph Jefferson. Brother Robert Lewis Jefferson preferred life as a planter, first farming in Buckingham County, then in southern Albemarle County at Porter's Precinct. Peter Field Jefferson's rise in Scottsville is well-documented. He did own small boats which ran on the James River before the coming of the canal and indeed made money in Virginia State Bonds. His house, which still sits on a bluff above the James River, was a bit less than one hundred years old in 1900. Known as Mount Walla, the date of construction is debated but does not predate 1828 and may have been built or elaborated by Peter Field Jefferson himself in about 1840. Additionally, the "beautiful farm" where old Albemarle Courthouse once sat was called Valmont, not Velmont.

The recollection of Peter Field Jefferson's loss of Snowden is extremely compressed and misleading, blending Capt. John Harris' purchase from Randolph Jefferson's estate and John L. Harris' purchase from Capt. John Harris' estate. If Peter Field Jefferson bid on Snowden, no evidence survives; however, he did purchase Winfrey's Tract, which turned out to be an unsatisfactory replacement for his birthplace.

The reference to an unclaimed debt of $35,000 is intriguing, though likely apocryphal. A pre-war inventory of Peter Field Jefferson's assets, taken in August of 1859, documents many loans but none of such magnitude. Nor was a loan of this size made from his estate before his death in 1861. There is no question that his fortune was devalued after the war, in part, because his executor accepted Confederate money for debts during the war years. To date, however, no one man's failure accounts for a missing $35,000.

The fanciful story of Thomas Jefferson's escape from Monticello, of course, did not involve Peter Field Jefferson, who was not yet born, but did incorporate Snowden and Randolph Jefferson. How convenient that the famous cave was destroyed during the creation of the canal, and how impossible. The canal ran on the north bank of the James River and the cave at Snowden, if it even existed, would have been located on the south bank.

The following is my analysis of the famous flight, originally published in the *Buckingham Beacon*.[5]

"Thomas Jefferson Did Not Sleep Here: The Cave at Snowden"

A few years ago, when I set out to write about Thomas Jefferson's only brother, Randolph, a heated discussion was in progress concerning the father of Sally Heming's son, Eston; both were the property of Thomas Jefferson. The DNA of Eston's descendants matched Jefferson family DNA and it quickly became apparent that I would be asked my opinion concerning Randolph Jefferson as a possible father of Sally Heming's youngest child. Indeed the question continues to come up and I am prepared with my answer.

What I was not prepared for was a smaller, though also thorny issue . . . the local attachment to a legend involving Randolph's plantation, Snowden, and Thomas Jefferson's flight from Monticello during June of 1781 when Lt. General Charles Cornwallis, Col. Banastre Tarleton, and the British troops were bearing down on central Virginia.

In 1969, Virginia Moore told an embellished version of this legend in her conversational history, *Scottsville on the James*. She began, "There is a tradition that Jefferson hid out in a cave under a bluff below Scott's Landing, about a mile downstream from his brother Randolph's plantation-house; the place is pointed out."[6] In the 18th century, Randolph Jefferson's Snowden consisted of about 2,000 acres covering both high and low grounds at the James River's Horseshoe Bend.

It was George W. Foland, a descendant of Randolph Jefferson's granddaughter, Frances (Jefferson) Foland, who related the family's oral history to Virginia Moore, who continued:

> *He says that Thomas Jefferson rode south along blind mountain paths. Striking Rockfish River, he followed it to a ford near Mount Alto, crossed, and stopped at a house where he told his story and asked for shelter. The owner thought this road, the only good one in the area, unsafe—Tarleton might gallop up. Conducted two miles upstream, ex-Governor Jefferson (his term had just expired) spent two weeks at the home of Mr. Thomas Farrar. Then pressed on to Scott's Landing, which he knew intimately, having for years, passed through it to visit Snowden, now his brother's. It was probably Randolph Jefferson who suggested the cliff-cave below Scott's Landing as a hideout. Provisions could be sent as long as there remained any danger of a Tarleton or Simcoe raid. Perhaps also such luxuries as pillow, quilt, towel. Already Scott's Landing had heard that Cornwallis was using Jefferson's Goochland seat Elk Hill below Point of Fork as British headquarters, news not calculated to make a cave more comfortable.*[7]

With the publication of *The Jefferson Brothers* (Slate River Press), I became the bearer of bad tidings. Randolph Jefferson had not come to the aid of his brother during his daring flight. Thomas had not hidden, even for a few hours, at Snowden. In fact, Jefferson's own writings made it perfectly clear what actually happened when he fled his home atop the little mountain. In his "Diary of Arnold's Invasion and Notes on Subsequent Events in 1781," Jefferson wrote:

> *I now sent off my family, to secure them from danger and was myself still at Monticello, making arrangements for my own departure, when Lt. [Christopher] Hudson arrived there at half speed, and informed me the enemy were ascending the hill of Monticello. I departed immediately, and knowing that I should be pursued if I followed the public road, in which too my family would be found, I took my course thro' the woods along the mountains and overtook my family at Colo. Cole's, dined there, and carried them on to Rockfish after dinner, and the next day to Colo. Hugh Rose's in Amherst, I left them there on the 7th. and returned to Monticello. . . . I then rejoined my family at*

Colo. Rose's and proceeded with them to Poplar Forest in Bedford 80. miles S.W. from Monticello.[8]

Jefferson's version of his methodical escape leaves no room for doubt. There was no two week-stay with Thomas Farrar, no time spent secluded in a cave at Snowden, and, certainly, no "pillow, quilt and towel" provided by his attentive brother, Randolph.

"Wait!" protested Buckingham and Scottsville locals. "There is a cave at Snowden!"

Indeed there is something like a cave at Snowden, and Virginia State Geologist David Spears has examined and described it, further putting an end to the myth.

Caves and sinkholes do not typically form in the geological formation exposed in the bluffs of the Horseshoe Bend at what was once Randolph Jefferson's Snowden. Spears believes that the extremely small "cave" which can be found there today is man-made. He suspects that the bluff may have been excavated by someone searching for mineralized calcium carbonate. Faint traces of calcite (lime) can be seen on the rock surface. A keen eye might have noticed the streaks and dug into the bluff hoping to find a pocket of lime, useful to farmers as fertilizer.

According to Spears, "There are very few sources of lime in the Piedmont. In the 19th century, a few thin bands of marble running along the James River between Scottsville and Lynchburg were exploited extensively for agricultural lime. The prospect at Snowden is not in a layer of marble; it's a rock we call phyllite, made mostly of mica and mica-like minerals, but it has just enough calcite in it to be noticeable. The hole in the rock face was probably made in a desperate attempt to scrape a little lime out of a lime-poor rock."[9]

There is no indication that this hole in Snowden's bluff dates back to 1781. Likewise, there is no way of knowing when the tale of Thomas Jefferson hiding there began to circulate though, following the publication of *The Jefferson Brothers*, I discovered a version in print in 1900, indicating it was cherished by the descendants of Randolph Jefferson long before it was repeated to Virginia Moore.

Snowden may have lost a legend but in its place I've discovered an actual mystery. This time, however, the Thomas Jefferson involved is Randolph Jefferson's son, Thomas Jefferson, Jr., not his famous namesake.

About 1807, Randolph Jefferson, his oldest sons, and his son-in-law, Zachariah Nevil, launched a business venture at Snowden called "Nevil and Jefferson." They purchased supplies at William Moon's store at Stony Point, located just above Scott's Ferry, now Scottsville. A surviving store ledger shows that they bought, among other things, "shoe brushes, 27 [units?] iron, a blacking ball, quires of paper and pencils, copperass, pit and hand saws, two orders of German steel, and black pepper."

What early 19th century endeavor might have utilized iron, copperass, and steel? Copperass is an antiquated term for ferrous sulfate which was used in the manufacture of inks, most notably iron gall ink. This process dated from the middle ages and was used until the end of the 18th century. It was also used in the dyeing of wool and in a material called harewood, used in parquetry.

Significantly, in 1808, Randolph's son, Thomas Jefferson, Jr., purchased an African-American slave named Gary who was skilled as a "rough" cooper. Did Gary make barrels for specialized containers for "Nevil and Jefferson?" What might they be selling that required barrels, tubs, casks, or other containers made of wood? Hogsheads were used for tobacco. Whiskey required barrels.

By 1810, the business had dissolved, Randolph Jefferson had remarried, and most of his children had dispersed from Snowden. At least for now, that's where the story of "Nevil and Jefferson" ends.

NOTES

"Thomas Jefferson, Jr.: The Enigmatic Jefferson"

1 Joanne L. Yeck, *The Jefferson Brothers* (Kettering, OH: Slate River Press, 2012), 301.

2 Nell C. Hailey, *Fluvanna County, Virginia. Death records, 1853–1896* (Athens, GA: Iberian Publishing Co., 1995), 133. The record of Thomas Jefferson, Jr.'s second marriage, which claimed he was seventy years old in January of 1858, placing his birth in 1787, is likely incorrect. He had good reason to reduce his age. His bride, Elizabeth W. (Siegfried) Barker, was only thirty-two years old. Records for Thomas Jefferson Jr.'s second and third marriages, in 1858 and 1868, both state that he was born in Albemarle County, Virginia.

3 Bernard Mayo, with additions by James A. Bear, Jr., *Thomas Jefferson and His Unknown Brother* (Charlottesville, VA: University Press of Virginia, 1981), 13. This comment indicates that Thomas Jefferson, Jr. may have been about seven years old in January of 1789.

4 Yeck, *The Jefferson Brothers*, 206.

5 "Thomas Jefferson to Philip Mazzei, 7 January 1792," *Founders Online,* accessed September 2017, https://founders.archives.gov/documents/Jefferson/01-23-02-0022.

6 Boynton Merrill, Jr., *Jefferson's Nephews: A Frontier Tragedy* (Lincoln, NE: University of Nebraska Press, 2004); "Craven Peyton," *Thomas Jefferson Encyclopedia,* accessed September 2017, https://www.monticello.org/site/research-and-collections/craven-peyton; R. E. Hannum, "Mount Eagle," 14 February 1938, Virginia Historical Inventory, Library of Virginia.

7 Merrill, "Shipwreck of Fortunes," 44–54.

8 Craven Peyton sent the sad news of Betsy Lewis' death to Thomas Jefferson, writing: "two of Col° Lewis Daughtars & myself was attacked with fevar about 15 days ago.— Betsy Lewis whom I carried to Bethlehem to school, with my little Daughter, was not receaved by the Director because she was two years Oalder than their rules admitted of. She expared on the twelvth day, her sustar & myself are both very low now." Betsy's unnamed sister is likely Polly. Peyton's ill daughter may be Margaret Gwatkins Peyton (b. abt. 1796), who later married her cousin, Isham Randolph Jefferson, in 1822. (Thomas Jefferson from Craven Peyton, 9 October 1806, *Founders Online,* accessed September 2017, http://founders.archives.gov/documents/Jefferson/99-01-02-4362.) Many members of this Lewis generation had no children of their own. Polly Lewis married, but died childless. Anna Marks and Elizabeth Lewis had no issue. Charles Lewis had no legitimate heirs, though he was allegedly the father of at least one mixed-race child. Isham Lewis was likely childless, as well. Martha A. C. (Lewis) Monroe raised her brother Randolph's child, Warren Lewis. See Joanne L. Yeck, "Lilburne Lewis," *Lost Jeffersons* (Slate River Press, 2018).

9   Marriage Bond, 3 October 1808, Albemarle County, VA; John Vogt, *Albemarle County Marriages, Volume 1* (Athens, GA: Iberian Publishing Co., 1991), 175; David Anderson, deposition, "Thomas Jefferson, Jr. and wife, etc. vs Craven Peyton and wife," 1818-001, Augusta County Superior Court, Augusta County, VA, Library of Virginia.

10   Yeck, "Anna Scott Jefferson," *Lost Jeffersons*.

11   Merrill, 54.

12   Yeck, *The Jefferson Brothers*, 261–63, 302–3; Joanne L. Yeck, "A Most Valuable Citizen: A Profile of Randolph Jefferson," *Magazine of Albemarle County History* (Albemarle Charlottesville Historical Society, 2011), 1-37. In 1808, Thomas Jefferson, Jr. owned a slave named Gary, a rough cooper, who came from an estate in Brunswick County. Gary's occupation as a barrel maker offers a possible clue as to the Snowden business venture. See Yeck, *Jefferson Brothers*, 210–11.

13   Federal Population Census, Albemarle County, VA, 1810; Personal Property Tax, Albemarle County, VA, 1810. In 1812, Thomas Jefferson, Jr. was taxed on nine slaves above the age of sixteen, paying $5.30 in tax. His was the highest tax on the page, with the outstanding exception of his uncle, Thomas Jefferson, who owed $43.66 in taxes on dozens of slaves, two giggs, and a phaeton.

14   In 1811, "Thomas Jefferson & Co." payed tax in Albemarle County on 333 ½ acres of land in the southern section of the county. Currently, his business partners are unknown, though one may have been Joseph Brand. See Land Tax, Albemarle County, VA, 1811.

15   Fluvanna County Deed Book 6, pp. 45–47, 260–61; Marriage Bond, Fluvanna County, VA. Mary Anne Henderson was the granddaughter of Elizabeth (Lewis) and Bennett Henderson. [See Yeck, "Isham Randolph Jefferson," *Lost Jeffersons*.] Thomas Jefferson, Jr. continued to expand his farmland in Fluvanna, purchasing an additional 174 acres in 1823 and another 25 ½ acres in 1828. Jefferson paid personal property tax exclusively in Fluvanna from at least 1813–1826. In 1828, Thomas Jefferson, Jr. paid personal property tax in Albemarle County, Virginia. [See Fluvanna County Deed Book 8, pp. 438–39; Fluvanna County Deed Book 9, pp. 344–45; Personal Property Tax, Fluvanna County, VA, 1813–1826; Personal Property Tax, Albemarle, VA, 1828.] On January 21, 1818, Isham Randolph Jefferson purchased his own farm in Fluvanna County. See Fluvanna County Deed Book 7, pp. 186–87.

16   Albemarle Order Book, March 1810–August 1811, p. 472; Albemarle County Order Book, 1811–1813, pp. 173–74, 226. The nature of the business operated by Thomas Jefferson, Jr. and Joseph Brand is unknown. There was a Joseph Brand, originally of Hanover County, who settled in Albemarle County in 1779. In 1810, he owned twenty-five slaves and supported a large family. Upon his death, his executors sold his land opposite the town of Milton to Martin Dawson. He had a son, Joseph Brand, Jr., who was likely Jefferson's partner. James Monroe's political and domestic life had long been intertwined with Monticello and President Thomas Jefferson, including the purchase of some of Jefferson's slaves. In 1794, Monroe bought Thenia Hemings,

Sally Hemings' older sister, and Thenia's children: Mary, Lucy, Betsy, Susan, and Sally. The previous year, Monroe had acquired 3,500 acres adjacent to Monticello and, in 1799, his dwelling house, called Highland, was completed. Later, in September of 1816, Monroe purchased Limestone Farm, which was convenient to Milton and would later play a role in the life of Thomas Jefferson, Jr. For an account of James Monroe's Albemarle land holdings, see "Limestone Farm, Albemarle County," accessed September 2017, http://www.histarch.uiuc.edu/highland/ashlawn4.html.

17   *Richmond Enquirer*, 18 February 1812, p. 1.

18   Merrill, "Peyton, Jefferson, and the Hendersons," 55–70; John Henderson Mill (Milton), Mutual Assurance Policy #335, 4 May 1799, Library of Virginia; Robert Haggard, "Thomas Jefferson v The Heirs of Bennett Henderson, 1795–1818: A Case Study in Caveat Emptor" (*Albemarle County Magazine of History*, 2005), 1–29. The heirs of Bennett Henderson owned over a thousand acres at Milton, with access to the Rivanna River. In 1801, President Thomas Jefferson asked Craven Peyton to buy and manage that land until he left public office. It became an ill-fated investment. See "Craven Peyton," *Thomas Jefferson Encyclopedia*.

19   Rev. Edgar Woods, *Albemarle County in Virginia* (Baltimore, MD: Clearfield Co., 1997), 57–58.

20   Yeck, "Lilburne Lewis," *Lost Jeffersons*; Craven Peyton, answer, "Thomas Jefferson, Jr. and wife, etc. vs Craven Peyton and wife."

21   Land deed, Charles and Lucy Lewis to Charles Lewis, Jr., "Thomas Jefferson, Jr. and wife, etc. vs Craven Peyton and wife;" Albemarle County Deed Book 14, pp. 506–07. This land was deeded to Charles Lewis, Jr. at the time he was engaged to Anna Scott Jefferson. See Yeck, "Anna Scott Jefferson," *Lost Jeffersons*.

22   Merrill, 314–15; Livingston County Deed Book B, 504. A document representing Ann M. Lewis dated November 9, 1814, and recorded in Livingston County, Kentucky, was recorded again in Fluvanna County on November 25, 1822, gave Thomas Jefferson, Jr. Esq. the following powers: "my attorney in fact for me and in my name . . . to recover any money to myself for the rent of land in the County of Albemarle in the state of Virginia and in any other county and said state and in my name to prosecute any suit or suits and prosecute the same to Judgment." See Fluvanna County Deed Book 8, pp. 198–99.

23   In 1815, Martha A. C. Lewis married Daniel Monroe and, sometime after 1817, moved to New Orleans. Ann Marks Lewis eventually joined the Monroes in New Orleans. Lucy B. Lewis, who married Washington A. Griffin, settled in Shelbyville, Kentucky. About 1830, the Griffins moved to New Albany, Indiana. See Merrill, 35, 339, 342, 347.

24   Lucy Jefferson Lewis to Thomas Jefferson, 19 November 1807, *Founders Online*, accessed September 2017, http://founders.archives.gov/documents/Jefferson/99-01-02-6810.

25 David Anderson, deposition, "Thomas Jefferson, Jr. and wife, etc. vs Craven Peyton and wife;" Merrill, 314–15.

26 Craven Peyton, answer, "Thomas Jefferson, Jr. and wife, etc. vs Craven Peyton and wife."

27 Ibid. Despite this battle over Charles Lewis, Jr.'s Buck Island land, the Peytons did not hold a grudge against the Jeffersons. On July 2, 1822, Isham Randolph Jefferson (a.k.a. Randolph Jefferson, Jr.) married their daughter, Margaret Gwatkins Peyton. The Jeffersons had two daughters before Margaret's death c. 1833. The girls were remembered in Craven Peyton's 1837 will. See Marriage Records, Albemarle County, Virginia; Craven Peyton Will, Albemarle County Will Book 12, pp. 381–83.

28 Merrill, 319; *Atlanta Constitution*, 28 November 1874, p. 1; Personal Property Tax, Fluvanna County, VA, 1815. In 1820, the one male over forty-five years old living with the Thomas Jeffersons in Fluvanna County is likely Charles L. Lewis. See Federal Population Census, Fluvanna County, VA, 1820.

29 *Virginia Advocate*, 1 September 1827, p. 1. Note that President Thomas Jefferson had died in 1826, thus his nephew was no longer identified as "Thomas Jefferson, Jr." in 1827.

30 Fluvanna County Deed Book 11, pp. 278–81; Fluvanna County Deed Book 12, pp. 72–3.

31 Federal Population Census, Albemarle County, VA, 1830; Personal Property Tax, Albemarle County, VA, 1830, 1831; Agricultural Census, Albemarle County, VA, 1850. This farm combined two parcels: 242 acres from Ludlow Branham and 183 3/4 acres from Martin Dawson. See Land Tax, Albemarle County, VA, 1829.

32 Federal Population Census, Albemarle County, VA, 1830; Death Record, Albemarle County, VA. Mary R. Jefferson's cause of death (probably paralysis) is nearly illegible on two separate death registers. In 1830, an unidentified white female, possibly a niece, age sixteen to twenty, lived in the Jefferson household. See Federal Population Census, Albemarle County, VA, 1830.

33 Albemarle County Deed Book 56, p. 413; Albemarle County Deed Book 59, pp. 567–68, recorded 4 November 1861. John O. Lewis lived at Cliffside, located on what is now Warren Street in Scottsville. According to Scottsville Museum: "[George Walden] Dillard owned various properties in Scottsville, including the old Eagle Hotel (later known as the Carleton House) on Valley Street from 1872–1880." See "Cliffside," Scottsville Museum website, accessed September 2017, http://scotts-villemuseum.com/homes/homeEEcdEE01.html; "Dr. Benjamin Lewis Dillard," Scottsville Museum website, accessed September 2017, http://scottsvillemuseum.com/portraits/homeB114cdB17.html.

34 Marriage Record, 4 January 1858, Albemarle County, VA.

35 Jennings L. Wagoner, Jr., *Jefferson and Education* (Charlottesville, VA: University of Virginia Press, 2011), 134; Kenneth Silverman, *Edgar A. Poe: Mournful and*

Never-ending Remembrance (New York, NY: Harper Perennial, 2008), 29–30; "Missouri, Marriage Records, 1805–2002," ancestry.com.

36   Albemarle County Deed Book 59, pp. 141–42.

37   Anna C. Siegfried out-lived her daughter by several years. Her will, written in her own hand, on July 20, 1871, was recorded in Albemarle County both in its original German and in English translation. See Albemarle County Will Book 29, pp. 309–11.

38   *Richmond Dispatch*, 23 March 1865, p. 2.

39   Richard L. Nicholas, "War Comes to Scottsville," Scottsville Museum website, accessed September 2017, http://scottsvillemuseum.com/war/1865WarInScottsville/ WarComesToScottsville.pdf; Albemarle County Deed Book 61, p. 196.

40   Marriage record, Fluvanna County, VA.

41   Fluvanna County Deed Book 20, pp. 257–58; Thomas Jefferson Will, written 26 September 1869, recorded 27 March 1877, Fluvanna County Will Book 11, pp. 200–01.

42   Federal Population Census, Fluvanna County, VA, 1850–1880. Robert and Elizabeth A. Ligon were the children of Robert Ligon and Nancy W. Jefferson's sister, Leah M. Pollard. Like the Jefferson–Lewis family, the Pollard family may have suffered from too much cousin marriage, a sad legacy pervasive throughout Virginia's planter class. See Fluvanna County Marriage Bonds, Fluvanna County, VA; "Fluvanna County Marriage Bonds, 1777–1858," accessed September 2017, http://files.usgwarchives.net/ va/fluvanna/vitals/marriages/marr7758.txt.

43   Rev. John A. Doll, deposition, "Albert Gantt and wife vs John Noel, etc.," 1871-066 Cc, Albemarle County Chancery Case, Library of Virginia.

44   Fluvanna County Deed Book 21, pp. 156–57; Death Record, Fluvanna County, VA; Federal Population Census, Fluvanna County, VA, 1880.

45   Woods, 237. Peter Field Jefferson's daughter, Fanny, married Valentine Foland, not Peter Foland, who was her son. This error would be repeated over the years.

"Isham Randolph Jefferson: "A Striking Resemblance"

1   *Buffalo Evening Post*, 9 August 1862, p. 3. Called Randolph, Jr. by his family, he appears on most public documents as Isham, Isham R., or I. R. Jefferson. The obituary for Isham Randolph Jefferson places his birth about 1791, though he was likely born earlier, probably the second son of Randolph and Anne (Lewis) Jefferson. In 1809, Randolph, Jr. paid personal property tax in Buckingham County, indicating his birth was prior to 1788.

2   *Evening Courier and Republic* (Buffalo, NY), 12 August 1862, p. 1.

3   J. H. Battle, editor, "Dr. Walter B. Jefferson," *History of Todd County, Kentucky* (Chicago, IL & Louisville, KY: F. A. Battey Publishing Co., 1884), accessed October

2017, https://www.accessgenealogy.com/kentucky/biography-of-dr-walter-b-jefferson.htm.

4   In Thomas Jefferson's *Memorandum Books*, there is not a single clear reference to Isham Randolph Jefferson, while there are multiple references to his sister, Nancy, and his brothers, Thomas Jefferson, Jr. and James Lilburne. Since the family called him "Randolph," it is possible that some of the entries which are attributed to Thomas Jefferson's brother actually concern his nephew. Thomas sometimes notes "my brother" and sometimes "R. J."—as well as entries which refer to Randolph and Randolph Jefferson. Three entries, written between 1802–1806, might apply to Randolph, Jr., however, when compared to the entries for niece Nancy and nephew Thomas, which are clearly for "outfitting" and education, they more likely concern his father, Randolph, Sr. See James A. Bear, Jr., and Lucia C. Stanton, eds., *Jefferson's Memorandum Books: Accounts, with Legal Records and Miscellany, 1767-1826, Volume ii* (Princeton, NJ: Princeton University Press, 1997), 1081, 1163, 1192.

5   "Thomas Jefferson's Deposition Regarding Randolph Jefferson's Estate, 15 September 1815," *Founders Online*, accessed September 2017, https://founders.archives.gov/documents/Jefferson/03-09-02-0017.

6   Recorded as Mary Anne, Mariann, Marianne, and Meriam Henderson, she is "Mary Ann" in her obituary, which ran in Virginia's *Central Gazette* on December 14, 1821, and was twenty-seven years old at the time of her death. Mary Anne's father, John Henderson, was the son of Bennett and Elizabeth (Lewis) Henderson. Bennett Henderson's death in 1793 left Elizabeth a widow with twelve children. Mary Anne's mother was born Ann Barber "Nancy" Hudson. Her ancestor, Charles Hudson, was an early Albemarle County patentee and settled along the Hardware below Carter's Bridge. Bennett's brother, Charles Hudson Henderson, married Jane Lewis, Anne (Lewis) Jefferson's sister. See Rev. Edgar Woods, *Albemarle County in Virginia* (Baltimore, Maryland: Clearfield Co., 1997), 226–28, 230–31.

7   Rev. Edgar Woods writes about John Winn, who came from Fluvanna County and settled in Charlottesville. "As the partner of Twyman Wayt, he was for a long time one of the principle merchants of the town, and its Postmaster. He also dealt considerably in real estate. In 1813 he purchased from John Carr his seat at Belmont, where he resided until his death." See Woods, 346–47.

8   Fluvanna County Deed Book 7, pp. 186–87; "Central Gazette Obituaries," *Papers of the Albemarle County Historical Society, Volume X, 1949–1950* (Charlottesville, VA: Albemarle County Historical Society, 1950), 35. In 1814, Isham Randolph Jefferson paid personal property tax in Fluvanna County. He was listed as "Randolph Jefferson." This may be the basis of the long-repeated error that Randolph Jefferson, brother to President Jefferson, lived in Fluvanna County. During the period from 1814–1818, Randolph, Jr. owned about half a dozen slaves and a horse or two. Interestingly, records from Todd County, Kentucky, where his son, Thomas Jefferson, spent most of his life, indicate he was born in Albemarle County, not in Fluvanna County. See Personal Property Tax, Albemarle County, Virginia, 1814; Personal Property Tax,

Fluvanna County, VA, 1815, 1816, 1819; Personal Property Tax, Buckingham County, VA, 1817.

9   John Vogt, *Albemarle County Marriages, Volume 1* (Athens, GA: Iberian Publishing Co., 1991), 175; Woods, 135.

10   Federal Population Census, Fluvanna County, VA, 1830.

11   Land Tax, Fluvanna County, VA, 1830.

12   Fluvanna County Deed Book 10, p. 294; Albemarle County Deed Book 38, pp. 119–20. This deed, recorded in 1833, describes I. R. Jefferson as "of Fluvanna." According to the Scottsville Museum, the congregation purchased lot #26 in Scottsville for $150.00 in 1832 and completed the building of their new church in 1833. See "Scottsville Methodist Church," Scottsville Museum website, accessed September 2017, http://scottsvillemuseum.com/church/homeB58dcdB16.html.

13   *Courier-Journal* (Louisville, KY), 29 January 1995, p. 1; Frances Marion Williams, *The Story of Todd County, Kentucky, 1820-1970* (Nashville, TN: Parthenon Press, 1972); Personal Property Tax, Fluvanna County, VA, 1826; Federal Population Census, Fluvanna County, VA, 1830; Federal Population Census, Todd County, KY, 1840.

14   Marriage Record, Todd County, KY; Yeck, *The Jefferson Brothers*, pp. 289–318. Currently the details of Margaret G. (Peyton) Jefferson's death are unknown; it likely occurred 1832–1834. It is doubtful that she lived to travel to Kentucky with her family and was probably deceased when I. R. Jefferson sold his lot in Scottsville on September 30, 1833. In 1870, Sarah A. Jefferson (age sixty) was enumerated as Isham Randolph's widow, living with some of her children. See Federal Population Census, Todd County, KY, 1850–1870.

15   Isham Randolph Jefferson obituary, *Weekly Oreganian* (Portland, OR), 11 October 1862, p. 2.

16   *Cincinnati Daily Enquirer*, 11 December 1862, p. 2.

17   Marriage Record, Logan County, KY. Thomas Jefferson died on February 1, 1885 and is buried in Glenwood Cemetery, Elkton, Todd County, Kentucky. See Find A Grave, accessed October 2017, https://www.findagrave.com/memorial/47465698.

18   Albemarle County Will Book 12, pp. 381–83.

19   Federal Population Census, Logan County, KY, 1850–1860; Mary Broach, McLean Family Tree, ancestry.com.

20   Battle, "Paul H. Salmon," *History of Todd County, Kentucky*, 281–82. The brief biography contains several errors. The Salmons were married on February 6, 1849 in Todd County, Kentucky. In 1850, their son George Randolph was five months old. [See Marriage Records, Todd County, KY; Federal Population Census, Todd County, KY, 1850.] Additionally, L. J. Jefferson's mother was Margaret G. Peyton.

21   "Death of Minister.," *Hopkinsville Kentuckian*, 16 September 1902, p. 1.

22   Battle, "Frank Byars," *History of Todd County, Kentucky*, 290. Other sources state that Nannie and Frank M. Byars had seven children, five of whom were living in 1900. At the time of Frank's death in 1905, his surviving children were: "Misses Jimmie, Nannie and "Manie" Byars and Sandy Byars, of [Hopkinsville, KY], and Frank M. Byars, Jr., operator of the Postal Telegraph Company at Shelbyville, Ky." See Federal Population Census, Hopkinsville, KY, 1900; Frank M. Byars, obituary, *Hopkinsville Kentuckian*, 16 February 1905, p. 1.

23   Frank M. Byars, obituary, *Hopkinsville Kentuckian*, 16 February 1905, p. 1; Mrs. Nannie Jefferson Byars, obituary, *St. Louis Post-Dispatch*, 29 May 1934, p. 19.

24   James M. Jefferson died of typhoid fever in May of 1859. See Kentucky Death Records 1852–1964, ancestry.com.

25   Battle, "Walter B. Jefferson," *History of Todd County, Kentucky*, accessed December 2017, https://www.accessgenealogy.com/kentucky/biography-of-dr-walter-b-jefferson.htm.

26   Find A Grave, Randolph Jefferson, accessed December 2017, https://www.findagrave.com/memorial/48348164; Find A Grave, Marion Jefferson, accessed December 2017, https://www.findagrave.com/memorial/48348118.

27   *Courier-Journal* (Louisville, KY), 5 February 1884, p.1.

28   Death Record, Hopkinsville, KY.

29   *Richmond Times*-Dispatch, 12 April 1943, p. 5. Apparently, this Jefferson line displayed President Thomas Jefferson's height. In 1943, when Edwin R. Jefferson attended the dedication of the Jefferson Memorial in Washington, D.C., it was reported that he was white-haired and 6' 1" tall. [Ibid.] Edwin was born on January 25, 1887 in Kentucky and died of asthma on May 12, 1958 in Nashville, Tennessee. See Death Record, Nashville, TN; *Hood County News-Tablet* (Granbury, TX), 10 January 1957, p. 7; *Tennessean* (Nashville, TN), 14 May 1958, p. 30.

"James Lilburne Jefferson: A Young Man Adrift"

1   In 1818, James Lilburne Jefferson paid personal property tax, placing his birth in about 1797. See Personal Property Tax, Fluvanna County, VA, 1818; Personal Property Tax, Albemarle County, VA, 1818.

2   Thomas Jefferson to Randolph Jefferson, 25 May 1813, *Founders Online*, accessed October 2017, https://founders.archives.gov/documents/Jefferson/03-06-02-0134; Randolph Jefferson to Thomas Jefferson, 26 May 1813, *Founders Online*, accessed October 2017, http://founders.archives.gov/documents/Jefferson/03-06-02-0136; Randolph Jefferson to Thomas Jefferson, 21 June 1813, *Founders Online*, accessed October 2017, https://founders.archives.gov/documents/Jefferson/03-06-02-0195; Virginia Auditor's Office, *Virginia Militia in the War of 1812, Volume 1* (Baltimore, MD: Genealogical Publishing Company, 2001), 329–30. Captains Boaz Ford, William Freeland, and William M. Holman headed companies from Buckingham County. According to Stuart Lee Butler, "Buckingham county soldiers participated in the

defense of Norfolk and Richmond." Officers included Mitchie B. (Pryor) Jefferson's brother, Lt. Langston Pryor. See Stuart Lee Butler, *A Guide to Virginia Militia Units in the War of 1812* (Athens, GA: Iberian Publishing Company, 1988), 59–60, 253.

3   James Lilburne Jefferson to Thomas Jefferson, 18 February 1816, *Founders Online*, accessed September 2017, http://founders.archives.gov/documents/ Jefferson/03-09-02-0327. In 1816, John Scott III still owned the ferry at Scott's Landing. In 1821, he sold it to Thomas O. Henley for $750. (Albemarle County Deed Book No. 22, p. 428.) In April of 1816, Lilburne wrote to Thomas Jefferson from Warren, upriver from Scottsville. Perhaps, this is where he had rented "the ferry." See James Lilburne Jefferson to Thomas Jefferson, 19 April [1816], *Founders Online*, accessed September 2017, http://founders.archives.gov/documents/ Jefferson/03-09-02-0467.

4   "Memorandum Books, 1816," *Founders Online*, accessed September 2017, http:// founders.archives.gov/documents/Jefferson/02-02-02-0026; "Memorandum Books, 1817," *Founders Online*, accessed September 2017, http://founders.archives.gov/ documents/Jefferson/02-02-02-0027.

5   Albemarle County Deed Book 21, pp. 259, 340–41. Edith F. Axelton, *Virginia Postmasters and Post Offices, 1789–1832* (Athens, GA: Iberian Publishing Co., 1991), 6. In 1818, Lilburne appeared on both the Albemarle and the Fluvanna County personal property tax records. See Personal Property Tax, Albemarle County, VA, 14 April 1818; Personal Property Tax, Fluvanna County, VA, 22 May 1818.

6   James L. Jefferson, clipping file, Fluvanna Historical Society.

7   Federal Population Census, Fluvanna County, VA, 1820; Personal Property Tax, Fluvanna County, VA, 1820.

8   Fluvanna County Deed Book 7, pp. 679–80; Personal Property Tax, Nelson County, VA, 1822; Personal Property Tax, Buckingham County, VA, 1823–1825. The Scottsville lot was described as bounded by the James River on the south; by Walter and John Coles on the west; Jacob Moon on the north; and by William Moon and Samuel Dyer on the east. It was the same lot which was transferred to James Lilburne Jefferson from Randolph Turner for $700. Martin B. Tutwiler would become a significant local businessman, owning numerous properties in and around Scottsville, including the Eagle Hotel. In 1823, he bought the ferry from Thomas O. Henley. See Richard L. Nicholas, "The Early History of the Founding of Scottsville, Virginia and Surrounding Area 1732–1830," (Unpublished manuscript, 2009), 171.

9   Albemarle County Deed Book 23, p. 457; Land Tax, Albemarle County, VA, 1825.

10 Personal Property Tax, Lynchburg, VA, 1825–1836; Federal population census, Lynchburg, VA, 1830; "Peter F. Jefferson vs Thomas Jefferson, Robert L. Jefferson, Isham R. Jefferson, Lafayette Nevil, James L. Nevil, Jefferson M. Nevil, Jesse Mundy & Louisiana his wife, late Louisiana Nevil, who are children and heirs of Ann S. Nevil formerly Ann S. Jefferson," Albemarle County Chancery Case, 1843-007, Library of Virginia. In 1825, James Lilburne Jefferson owned two slaves and one horse,

while Robert Lewis Jefferson was responsible for fourteen slaves and five horses, a percentage of which was likely property still held in Randolph Jefferson's estate and would be distributed during 1825–1826. See Personal Property Tax, Buckingham County, VA, 1825.

11 *Lynchburg Virginian*, 24 October 1836, p. 3; *Springfield Republican* (Springfield, MA), 26 November 1836, p. 2; *Public Ledger* (Philadelphia, PA), 22 November 1836, p. 2.

12 *Republican Farmer and Democratic Journal* (Wilkes-Barre, PA), 4 January 1837, p. 3.

"Anna Scott Jefferson: The Rise and Fall of the Nevils of Nelson County"

1 There is no public record documenting the birth of Anna Scott Jefferson. Martha (Jefferson) Randolph and her daughter, Ellen (Randolph) Coolidge, referred to her as "Nanny Dish," an odd nickname yet to be explained. Her aunt, Anna Scott (Jefferson) Marks, had no children of her own, so Nancy Jefferson may have been a particular favorite. Charles Lilburne and Lucy (Jefferson) Lewis also honored Anna Scott (Jefferson) Marks, naming one of their daughters, Ann Marks Lewis. See Martha (Jefferson) Randolph to Ellen W. (Randolph) Coolidge, 1 September 1825, MSS 9090, Small Special Collections, University of Virginia.

2 Thomas Jefferson to John Wayles Eppes, 8 April 1801, *Founders Online*, accessed September 2017, http://founders.archives.gov/documents/Jefferson/01-33-02-0479.

3 "Memorandum Books, 1801," *Founders Online*, accessed September 2017, http://founders.archives.gov/documents/Jefferson/02-02-02-0011.

4 "Inoculation," *Thomas Jefferson Encyclopedia*, accessed September 2017, https://www.monticello.org/site/research-and-collections/inoculation. Former Snowden slaves, Ben and Cary, and several members of the Hemings family were also treated. For more about Ben and Cary, see Joanne L. Yeck, *The Jefferson Brothers* (Kettering, OH: Slate River Press, 2012), 152–54; 217–22.

5 Boyton Merrill, Jr., *Jefferson's Nephews: A Frontier Tragedy* (Lincoln, NE: University of Nebraska Press, 2004), 48–49.

6 Albemarle County Deed Book 14, pp. 506–07; Merrill, 51.

7 It is likely that Nancy Jefferson's mother, Anne (Lewis) Jefferson, was deceased at the time of the engagement.

8 Merrill, 84–87.

9 Ibid., 49.

10 Ibid., 240–41, 316, 417; Pam Smith to Joanne Yeck, emails, 2011. Matilda was actually the great-niece of Thomas Jefferson. According to the article which appeared in *The Crittenden Press*, "Aunt" Matilda Threlkeld lived in a "miserable hovel." See Merrill, "An Interview with Matilda," 351–52.

11 Thomas Jefferson from Charles L. Lewis, 29 April 1806, *Founders Online*, accessed September 2017, http://founders.archives.gov/documents/Jefferson/99-01-02-3662;

Thomas Jefferson to Col. Charles Lewis, 7 October 1806, Massachusetts Historical Society.

12 Marriage Record, Albemarle County, VA.

13 Rev. Edgar Woods, *Albemarle County in Virginia* (Baltimore, Maryland: Clearfield Co., 1997), 9; "Virginia Land Office Patents and Grants/Northern Neck Grants and Surveys," Library of Virginia; Eric G. Grundset, *Land lying in the County of Albemarle: Albemarle County, Virginia Surveyors' Plat Books Volume I, Parts 1 and 3, and Volume 2, 1744–1853 [and 1892]* (Privately published, 1998), 8, 35, 54, 61; James Nevill [sic] Will, Albemarle County Will Book 2, p. 1; "Notes and Queries," *The Virginia Magazine of History and Biography* (April 1929), 161–70.

14 James Nevil Will, Amherst County Will Book 2, pp. 211–20; 224–216; Amherst County Will Book 3, pp. 20, 121; Amherst County Will Book 4, p. 1 [indexed as p. 4]. On October 21, 1799, Zachariah Nevil became Ethel Nevil's legal guardian, apparently delayed his own marriage until after she married Samuel Edmunds, in Amherst County, Virginia, on August 5, 1802. On November 28, 1808, Mary Nevil and her son, Cornelius, granted 412 acres on the Rockfish River to John Syme. On October 22, 1810, Zachariah Nevil purchased the land from John Syme and his wife, Ann. See "Marriage Records from Amherst, Virginia through 1850," ancestry.com; Nelson County Deed Book 1, pp. 43, 82, 250, 265, 321.

15 Alexander Brown, *The Cabells and Their Kin: A Memorial Volume of History, Biography, and Genealogy* (Boston, MA: Houghton, Mifflin and Company, 1895), 190–91.

16 "The United States in account with Zachariah Nevil," 27 January 1794, Papers of the War Department, 1783–1800, accessed September 2017, http://wardepartmentpapers. org/searchresults.php?searchClass=fulltextSearch&fulltextQuery=Private+Zachariah+Nevil; Yeck, *The Jefferson Brothers*, 111–23.

17 During the early years of her marriage, Nancy Nevil visited her extended family in Albemarle County. In a letter written on April 21, 1808 from Ellen Wayles Randolph to Thomas Jefferson, Ellen describes the springtime in Albemarle County to her grandfather in Washington, D.C., mentioning that "Uncle Randolph Jefferson" was staying with her family at Edgehill, the Thomas Mann Randolph plantation, and adding that "Cousin Nancy Neville" was in the neighborhood. See Thomas Jefferson from Ellen Wayles Randolph Coolidge, 21 April 1808, *Founders Online*, accessed September 2017, http://founders.archives.gov/documents/Jefferson/99-01-02-7879.

18 In 1804, Zachariah Nevil was taxed in the section of Amherst County which would become Nelson County in 1809. In 1805, he paid tax in both Amherst and Buckingham counties and, in 1809, was taxed in both Buckingham and Nelson counties. In Nelson, Nevil was charged for one white male (himself), eight slaves above age sixteen; four slaves above age fourteen; and six horses. See Personal Property Tax, Amherst County, VA, 1804–1805; Personal Property Tax, Buckingham County, VA, 1805, 1809; Personal Property Tax, Nelson County, VA, 1809.

19   Federal Population Census, Nelson County, VA, 1810. From 1811 until 1827, Zachariah
      Nevil's post as Tobacco Inspector was renewed annually by a series of Virginia
      Governors. See Nelson County Will Book A (1808–1818); Nelson County Will
      Book B (1818–1822); Nelson County Will Book C (1822–1829); Nelson County
      Minute Book (1825–1826).

20   "Lebanon," Mutual Assurance Society, policy #455, 13 October 1812, Library of
      Virginia. In 1842, an advertisement called the farm "Mount Lebanon." In family
      documents, it was referred to as Locust Grove. The same day that Zachariah Nevil
      took out his new policy, he and James Murphy witnessed the Mutual Assurance
      Society policy declaration #435 for George Cabell, Jr.'s home, Bonair (a.k.a. Bon Air
      and Bon Aire), on the James River. A total of four structures were valued at $6,250.
      Fourteen years later, Nevil bought Cabell's Bonair. See "Jesse Mundy and Wife vs
      Lafayette Neville, Committee, etc.," Nelson County Chancery Case 1845-001, Library
      of Virginia; "Jesse Mundy and Wife vs Administrators of Zachariah Neville, etc.,"
      1872-052, Nelson County Chancery Case, Library of Virginia.

21   Yeck, *The Jefferson Brothers*, 261–63; 302; 327–28. In the accounts of Zachariah Nevil's
      estate, there are references to distributions made from Randolph Jefferson's estate to
      the Nevil children. See Mr. James L. Jefferson in account with Jesse Jopling adm. of
      Z. Nevil dec[d], "Jesse Mundy and Wife vs Administrators of Zachariah Neville, etc."

22   Charles Lewis, Jr. Will, Albemarle County Will Book 2, pp. 399–400; Peter Jefferson
      Will, Albemarle County Will Book 2, pp. 32–35.

23   Nelson County Will Book D, 415; "Valuable James River Land For Sale," *Richmond
      Enquirer*, 15 October 1822, p. 4. Zachariah Nevil went to court in Albemarle County,
      attempting to collect debts for Randolph Jefferson's legatees. Additionally, in 1830,
      Nevil's own estate shows that as Administrator for Randolph Jefferson he did business
      with "Rives & Brown" using funds from the Jefferson estate. Nevil's Administrators
      paid two debts to "Rives & Brown" in October of 1830: $40.06 from the Estate of
      Cornelius Nevil, dec[d] (Zachariah Nevil's younger brother) and $450.34 due from
      "the administrator of the estate of Randolph Jefferson." Nevil engaged in several
      partnerships, including "Nevil and Jefferson," which was taxed on three slaves in
      1825. See Personal Property Tax, Nelson County, VA, 1825.

24   "List of Subscribers, Contributors, and Founders of the Central College," 1 August
      1818, *Founders Online*, accessed September 2017, https://founders.archives.gov/
      documents/Madison/04-01-02-0287.

25   Zachariah Nevil Estate Inventory, Nelson County Will Book D, 39.

26   Federal Population Census, Nelson County, VA, 1820; Zachariah Nevil Inventory,
      Nelson County Will Book D, 38–42; Zachariah Nevil obituary, *Richmond Enquirer*,
      20 April 1830, p. 3.

27   Martha (Jefferson) Randolph to Ellen W. (Randolph) Coolidge, 1 September 1825,
      Acc. 9090, University of Virginia; Edwin Morris Betts and James Adam Bear, Jr.,

editors, *The Family Letters of Thomas Jefferson* (Columbia, MO: University of Missouri Press, 1966), 343.

28 Land Tax, Nelson County, VA, 1829; "Jesse Mundy & Wife vs Administrators of Zachariah Neville, etc.;" Nelson County Will Book C, 315–16, 362, 426.

29 Nelson County Deed Book 6, p. 89; Mutual Assurance Society, policy #435, 13 October 1812, Library of Virginia; Brown, *The Cabells and Their Kin*, 281–82. Dr. George Cabell lived at Bonair until 1817, the year his first wife, Susannah (Wyatt) Cabell, died. Cabell and his second wife, Elizabeth Fitzhugh May, were residing in Richmond, Virginia when the deed for Bonair was recorded in November of 1826. Bonair remained in Zachariah Nevil's estate until March of 1836, when it was sold by his children to James T. Smith of Buckingham County for $10,000. In 1937, Bonair was the subject of a survey for the Virginia Historical Inventory and, in 1980, the owners applied to have the property listed on the National Register of Historic Places. See Nelson County Deed Book 8, pp. 410, 415; Annie L. Harrower, "Bon Aire," Virginia Historical Inventory, Library of Virginia; "Bon Aire," National Register of Historic Places Inventory Nomination Form, 30 July 1980.

30 "Bon Air," n. d., clipping file, Nelson County Historical Society, Nelson Memorial Library, Lovingston, VA.

31 Brown, *The Cabells and Their Kin*, 422.

32 *Richmond Enquirer*, 20 April 1830, p. 3.

33 Administrator's Bond, Nelson County Will Book D, 26. Jesse and Louisa (Nevil) Mundy challenged the administrators of Zachariah Nevil's estate in the Nelson County Court. The dispute was not settled until 1872. Numerous papers pertaining to Nevil's estate were filed during the chancery case and are preserved at the Library of Virginia. See "Jesse Mundy & Wife vs Administrators of Zachariah Neville, etc."

34 Marriage Record, Albemarle County, VA; Mr. James L. Nevil in account with Jesse Jopling, January 1835, "Jesse Mundy & Wife vs Administrators of Zachariah Neville, etc.;" Albemarle County Will Book 22, p. 362; Nelson County Will Book G (1843–1847), 73–74.

35 John Vogt & T. William Kethley, Jr., *Nelson County Virginia Marriages 1808–1850*, p. 107; Federal Population Census, Amherst County, VA, 1850; "Jesse Mundy & Wife vs Administrators of Zachariah Neville, etc." In 1871, the Mundys' daughter, Lue, married Paul C. Cabell, who briefly represented Amherst County in the Virginia House of Delegates. See "Cabells in the Virginia General Assembly," Small Special Collections Library, University of Virginia, accessed September 2017, http://small.library.virginia.edu/collections/featured/the-cabell-family-papers-2/contributions/statesmen/cabells-general-assembly/.

36 Nelson County Will Book D, 28; Nelson County Minute Book, 1830–1835, p. 11; Yeck, *The Jefferson Brothers*, 111–23.

37   Joseph C. Cabell to Col. Zachariah Nevil, MS 38-764, Small Special Collections, University of Virginia.

38   Nelson County Will Book D, 17. In this document, Madison's name was recorded as James M. Nevil, likely a clerical error. In 1832, he matriculated at Washington College as Jefferson M. Nevil. See "Matriculation List: Winter Session, 1832-3," Manuscripts Collection, James Graham Leyburn Library, Washington and Lee University.

39   "Accounting for M. Nevil, with Robert L. Jefferson, his Guardian," Nelson County Will Book D, 482–484; "Jesse Mundy & Wife vs Administrators of Zachariah Neville, etc.;" Joanne L. Yeck, "Elbridge G. Jefferson," *Lost Jeffersons* (Slate River Press, 2018).

40   The accounts for Zachariah Nevil's estate indicate that on December 21, 1830, $.79 was paid for Madison's "ferriage to Maj. Yancey's school." Maj. Charles Yancey (1770–1857), mentioned elsewhere in the estate accounts of Zachariah Nevil, owned land adjacent Nevil tracts on the Rockfish River, in addition to thousands of acres across the James River in Buckingham County. Madison Nevil's accounts reveal multiple payments for education including: Peter White ($29.25 for tuition and board); James Walker; and "Kilbourne." See "Accounting for M. Nevil, with Robert L. Jefferson, his Guardian," Nelson County Deed Book 1, p. 43; "Major Charles Yancey," accessed September 2017, http://yanceyfamilygenealogy.org/cxypic.htm.

41   Joseph Martin, *A New and Comprehensive Gazetteer of Virginia and the District of Colombia* (Charlottesville, VA, 1835), 427.

42   Calder Conrad Loth, "The Ante Bellum Architecture of Washington and Lee University," (Thesis, University of Virginia, May, 1967), 28–29.

43   Charles F. Hoffman, *Winter in the West: By a New Yorker, Volume II* (New-York, NY: Harper & Brothers, 1835), 311–12. Despite Hoffman's idyllic description, the early 1830s were challenging for Washington College, particularly due to President Marshall's radical educational philosophies. Enrollment decreased as a result. See Calder Conrad Loth, "The Ante Bellum Architecture of Washington and Lee University;" Ollinger Crenshaw, *General Lee's College: The Rise and Growth of Washington and Lee University* (NY: Random House, 1969).

44   "Matriculation List: Winter Session, 1832–1833," Washington and Lee University; Cornelius Thomas, deposition, "Jesse Mundy and Wife vs Lafayette Neville, Committee, etc.," Nelson County Chancery Case, 1845-001, Library of Virginia. In 1833, Lafayette Nevil rented Locust Grove from his father's estate. Cornelius Thomas was Nevil's overseer. See "Jesse Mundy & Wife vs Lafayette Neville, Committee, etc."

45   Minutes, "Washington Literary Society Records," Collection 159, James Graham Leyburn Library, Washington and Lee University.

46   Manuscripts Collection, James Graham Leyburn Library, Washington and Lee University.

47 Nelson County Minute Book, 1830–1835, p. 254; Nelson County Minute Book, 1835–1840, pp. 124, 384; "Jesse Mundy & Wife vs Administrators of Zachariah Neville, etc."

48 John W. Thomas, deposition, "Jesse Mundy and Wife vs Lafayette Neville, Committee, etc."

49 *Richmond Whig*, 17 July 1835, p. 3. Bonair was purchased by James T. Smith of Buckingham County for $10,000. See Nelson County Deed Book 8, p. 410, 415.

50 Locust Grove, Nelson County Deed Book 8, pp. 446–48.

51 "Virginia, Select Marriages, 1785-1940," ancestry.com; Personal Property Tax, Nelson County, VA, 1837; "Pleasant Labby (1792–1869)," Old City Cemetery website, accessed September 2017, http://www.gravegarden.org/pleasant-labby1792-1869/. At the time of the Nevil's marriage, Lafayette Nevil's uncle, James Lilburne Jefferson, was still alive and living in Lynchburg.

52 John W. Thomas, deposition, "Jesse Mundy and Wife vs Lafayette Neville, Committee, etc.;" Cornelius Thomas, deposition, ibid.; Lafayette Nevil, response, ibid. Despite Madison Nevil's mental decline, he was able to conduct some business at the Nelson County Court. On January 11, 1836, Madison signed off on his guardian's accounting from December 1831–1835. He was due $369.48 in cash. See "Accounting for M. Nevil, with Robert L. Jefferson, his Guardian," Nelson County Will Book D, 482–84. In March 1837, along with his siblings, Madison sold his share of Bonair (a.k.a. "The River Plantation") and, in May, he sold his share of the homeplace, Locust Grove, to his brother Lafayette. See Nelson County Deed Book 8, pp. 410, 415; Nelson County Deed Book 8, p. 447.

53 Personal Property Tax, Albemarle County, VA, 1834–1835; Yeck, "Elbridge Gerry Jefferson," *Lost Jeffersons.*

54 John W. Thomas, deposition, "Jesse Mundy and Wife vs Lafayette Neville, Committee, etc."

55 Lafayette Nevil, response, ibid.; James Powell, deposition, ibid.; John W. Thomas, deposition, ibid.

56 Cornelius Thomas, deposition, ibid.; Elizabeth Murphy, deposition, ibid.; Pauline Thomas, deposition, ibid.; Norborne M. Thomas, deposition, ibid.; John W. Thomas, deposition, ibid.

57 "A Guide to the Records of Western State Hospital, 1825–2000," Library of Virginia, accessed September 2017, http://ead.lib.virginia.edu/vivaxtf/view?docId=lva/vi00937.xml.

58 Cornelius Thomas, deposition, "Jesse Mundy and Wife vs Lafayette Neville, Committee, etc.;" John W. Thomas, deposition, ibid.; John W. Thomas, deposition, ibid.

59 "Jesse Mundy and Wife vs Lafayette Neville, Committee, etc."

60 Court order, "Jesse Mundy and Wife vs Lafayette Neville, Committee, etc."

61 Curator's bond, ibid.

62 Court order, ibid.

63 Lafayette Neville to Louisa Mundy, 21 August 1838, ibid.

64 Lafayette Neville to Louisa Mundy, 18 November 1838, ibid.

65 Lafayette Neville to Louisa Mundy, 25 December 1838, ibid.

66 Federal Census, Albemarle County, VA, 1860.

67 "Jesse Mundy and Wife vs Lafayette Neville, Committee, etc."

68 Nelson County Minute Book, 1835–1840, p. 276.

69 John W. Thomas, deposition, "Jesse Mundy and Wife vs Lafayette Neville, Committee, etc."

70 "Jesse Mundy and Wife vs Lafayette Neville, Committee, etc."

71 Lafayette Neville answer [mutilated], "Jesse Mundy & Wife vs Lafayette Neville, Committee, etc."

72 "Jesse Mundy & Wife vs Lafayette Neville, Committee, etc."

73 Ibid.

74 *Richmond Enquirer*, 15 January 1842, p. 1.

75 *Lynchburg Virginian*, 5 February 1849, p. 3.

"Elbridge Gerry Jefferson: Surrogate Son of Peter Field Jefferson"

1 Peter Field Jefferson Will, Albemarle County Will Book 26, pp. 245–46; Peter Field Jefferson, "1864 Estate Sale," Albemarle County Will Book 27, pp. 262–63.

2 In 1807, a letter from Randolph Jefferson to his brother Thomas Jefferson was addressed: "Mr. Thomas Jefferson; pr son Lewis; Monticello." There is no birth record for Lewis Jefferson, however, his death record, dated May of 1858, stated he was seventy-two. If this is correct, he was born in Buckingham County in about 1786. See Death Record, Albemarle County, VA.

3 Joanne L. Yeck, *The Jefferson Brothers* (Kettering, OH: Slate River Press), 302–306.

4 Robert Lewis Jefferson, advertisement, *Richmond Enquirer*, 18 June 1811, p. 1; Thomas Jefferson, Jr., advertisement, *Richmond Enquirer*, 18 February 1812, p. 1; Peter Field Jefferson, advertisement, *Richmond Enquirer*, 8 June 1816, p. 1.

5 John Vogt and T. William Kethley, Jr., *Nelson County Virginia Marriages 1808–1850* (Athens, GA: Iberian Publishing Co., 1985), 37; Amherst County Deed Book M, 494–95. In 1814, Lewis Jefferson purchased 110 acres of land located on Water Park Branch and Elk Island Creek from John Scruggs for the sum of £80. Later that year, George Penn and his wife, Pamelia, transferred an additional 195 acres on the

branches of Elk Island Creek to Lewis Jefferson. The price was £425. On this deed, Jefferson is identified as "Robert Lewis Jefferson of Nelson County."

6   In 1813, Lewis Jefferson paid personal property tax on himself, one horse, and one slave. It was a modest beginning. In 1814, he paid tax on himself and a slave; the horse was gone. In 1815, he was taxed only on himself, his fortunes apparently declining. In 1821, Jefferson once again owned a horse and a slave, paying $.66 ½ tax. The following year, his wealth improved dramatically and now included three slaves (aged over sixteen) and a horse. The 1828 Buckingham land tax record shows the conveyance from Howel Lewis to Robert Lewis Jefferson. The farm was adjacent two slightly larger, Harris-owned plantations. Benjamin D. and John M. Harris were the sons of prominent Albemarle planter, Benjamin Harris, and social peers of Lewis Jefferson and his brothers. They were nephews of Capt. John Harris of Albemarle, who purchased Snowden. It is currently unknown whether Robert Lewis or Elbridge G. Jefferson named the farm Millbrook. It was definitely known as such when it was sold from Elbridge Jefferson's estate. Various deeds indicate that there once was a mill on the property. It may be a coincidence that Millbrook was the name of John Wayles Eppes' tobacco plantation in southern Buckingham County. Eppes was President Thomas Jefferson's son-in-law, who settled there in about 1811, after the death of his wife Maria (Jefferson) Eppes. Moving to Buckingham County was politically strategic. Thomas Jefferson wanted his son-in-law to run for Congress to oust a political nemesis, John Randolph, and Eppes succeeded in the 1813 election. See Personal Property Tax, Nelson County, VA, 1813–1815, 1821–1822. Personal Property Tax, Buckingham County, VA, 1823–1825; Land Tax, Buckingham County, VA, 1828; "Millbrook," *Thomas Jefferson Encyclopedia*, accessed September 2017, https://www.monticello.org/site/research-and-collections/millbrook.

7   Marriage Record, Albemarle County, VA; Yeck, "The Second Mrs. Jefferson," *The Jefferson Brothers*, 259–84; Albemarle County Deed Book 29, pp. 39–40, 530. On June 12, 1830, Robert Lewis Jefferson acquired the Robert Moorman homeplace on Totier Creek in Albemarle County, purchasing 437 acres from the Moorman heirs. It was a valuable piece of property, as tax records would later reveal.

8   Roger G. Ward, *Land Tax Summaries & Implied Deeds 1815–1830, Volume 2* (Athens, GA: Iberian Publishing Company, 1994), 185. In 1830, Lewis Jefferson owned fourteen male and thirteen female slaves. In 1832, Lewis Jefferson added another 133 1/3 acres to his Buckingham County farm. Purchased from Edward Robertson, this tract was described as being on Slate River, fifteen miles northeast of the courthouse. See Federal Population Census, Buckingham County, VA, 1830; Ward, *Land Tax Summaries & Implied Deeds 1815–1830, Volume 2*, p. 185.

9   Millbrook photographs, Jeremy Winfrey Collection. In 1829, the structures on Robert Lewis Jefferson's farm were valued at $500. In 1865, the structures on Elbridge G. Jefferson's land were still valued at $500. See Land Tax, Buckingham County, VA, 1829–1865.

10   S. Allen Chambers to Joanne Yeck, email, May 2009. The house at Millbrook is still remembered by citizens in the Slate River District, however, it burned many years ago, making any further evaluation of the dwelling impossible.

11   Roger G. Ward, *Land Tax Summaries & Implied Deeds 1841–1870, Volume 3* (Athens, GA: Iberian Publishing Company, 1995), 149; *Nelson County Virginia Marriages 1808–1850*, p. 37. Mary C. Horsley was the daughter of William and Sarah "Sally" (Christian) Horsley, of Nelson County. Her father was named a Magistrate when Nelson County was formed in 1809. The Horsleys and Jordans intermarried with the Cabell family and established themselves along the north side of the upper valley of the James River. Sally was a descendant of Mary Cabell and William Horsley of Center Hill. Col. William Cabell of Union Hill married Margaret Jordan. Robert Lewis Jefferson engaged in business with the larger Christian–Horsley family. In a bond dated December 20, 1819 (recorded March 23, 1830, Nelson County, VA) between Charles Christian, Robert Lewis Jefferson, William Horsley, and Henry H. Watts, Christian transferred thirteen of his "negro" slaves to the three men as trustees. Among them were slaves named Jordan and Lewis, indicating tight family connections. In the bond, Christian named his sister Sally, wife of William Horsley; his sister Elizabeth, wife of James Murphy; and his brother James Christian. See Nelson County Deed Book 1, pp. 41–42; Alexander Brown, *The Cabells and Their Kin: A Memorial Volume of History, Biography, and Genealogy* (Boston, MA: Houghton, Mifflin and Company, 1895), 61, 190–191, 274.

12   William Jordan Will, Nelson County Will Book G (1844–1847), 271–74. The will was written on December 13, 1840, with a codicil dated April 21, 1846, and proved in Nelson County on October 26, 1846. William Jordan's inventory, recorded in October of 1846, indicates his personal property totaled $8,770.89 at the time of his death. See William Jordan Inventory, Nelson County Will Book G (1844–1847), 305–07.

13   Federal Population Census, Buckingham County, VA, 1850–1860; Slave Census, Buckingham County, VA, 1850–1860; Agricultural Census, Buckingham County, VA, 1850–1860.

14   Federal Population Census, Buckingham County, VA, 1860. Jeanne Stinson, *Buckingham County Virginia Death Records, 1853-1868* (Atlanta, GA: Iberian Publishing Company, 2000), 87, 105.

15   Virginia Militia Commissions, Virginia Governors' Records, 1776-1998, Special Collections, Library of Virginia.

16   Gordon G. Ragland, Jr., *The Tie That Binds: The Stories of Sharon Baptist Church Buckingham County, Virginia*, (Privately Published, 2008), 27–29; Margaret A. Pennington and Lorna S. Scott, *The Courthouse Burned—Book II* (Buckingham Court House, VA: Historic Buckingham, 2002), 90; Federal Population Census, Buckingham County, VA, 1860. Three of the marriages Elbridge G. Jefferson performed are documented in *Lost Marriages of Buckingham County, Virginia*. See

James Randolph Kidd, *Lost Marriages of Buckingham County, Virginia* (Athens, GA: 1992).

17 Albemarle County Deed Book 51, p. 19; Rev. Edgar Woods, *Albemarle County in Virginia* (Baltimore, MD: Clearfield Co., 1997), 134. Rev. Martin Dawson conducted marriages for Anna Scott Jefferson and Zachariah Nevil (1803) and for Polly Lewis and Thomas Jefferson, Jr. (1808).

18 Death Record, Albemarle County, VA; Albemarle County Will Book 25, pp. 355–56. Elizabeth Ann (Moorman) Jefferson died after 1880. See Federal Population Census, Albemarle County, VA, 1880.

19 Federal Population Census, Albemarle County, VA, 1860.

20 Peter Field Jefferson Will, Albemarle County Will Book 26, pp. 245–46; Peter Field Jefferson Estate Sale (1864), Albemarle County Will Book 27, pp. 262–63.

21 Buckingham County Deed Book 4, pp. 368–69; Federal Industrial Census, Buckingham County, VA, 1860.

22 *Daily Progress*, no date, clipping file, Albemarle Charlottesville Historical Society.

23 *Scottsville Register*, 2 November 1867, p. 2, clipping file, Small Special Collections, University of Virginia.

24 Capt. John Clark Turner (23 September 1823–14 October 1906) was a Buckingham County native with many connections to the Jefferson family. Despite being a court appointed administrator, he likely was a trusted friend of E. G. Jefferson. In 1850, Turner headed an inclusive household. Living with his family were his nephew, John N. Tapscott (age 11), Fanny Goode (age 70), and a boarder, Dr. Lineaus Bolling (age 28). In 1872, H. B. Burnley was the guardian for these Jefferson brothers, who were still minors. A Buckingham County Chancery Case, still open in the June Term of 1874, revealed that Elbridge Jefferson's brother-in-law, Albert W. Gantt, served as the Administrator of Jefferson's estate. In 1873, the Buckingham County Chancery Case, "Jones vs Jones Executor," included Elbridge G. Jefferson, dec^d and John C. Turner, among many others. In September of 1875, "Tapscott and Jefferson Administrators vs Tapscott" included E. G. Jefferson dec^d and John C. Turner, among others. See Elizabeth A. Jefferson, deposition, "Elizabeth A. Jefferson vs A. W. Gantt and wife," Albemarle County Chancery Case, 1873-006, Library of Virginia; Buckingham Order Book 2, p.194; Jeanne Stinson, *Buckingham County Virginia Undetermined Chancery Files Index* (Athens, GA: Iberian Publishing Company, 1994), 38, 68.

25 Federal Population Census, Buckingham County, VA, 1870. The real estate was Millbrook Farm on Sharps Creek, however, the personal property value is difficult to interpret. In 1870, the Jefferson's wealthy neighbor, James Harris, for example, owned $28,000 in real estate and only $2,000 in personal property. Capt. John C. Turner was living handsomely, reporting $8,000 in real estate and $8,000 in personal property.

26 Eventually, the Jefferson brothers sold the farm in pieces to M. L. A. "Matt" Moseley. See Land Tax, Buckingham County, VA, 1886.

27 Federal Population Census, Buckingham County, VA, 1870, 1910; Death Record, Buckingham County, VA; Death Record, Albemarle County, VA. Interestingly, their great-grandfather, Randolph Jefferson, suffered from kidney stones.

"Lilburne Lewis: Virginia Gentry Gone Wrong"

1 Boyton Merrill, Jr., *Jefferson's Nephews: A Frontier Tragedy* (Lincoln, NE: University of Nebraska Press, 2004), 258–61.

2 In 1953, Southern literary giant Robert Penn Warren immortalized the Lewis murder in his book, *Brother to Dragons: A Tale in Verse and Voices*. See Robert Penn Warren, *Brother to Dragons: A Tale in Verse and Voices* (New York, NY: Random House, 1979).

3 *New National Era and Citizen*, 1 January 1874, p. 1.

4 Merrill, "A Mistaken Title," 341–42.

5 Thomas Jefferson to Col. Charles Lewis, 7 October 1806, Massachusetts Historical Society.

6 Jay Feldman, *When the Mississippi Ran Backwards: Empire, Intrigue, and the New Madrid Earthquakes* (New York, NY: Free Press, 2005), 95–96.

7 The original note is signed only "L. L.", with no reference to a "G. H." See Lilburne Lewis, will, 10 April 1812, Livingston County, Kentucky, Will Book A, 34.

8 *New National Era and Citizen*, 1 January 1874, p. 1.

9 *Indiana State Sentinel*, 6 January 1874, p. 6.

10 Elizabeth Jane Woodson (Lewis) Lewis, Find A Grave, accessed October 2017, https://www.findagrave.com/memorial/144848865.

11 Merrill, pp. 266–69.

12 *Hartford Weekly Herald*, (Hartford, KY), 18 January 1893, p. 4.

13 Robert Lewis (1807–1814) is buried in the Lewis cemetery in Birdsville, Livingston County, Kentucky. See Find A Grave, accessed September 2017, https://www.find-agrave.com/memorial/144849400.

14 Charles L. Lewis to Thomas Jefferson, 5 August 1813, *Founders Online*, accessed September 2017, https://founders.archives.gov/documents/Jefferson/03-06-02-0296.

15 Atlanta H. Taylor Pool, "Tragedies in Livingston," *Courier-Journal* (Louisville, KY), 10 June 1894, p. 18.

16 *Atlanta Constitution*, 28 November 1874, p. 1.

17 *Courier-Journal* (Louisville, KY), 6 October 1936, p.7. Otto A. Rothert's paper was published in the *Filson Club History Quarterly* in October, 1936. See The Filson Historical Society Index to the *Filson Club History Quarterly*," accessed December 2017, http://filsonhistorical.org/wp-content/uploads/FCHQ_index1.pdf.

18   Ibid.

19   Boynton Merrill, Jr., *Jefferson's Nephews: A Frontier Tragedy*; Robert Penn Warren, *Brother to Dragons: A Tale in Verse and Voices*.

"Jefferson Myths"

1   Virginia Moore, *Scottsville on the James: An Informal History* (Richmond, VA: The Dietz Press, 1994), 37.

2   *Richmond Dispatch*, 25 February, 1900, p. 9.

3   Susan Kern, *The Jeffersons at Shadwell* (New Haven, CT: Yale University Press, 2012).

4   Eric G. Grundset, *"Land lying in the County of Albemarle:" Albemarle County, Virginia Surveyors' Plat Books Volume 1, Parts 1 and 2, and Volume 2 1744–1853 [and 1892]*, (Privately published, 1998), 12; Goochland County Deed Book 2, p. 222; "Shadwell," *Thomas Jefferson Encyclopedia*, accessed September 2017, https://www.monticello.org/site/research-and-collections/shadwell.

5   Joanne L. Yeck, "Thomas Jefferson Did Not Sleep Here: The Cave at Snowden," *Buckingham Beacon* (September 2014), 8–9, 14. For the complete story of Thomas Jefferson's role as Governor of Virginia and his daring escape from Monticello, see Michael Kranish, *Flight from Monticello: Thomas Jefferson at War* (Oxford, England: Oxford University Press, 2010).

6   Virginia Moore, *Scottsville*, 37.

7   Ibid., 37–38.

8   "Diary of Arnold's Invasion and Notes on Subsequent Events in 1781: Versions of 1796 ?, 1805, and 1816," Founders Online, National Archives, accessed September 2017, https://founders.archives.gov/documents/Jefferson/01-04-02-0323-0002.

9   David Spears to Joanne Yeck, email, August 2014.

Appendix

Genealogy Chart: Randolph Jefferson Family

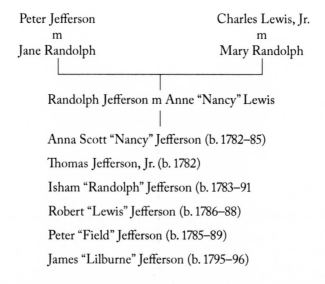

Peter Jefferson
m
Jane Randolph

Charles Lewis, Jr.
m
Mary Randolph

Randolph Jefferson m Anne "Nancy" Lewis

Anna Scott "Nancy" Jefferson (b. 1782–85)

Thomas Jefferson, Jr. (b. 1782)

Isham "Randolph" Jefferson (b. 1783–91)

Robert "Lewis" Jefferson (b. 1786–88)

Peter "Field" Jefferson (b. 1785–89)

James "Lilburne" Jefferson (b. 1795–96)

There are no known records of the births of Randolph and Anne (Lewis) Jefferson's children. These dates are a composite of census data and other sources, including Randolph Jefferson's will, letters, and chancery case exhibits. Five sons and one daughter are known to have survived to adulthood. Randolph Jefferson's last child with his second wife, Mitchie B. (Pryor) Jefferson, John Randolph Jefferson (1816–1845), was born seven months after his father's death and was raised in Tennessee apart from his Jefferson kinfolk.

Genealogy Chart: Peter Field Jefferson Family

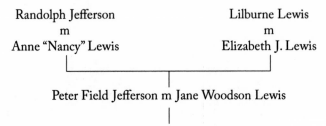

Randolph Jefferson   Lilburne Lewis
m   m
Anne "Nancy" Lewis   Elizabeth J. Lewis

Peter Field Jefferson m Jane Woodson Lewis

1. Frances Ann "Fanny" Jefferson m Valentine Foland

    i.   Peter Valentine Foland m Elizabeth "Bettie" Clarke Straton

2. Male Jefferson

3. Thomas Jefferson

4. Peter Field Jefferson, Jr. m Elizabeth A. Wood

    i.   Peter Jefferson

    ii.   Frances Anne Wade "Fannie" Jefferson m Hartwell Steven Moore

Will of Randolph Jefferson

I Randolph Jefferson of Buckingham county in Virginia being in sound health do make the following testamentary disposition of my estate.

I give all the negroes which I shall own at the time of my death to be equally divided between my five sons Thomas, Robert Lewis, Field, Randolph & Lilburne, each of them to whom I may have given slaves during my life time, bringing the value of those slaves into hotchpot with those to be divided, and ~~draw~~ taking from those to be divided only so much as with those before given shall make his portion of slaves equal to that of each of his other brothers. It is my will that all my lands and other property whatsoever be sold after my death, and the proceeds be equally divided among my said five sons, my son Thomas bringing into hotchpot with those proceeds

the sum of one thousand pounds (at which I estimate the advantages I have given him during my life) and taking from the proceeds only so much as, being added to the £s Thousand pounds, shall make his portion under this bequest equal to that of his other brothers.

~~I give to my son Lewis my violin, to my son~~

Lastly I make my friends Harding (sic) Perkins & Robert Craig, my son Robert Lewis, and my brother Thomas Jefferson executors of this my will, revoking all others heretofore made and ~~writing~~ in testimony hereof I have written the whole with my own hand this 27th day of

May 1808.*

* This surviving draft of Randolph Jefferson's 1808 will was held by his brother, Thomas Jefferson, one of the executors. In 1815, there was also a deathbed will, which was contested by Jefferson's sons. No copy of the last will is known to exist.

Will of Peter Field Jefferson

I. Peter F. Jefferson, considering the uncertainty of life, and the duty of being prepared for death, do make and ordain this to be my last will and testament, hereby revoking all former wills by me at anytime made.

I. I desire, that all my just debts shall be paid by my Executors.

II. I desire that all my property real and personal not herein specifically disposed of, to be sold by my executors.

III. I give and devise to my wife for and during her natural life, my tract of land and its appurtenances, situated in the County of Buckingham, and which was purchased by me from Winfree's estate, including the mill thereon. I also give to my wife my household and kitchen furniture at my residence in Scottsville, and fifteen hundred dollars.

IV. At the death of my wife I give and devise the track of land and appurtenances (including the mill) to William M. Wade & [Elbridge] Jefferson, or the survivor of them in trust for the exclusive use and benefit of my son Peter F. Jefferson and his wife, during their joint lives and the life of the survivor of them; and at the death of the survivor of them. I give the same to the children of the said Peter F. I also give to the said William M. Wade and [Elbridge] Jefferson, or the survivor of them, ten thousand dollars in trust for the use and benefit of my said son Peter F. and wife during their joint lives, and the life of the survivor of them; and at the death of the survivor I give the said ten thousand dollars to the children of the said Peter F. The said Peter F. should receive the interest on the said ten thousand dollars semi-annually; and in no case is the principle to be used. And the said Peter F. when he comes into possession of the said tract of land, is to have the privilege of cultivating the same and applying the profits thereof to the use and benefit of himself and wife; but should he not choose to cultivate the same the said William M. Wade & Elbridge Jefferson or the survivor of them, shall rent the same out, applying the rents to the use and benefit of the said Peter F. and wife.

V. I give and bequest fifteen thousand dollars to William M. Wade and [Elbridge] Jefferson or the survivor of them, in trust for the use and benefit, of my son Thomas Jefferson, for and during his natural life; and at his death I give the same to his children. The said Thomas is to receive the interest semi-annually; and in no case is the principle to be used.

VI. I give and devise all my real estate situated within the Town of Scottsville and immediately adjacent thereto, including the ferry, to my grandson Peter Foland but the said Peter Foland is not to take possession of the said property until he attains the age of twenty-one years; and in the meantime my executors are directed to rent the same out, and from year to year, or a term of years, until the said Peter Foland arrives at the age of twenty-one years; and the proceeds to be put out at interest and allowed to accumulate, until that said Peter Foland arrives at the age of twenty-one, and then to be paid over to him by my executors. But if my Executors shall deem it best my will and desire is that my said Scottsville property and property immediately adjacent thereto, shall be sold by them and the proceeds invested at interest, and allowed to accumulate until the said Peter Foland attains the age of twenty-one, and then my Executors shall pay the proceeds & its interest over to him in fee simple.

VII. I give to my nephew, [Elbridge] Jefferson all my property real and personal with in the County of Nelson to him & his heirs forever.

VIII. In case either of my sons die without issue, I direct that what is herein given to him dying without issue, shall go to the survivor of them, and if both die without issue, then my will is, that what is herein given to them shall go to, and be equally divided between the children of my brother Robert L. Jefferson. And if my grandson Peter Foland die without issue, before he attains the age of twenty-one years, I direct that what is herein given him shall go to and be equally divided between my two sons to be held on the same trusts, limitations and reservations as what I have given to them is held.

IX. All the rest and residue of my estate real and personal I give to my two sons and the children of my brother Robert L. Jefferson to be equally divided among them. But what is given my two sons under the 9th clause of my will is given to them upon the same trusts, limitations and reservations as what is herein before given to them.

X. I give my Negro man Winston to my wife for life, and at her death I give him to my son Peter F. Jefferson.

XI. I hereby nominate & appoint William M. Wade and [Elbridge] Jefferson, Executors of my last will and testament.

In testimony whereof I have hereto set my hand and seal this 9th day of September 1854.

Signed, sealed, published and declared, as and for the last will and testament of Peter F. Jefferson in our presence who at his request have witnessed the same.

B. F. Frye
Jno. O. Lewis
C. M. Ragland.

Recorded in Albemarle County Court September 2nd 1861.
Albemarle County Will Book 26, pp. 245–46.

Will of Lilburne Lewis

In the name of God Amen This my last Will &c.

1st It's my desire that all my Just debts be paid and then my property both real & personal be equally divided between my children Jane W. Lewis, Lucy J. Lewis, Lilburne L. Lewis, Elizabeth Lewis, Robert Lewis & James R. Lewis reserving to my beloved but cruel wife Letitia G. Lewis her Lawful part of said property during her natural life.

2nd It's my desire that my beloved father Charles L. Lewis be possessed of the riding horse which I purchased of Hurley my rifle & shot bag during his natural life also my walking cane and that my beloved sisters Martha C. Lewis, Lucy B. Lewis & Nancy M. Lewis may be comforted from the perquisites of sd estate by my executor as prudence may require or in other words so as to do my children and themselves entire Justice.

3rd I do hereby constitute my beloved father Charles L. Lewis the revd. Wm. Woods near Salem, Saml C. Harkins, James McCawley & Richd Ferguson my executors, whom I must remind that Henry F. Dealny has received a fee from me for the prosecution in a Trespass against James Rutter senr, James Rutter Jnr , James Young & Thomas Terry given under my hand this & revoking all and every other will heretofore made/ ninth day of Apl. Eighteen hundred and Twelve. Lilburne Lewis (seal)

NB. my dog nero I do hereby bequeath to my beloved father.

L. L.   Rocky Hill Apl. 9th 1812

Mr. James McCawley I have fallen a victim to my beloved but cruel Letitia. I die in the hope of being united to my other wife in heaven. take care of this will & come here that we may be decently buried.

Adieu. L. Lewis

NB. within this inclosure myself and brother requests be entered (sic) in the same coffin and in the same ground grave.

Rocky Hill Apl. 10th 1812 my beloved but cruel Letitia receive this as a pledge of my forgiveness to your connection the day of Judgement is to come. I owe you no malice but die on account of your absence and my dear little son James

Adieu my love Lilburne Lewis
Livingston county Sct. May county court 1812

The within will was proved to be the hand writing of Lilburne Lewis by William Rice, James McCawley and Lilburne Lewis senr. and ordered to be recorded.

Test. Enoch Prince Ch C
Livingston County, Kentucky Will Book A, 34.

Acknowledgments

Any work of non-fiction relies on a small army of helpful clerks, librarians, archivists, scholars, and other devotees of history. Over several years, expert staffs at the following institutions lent their collective knowledge to this project: Albemarle Charlottesville Historical Society; Albert and Shirley Small Special Collections Library (University of Virginia); Housewright Museum (Historic Buckingham); Library of Virginia; Virginia Historical Society; and Special Collections (Washington and Lee University). Albemarle, Fluvanna, and Nelson County courthouses provided access to many critical documents, and, at Buckingham County's courthouse, Brenda Kitchen, Margaret Thomas, and Diane Boggs were of invaluable assistance, locating and retrieving pertinent chancery cases.

Digitalized chancery records at the Library of Virginia's Virginia Memory filled in many gaps and the National Archives, via "Founders Online," provided core source material. In Ohio, I relied on Greg Estes and Jeanne Waselewski (Dayton Metro Library) and Chris May (Washington-Centerville Library) for assistance with interlibrary loan services. In Richmond, Bibb Edwards always had time for just one more "lookup" at the Library of Virginia.

The availability of searchable, historic newspapers online is fueling new and revised histories. These constantly growing collections of digital resources were fundamental to this endeavor. Special thanks to Errol Somay and "the gang" at Virginia Chronicle (Library of Virginia), who are particularly dedicated to making Virginia's historic newspapers accessible to all.

For assistance with images, thanks goes to the Library of Congress' Digital Collections; Dale Neighbors, Meghan Townes, and Mark Fagerburg (Library of Virginia); Connie Geary (Scottsville Museum); Quatro Hubbard and Randy Jones (Virginia Department of Historic Resources); and Mary Broach, Charles Culbertson, Jane Eaton, Richard Nicholas, Raymon Thacker, and Jeremy Winfrey for sharing their private collections.

Many individuals devoted to the preservation of Scottsville's history lent their expertise to this work. Connie Geary, Scottsville Museum's digital archivist and webmaster, answered question after question. Ruth Klippstein, Steven Meeks, Randolph Moulton, Gordon Ragland, and the encyclopedic Raymon Thacker made my work lighter and more fun. One rainy day, Judy Brown kindly escorted me up the hill to Mount Walla and, at Snowden, the Goodwin, Moseley, and Tyson families opened their homes and walked their land with me.

As this project was coming to a close, Mary Broach, a descendant of Isham Randolph Jefferson, came to my aid with rich information about the Jeffersons who removed to Kentucky. Also, the generous volunteers at Find A Grave helped locate the burial places of many Jeffersons.

I am deeply indebted to Boynton Merrill's well-documented scholarship and his book, *Jefferson's Nephews: A Frontier Tragedy*, which follows the lives of the Lucy (Jefferson) and Charles L. Lewis family and to Richard Nicholas' meticulous research which provided an essential foundation concerning Scottsville's founding and evolution.

In 2010, a Jefferson Fellowship at the Robert H. Smith International Center for Jefferson Studies not only supported research for *The Jefferson Brothers* (Slate River Press, 2012) but also gave me the opportunity and resources to delve into the lives of Randolph Jefferson's children. My on-going thanks to Anna Berkes, Research Librarian at Jefferson Library, who along with many other tasks, maintains the ever-expanding *Thomas Jefferson Encyclopedia*.

My production team included knowledgeable readers Mary Carolyn Mitton and Richard Nicholas; editor Zan McGreevey; designer Craig Ramsdell; and the tireless David Braughler who managed this project from soup to nuts to coffee. Above all, gratitude goes to my colleagues, my family, and my always hospitable Virginia cousins, who fed and housed me, driving me to places only trucks should go.

About the Author

After earning her doctorate in cinema studies at the University of Southern California, Joanne Yeck taught and wrote about film history for many years. She is the author of numerous articles concerning Classic Hollywood and American Popular Culture, and is the co-author of *Movie Westerns* and *Our Movie Heritage*. Since 1995, her interest in Virginia history has become a full-time occupation. Years of research resulted in *"At a Place Called Buckingham"* (2011), which celebrated the county's 250th anniversary, followed by *"At a Place Called Buckingham," Volume Two* (2015). In 2010, she was awarded a Jefferson Fellowship at the International Center for Jefferson Studies which supported her research for *The Jefferson Brothers* (2012), a biography of President Thomas Jefferson's only brother, Randolph Jefferson. Her blog, Slate River Ramblings, attracts a growing community interested in Buckingham County and its environs. When not exploring the back roads of Virginia, she lives in Kettering, Ohio. Visit her online at joannelyeck.com and slateriverramblings.com.

PHOTO BY ANDY SNOW

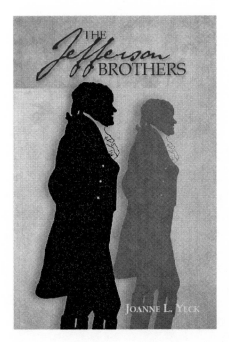

CPSIA information can be obtained
at www.ICGtesting.com
Printed in the USA
FFOW02n0927130318
45561173-46337FF